Practical Cooking

Baking

Practical Cooking

Baking

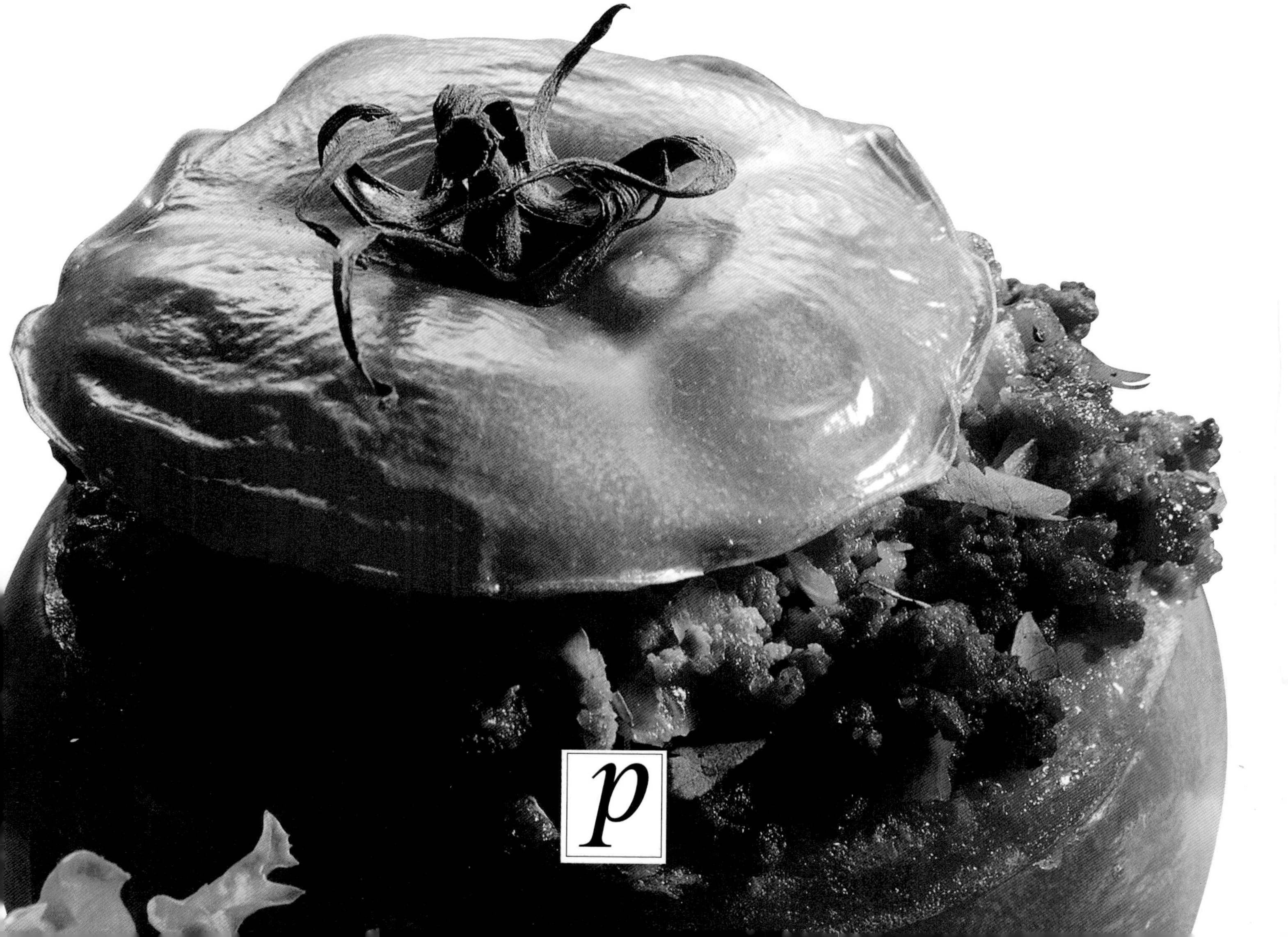

This is a Parragon Publishing Book
This edition published in 2002

Parragon Publishing
Queen Street House
4 Queen Street
Bath BA1 1HE, UK

ISBN: 0-75258-322-0

Printed in China

NOTE

Cup measurements in this book are for American cups. Tablespoons are assumed tobe 15ml. Unless otherwise stated, milk is assumed to be full fat, eggs are medium and pepper is freshly ground black pepper.

Recipes using uncooked eggs should be avoided by infants, the elderly, pregnant women and anyone suffering from an illness.

Contents

Appetizers & Snacks

Savory Meals

Savory Meals (continued)

Vegetarian & Vegan Dishes

Desserts

Cakes & Bread

Cookies

Introduction

It may be a daunting prospect to bake your own bread, pastries, cookies, and cakes instead of buying them at the supermarket, but once you have acquired the basic skills—and armed yourself with a few of the "tricks"—it becomes fun, versatile, and rewarding.

There are a few points that will ensure your baking session is successful, regardless of the type of recipe you have chosen. So, before you start:

- Read through the recipe carefully, and make sure you have the right ingredients—using all-purpose flour when self-rising flour is specified, for example, may not produce the result you were expecting!
- Remember to preheat the oven to the required temperature.
- Make sure you are using the correct size and shape of pan or dish, because the quantities given in the recipe are for the size of the pan specified.
- Prepare the cookware before you start assembling the ingredients—grease or line pans, dishes, or cookie sheets as directed in the recipe.
- Measure the ingredients accurately, and do any basic preparation, such as chopping, slicing, or grating, before you start cooking.
- Once you start cooking, follow the recipe step-by-step, in the order given. Using high-quality ingredients will give the best results—unbleached flours and unrefined sugars are readily

available for baking, while fresh vegetables, fish, and good-quality meat from a reliable supplier, and a good, extra virgin olive oil will make all the difference to your savory bakes.

A few very simple principles apply to making successful pie dough, bread, and cakes.

Pie Dough

- Metal pans, not porcelain dishes, are best for quiches and pies.
- Use fat at room temperature, cut into small pieces.
- Use ice water for mixing.
- Pie dough benefits from cool ingredients, and cold hands.
- Always strain the dry ingredients into a large mixing bowl, to incorporate air.
- Wrap the dough in foil and allow it to "rest" in the refrigerator for 30 minutes before using.

Bread

- Plan ahead—most bread recipes include one or two "provings" (leaving the dough in a warm place to double its bulk).
- If the flour feels cool, warm it gently in an oven at a low temperature.
- Make sure the liquid is lukewarm, to activate the yeast.
- To knead dough, stretch it away from you with one hand while pulling it toward you with the other, then fold in the edges, give it a quarter turn, and repeat.
- To test whether bread is cooked, tap the base—it should sound hollow if it is done.

Cakes

- Using a loose-based pan will make it easier to turn out any type of cake.
- Bring all the ingredients to room temperature before assembling.
- If possible, use a hand-held electric mixer for "creaming" (beating together the butter and sugar until the mixture has a "soft dropping" consistency).
- "Fold in" the dry ingredients very gently, using a metal spoon or spatula in a figure-eight movement. This lets the air get to the mixture and stops the cake becoming too heavy.
- When the cake is cooked, it should feel springy when pressed lightly. Alternatively, when a toothpick is inserted into the centre of the cake, it should come out clean if the cake is done.

Regional Cooking

Trends in eating have changed enormously in recent years to fit in with a greater awareness of health and a busier lifestyle, becoming lighter, healthier, and far more cosmopolitan. But one tradition has survived—the British afternoon tea—which many people around the world still enjoy today. Although it is often restricted to rest days and holidays, the aroma of freshly baked biscuits, cookies, teabreads, and cakes is as enticing as ever.

Teatime enthusiasts can progress through the year enjoying treats made with seasonal ingredients. Dark winter evenings may be cheered by a deliciously moist Orange, Banana & Cranberry Loaf; home-made Teacakes, laced with dried fruit and glazed with honey, served toasted, perhaps over a log fire; or a buttery, spicy Caraway Madeira.

Later in the year, the arrival of summer is celebrated by a leisurely tea in the garden. Cherry Scones, still warm from the oven, might be followed by Strawberry Roulade, a light sponge with a fruity mascarpone cheese filling, topped with toasted almonds and dusted with confectioners' sugar.

The onset of the cooler fall days are lightened by the year's harvest. A glut of apples can be turned into a Spiced Apple Ring, or Apple Shortcakes—light scones filled with braised apples and whipped cream—while the addition of roasted pumpkin flesh to a recipe makes an unusual and flavorsome Pumpkin Loaf.

At any time of year, the tea table can be enhanced by a plate of crisp, melting Shortbread Fantails, or one of the many fruitcake recipes—surely a good reason to start baking.

Equally appetizing, but in a totally different way, are the

Regional Cooking

Teatime enthusiasts can progress through the year enjoying treats made with seasonal ingredients. Dark winter evenings may be cheered by a deliciously moist Orange, Banana & Cranberry Loaf; home-made Teacakes, laced with dried fruit and glazed with honey, served toasted, perhaps over a log fire; or a buttery, spicy Caraway Madeira.

Later in the year, the arrival of summer is celebrated by a leisurely tea in the garden. Cherry Scones, still warm from the oven, might be followed by Strawberry Roulade, a light sponge with a fruity mascarpone cheese filling, topped with toasted almonds and dusted with confectioners' sugar.

The onset of the cooler fall days are lightened by the year's harvest. A glut of apples can be turned into a Spiced Apple Ring, or Apple Shortcakes—light scones filled with braised apples and whipped cream—while the addition of roasted pumpkin flesh to a recipe makes an unusual and flavorsome

Pumpkin Loaf.

At any time of year, the tea table can be enhanced by a plate of crisp, melting Shortbread Fantails, or one of the many fruitcake recipes—surely a good reason to start baking.

Equally appetizing, but in a totally different way, are the baking aromas that float from the kitchen of an Italian cook. Here,

pasta—in the form of lasagna, cannelloni, or any of the wide variety of shapes—is often served mixed with a sauce of vegetables, fish, or meat, topped with cheese and baked until golden. Spinach & Exotic Mushroom Lasagna, Pasticcio, and Shrimp & Tuna Pasta Bake

Basic Recipes

Savory Pie Dough

Makes 1 20-cm/8-inch savory flan base

6 tbsp butter, plus extra for greasing

1½ cups all-purpose flour

pinch of salt

2–3 tbsp water

1 Combine the flour and salt in a bowl, then rub in the butter. Add the water and work the mixture to a soft dough. Wrap in plastic wrap and leave to chill for 30 minutes

2 Grease a 20-cm/8-inch flan pan. Roll out the dough and line the pan with it. Prick the dough with a fork, then cover with plastic wrap and chill again for 30 minutes.

3 Preheat the oven to 200°C/400°F/Gas Mark 6. Line the pie shell with foil and then fill with baking beans. Bake in the preheated oven for 10–12 minutes, until golden.

4 Remove from the oven, discard the baking beans and foil, then bake in the oven for a further 10 minutes.

5 Remove from the oven, add your chosen filling, and cook as directed.

Sweet Pie Dough

Makes 1 24-cm/9½-inch sweet flan base.

1¼ cups all-purpose flour

2 tbsp superfine sugar

½ cup butter

1 tbsp water

1 Combine the flour and sugar in a bowl, then rub in the butter. Add the water and work the mixture to a soft dough. Wrap in plastic wrap and leave to chill for 30 minutes.

2 Grease a 24-cm/9½-inch flan pan. Roll out the dough and line the tin with it. Prick the dough with a fork, then cover with plastic wrap and chill again for 30 minutes.

3 Preheat the oven to 190°C/375°F/Gas Mark 5. Line the pie shell with foil and then fill with baking beans. Bake in the preheated oven for 15 minutes.

4 Remove from the oven, discard the baking beans and foil, then bake for a further 15 minutes.

5 Remove from the oven, then add your chosen filling and cook as directed.

Basic Pizza Dough

Makes one 25-cm/10-inch pizza

1½ cups all-purpose flour

1 tsp salt

1 tsp active dry yeast

6 tbsp lukewarm water

1 tbsp olive oil

1 Strain the flour and salt into a large bowl and add the yeast. Pour in the water and oil and mix to a dough. Knead for 5 minutes, then leave to "prove" until doubled in size.

2 Punch the air out from the dough, then knead lightly. Roll it out on a lightly floured surface, ready for use.

Basic Pasta Dough

Makes about 250 g/9 oz pasta

1 cup white bread flour, plus extra for dusting

⅔ cup fine semolina

1 tsp salt

1 tbsp olive oil

2 eggs

1–2 tbsp hot water

1 Sieve together the flour, semolina, and salt in a bowl and make a well in the centre. Pour in the oil and add the eggs. Add 1 tablespoon of hot water and, using your fingertips, work to form a smooth dough. Sprinkle on a little more water if necessary to make the dough pliable.

2 Lightly dust a clean board with flour, then knead the dough until it is elastic and silky. This can take 10–15 minutes. Dust the dough with more flour if your fingers become sticky.

3 Divide the dough into 2 equal pieces. Cover a counter with a clean cloth or dish cloth and dust it liberally with flour. Place one portion of the dough on the floured cloth and roll it out as thinly and evenly as possible, stretching the dough gently until the pattern of the weave shows through. Cover it with a cloth, then roll out the second piece of dough in the same way.

4 Use a ruler and a sharp knife to cut long, thin strips for noodles, or small confectionery cutters to cut rounds, star shapes, or an assortment of other decorative shapes. Cover the dough shapes with a clean cloth and leave them in a cool place (not a refrigerator) for 30–45

minutes to become partly dry. To dry ribbons, place a dish cloth over the back of a chair and hang the ribbons over it. Use this fresh pasta in the recipe of your choice.

Ragù Sauce

Makes about 1 pint/500 ml

3 tbsp olive oil

3 tbsp butter

2 large onions, chopped

4 celery sticks, thinly sliced

1 cup chopped bacon

2 garlic cloves, chopped

4½ cups ground beef

2 tbsp tomato paste

1 tbsp flour

14 oz/400 g can chopped tomatoes

⅔ cup beef stock

⅔ cup red wine

2 tsp dried oregano

½ tsp freshly grated nutmeg

salt and pepper

1 Heat the oil and butter in a pan over a medium heat. Add the onions, celery, and bacon and fry for 5 minutes, stirring constantly.

2 Stir in the garlic and ground beef and cook, stirring, until the meat has lost its redness. Lower the heat and simmer for 10 minutes, stirring occasionally.

3 Increase the heat to medium, stir in the tomato paste and the flour, and cook for 1–2 minutes. Add the tomatoes, stock, and wine and bring to the boil, stirring constantly. Season to taste, then stir in the oregano and nutmeg. Lower the heat, then cover and simmer for 45 minutes, stirring occasionally. The sauce is now ready to use.

Italian Cheese Sauce

Makes about 10 fl oz/300 ml

2 tbsp butter

¼ cup all-purpose flour

1¼ cups hot milk

pinch of nutmeg

pinch of dried thyme

2 tbsp white wine vinegar

3 tbsp heavy cream

½ cup grated mozzarella cheese

⅔ cup grated Parmesan cheese

1 tsp English mustard

2 tbsp sour cream

salt and pepper

1 Melt the butter in a pan and stir in the flour. Cook, stirring constantly, over a low heat until the roux is light in color and crumbly in texture. Stir in the hot milk gradually then cook over a low heat, still stirring, for 10 minutes until thick and smooth.

2 Add the nutmeg, thyme, and white wine vinegar and season to taste. Stir in the heavy cream and mix well, then add the cheeses, mustard, and sour cream. Mix until the cheeses have melted and blended into the sauce.

Pesto Sauce

Makes about 10 fl oz/300 ml

2 cups finely chopped fresh parsley

2 garlic cloves, crushed

½ cup pine nuts, crushed

2 tbsp chopped fresh basil leaves

⅔ cup freshly grated Parmesan cheese

⅔ cup olive oil

white pepper

1 Put all the ingredients in a blender or food processor and process for 2 minutes. Alternatively, you can blend by hand using a pestle and mortar.

2 Season with white pepper, then transfer to a pitcher, cover with plastic wrap, and store in the refrigerator before using.

How to Use This Book

Each recipe contains a wealth of useful information, including a breakdown of nutritional quantities, preparation and cooking times, and level of difficulty. All of this information is explained in detail below.

This amount of time represents the actual cooking time.

The nutritional information provided for each recipe is per serving or per portion. Optional ingredients, variations, or serving suggestions have not been included in the calculations.

The number of chef's hats represents the difficulty of each recipe, ranging from easy (1 chef's hat) to difficult (5 chef's hats).

This amount of time represents the preparation of ingredients, including cooling, chilling, and soaking times.

The ingredients for each recipe are listed in the order that they are used.

Baking 107

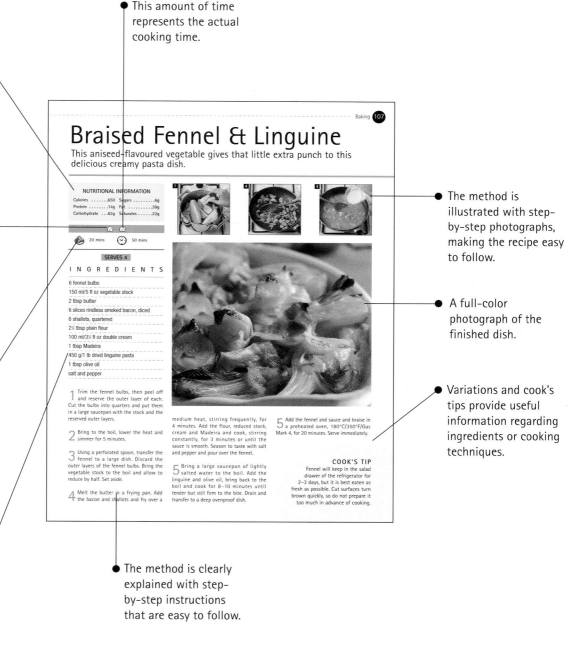

Braised Fennel & Linguine

This aniseed-flavoured vegetable gives that little extra punch to this delicious creamy pasta dish.

NUTRITIONAL INFORMATION

Calories	650	Sugars	6g
Protein	14g	Fat	39g
Carbohydrate	62g	Saturates	22g

20 mins 50 mins

SERVES 4

INGREDIENTS

6 fennel bulbs
150 ml/5 fl oz vegetable stock
2 tbsp butter
6 slices rindless smoked bacon, diced
6 shallots, quartered
2½ tbsp plain flour
100 ml/3½ fl oz double cream
1 tbsp Madeira
450 g/1 lb dried linguine pasta
1 tbsp olive oil
salt and pepper

1 Trim the fennel bulbs, then peel off and reserve the outer layer of each. Cut the bulbs into quarters and put them in a large saucepan with the stock and the reserved outer layers.

2 Bring to the boil, lower the heat and simmer for 5 minutes.

3 Using a perforated spoon, transfer the fennel to a large dish. Discard the outer layers of the fennel bulbs. Bring the vegetable stock to the boil and allow to reduce by half. Set aside.

4 Melt the butter in a frying pan. Add the bacon and shallots and fry over a medium heat, stirring frequently, for 4 minutes. Add the flour, reduced stock, cream and Madeira and cook, stirring constantly, for 3 minutes or until the sauce is smooth. Season to taste with salt and pepper and pour over the fennel.

5 Bring a large saucepan of lightly salted water to the boil. Add the linguine and olive oil, bring back to the boil and cook for 8–10 minutes until tender but still firm to the bite. Drain and transfer to a deep ovenproof dish.

5 Add the fennel and sauce and braise in a preheated oven, 180°C/350°F/Gas Mark 4, for 20 minutes. Serve immediately.

COOK'S TIP

Fennel will keep in the salad drawer of the refrigerator for 2–3 days, but it is best eaten as fresh as possible. Cut surfaces turn brown quickly, so do not prepare it too much in advance of cooking.

The method is illustrated with step-by-step photographs, making the recipe easy to follow.

A full-color photograph of the finished dish.

Variations and cook's tips provide useful information regarding ingredients or cooking techniques.

The method is clearly explained with step-by-step instructions that are easy to follow.

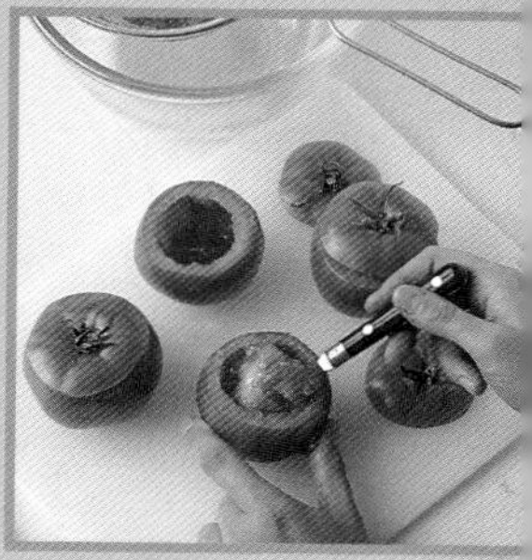

Appetizers & Snacks

With so many fresh ingredients readily available, it is very easy to create some deliciously different appetizers to make the perfect introduction to any meal. The ideas in this chapter are an inspiration to cook and a treat to eat,

and they give an edge to the appetite that makes the main course even more enjoyable. When choosing an appetizer, make sure that you provide a good balance of flavors, colors, and textures that offer variety and contrast. Balance the nature of the recipes too —a rich main course is best preceded by a light starter to stimulate the tastebuds.

Eggplant Bake

This dish combines layers of succulent eggplant, tomato sauce, mozzarella, and Parmesan to create a very tasty appetizer.

NUTRITIONAL INFORMATION

Calories	232	Sugars	8g
Protein	10g	Fat	18g
Carbohydrate	8g	Saturates	6g

5 mins 45 mins

SERVES 4

INGREDIENTS

- 3–4 tbsp olive oil
- 2 garlic cloves, crushed
- 2 large eggplants
- 3½ oz/100 g mozzarella cheese, sliced thinly
- generous ¾ cup passata (strained tomatoes)
- scant ⅔ cup freshly grated Parmesan cheese

1 Heat 2 tablespoons of the olive oil in a large skillet. Add the garlic and sauté for 30 seconds.

2 Slice the eggplants lengthwise. Add the slices to the skillet and cook in the oil for 3–4 minutes on each side or until tender. (You will probably have to cook them in batches, so add the remaining oil as necessary.)

3 Remove the eggplants with a perforated spoon and drain on absorbent paper towels.

4 Place a layer of eggplant slices in a shallow ovenproof dish. Cover the eggplants with a layer of mozzarella, and then pour over a third of the passata. Continue layering in the same order, finishing with a layer of passata on top.

2

2

4

5 Generously sprinkle the grated Parmesan cheese evenly over the top of the dish and bake in a preheated oven, 400°F/200°C, for 25–30 minutes or until the top is golden and bubbling.

6 Transfer the bake to serving plates and serve warm or let cool, then chill and serve cold.

Baked Fennel

Fennel is used extensively in northern Italy. It is a very versatile vegetable, which is good cooked or used raw in salads.

1

3

4

NUTRITIONAL INFORMATION

Calories	111	Sugars	6g
Protein	7g	Fat	7g
Carbohydrate	7g	Saturates	3g

10 mins   35 mins

SERVES 4

INGREDIENTS

- 2 fennel bulbs
- 2 celery stalks, cut into 3-inch/7.5-cm pieces
- 6 sun-dried tomatoes, halved
- generous ¾ cup passata (strained tomatoes)
- 2 tsp dried oregano
- scant ⅔ cup freshly grated Parmesan cheese

1 Using a sharp knife, trim the fennel, discarding any tough outer leaves, and cut the bulb into quarters.

2 Bring a large pan of water to a boil, add the fennel and celery, and cook for 8–10 minutes or until just tender. Remove with a perforated spoon.

3 Place the fennel pieces, celery, and sun-dried tomatoes in a large ovenproof dish.

4 Mix the passata and oregano and pour the mixture over the fennel.

5 Sprinkle with the Parmesan cheese and bake in a preheated oven, 375°F/190°C, for 20 minutes or until hot. Serve as a starter with crusty bread or as a vegetable side dish.

Onion & Mozzarella Tarts

These individual tarts are delicious served either hot or cold and are great for school lunches or picnics.

NUTRITIONAL INFORMATION

Calories	327	Sugars	3g
Protein	5g	Fat	23g
Carbohydrate	25g	Saturates	9g

45 mins 45 mins

SERVES 4

INGREDIENTS

- 9 oz/250 g packet puff pie dough, thawed if frozen
- 2 red onions
- 1 red bell pepper
- 8 cherry tomatoes, halved
- 3½ oz/100 g mozzarella cheese, cut into chunks
- 8 sprigs thyme

1 Roll out the pie dough on a lightly floured surface to make 4 squares, each 3 inches/7.5 cm wide. Using a sharp knife, trim the edges of the dough, reserving the trimmings. Chill the dough squares in the refrigerator for about 30 minutes.

2 Place the dough squares on a cookie sheet. Brush a little water along the edge of each square and use the reserved dough trimmings to make a rim around each tart.

3 Cut the red onions into thin wedges and halve and seed the bell pepper.

4 Place the onions and bell pepper in a roasting pan. Cook under a preheated broiler for 15 minutes or until the bell pepper skin is blackened and charred.

5 Place the roasted bell pepper halves in a plastic bag and set aside to sweat for 10 minutes. Peel off the skin from the bell pepper and cut the flesh into strips.

6 Line the dough squares with squares of foil. Bake in a preheated oven, 400°F/200°C, for 10 minutes. Remove the foil squares and bake the squares for a further 5 minutes.

7 Divide the onions, bell pepper strips, tomatoes, and cheese among the tarts and sprinkle with the fresh thyme.

8 Return to the oven for 15 minutes or until the tarts are golden. Transfer to warm serving plates and serve hot.

1
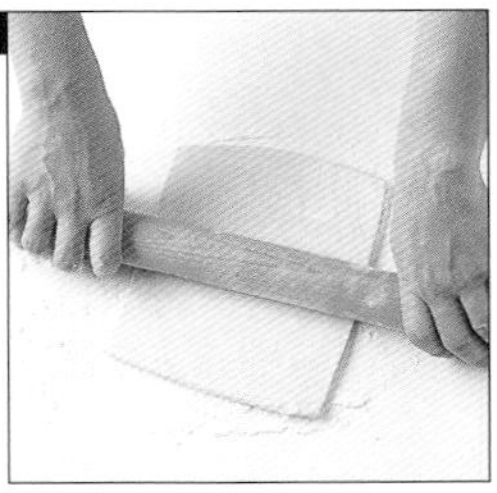

3

6

Stuffed Tomatoes

This is an impressive dinner-party dish—serve it as an appetizer. You will find large tomatoes are easier to fill.

NUTRITIONAL INFORMATION

Calories	290	Sugars	5g
Protein	17g	Fat	23g
Carbohydrate	8g	Saturates	9g

5 mins
45 mins

SERVES 4

INGREDIENTS

- 6 large, firm tomatoes
- 4 tbsp sweet butter
- 5 tbsp vegetable oil
- 1 onion, finely chopped
- 1 tsp finely chopped fresh ginger root
- 1 tsp crushed fresh garlic
- 1 tsp pepper
- 1 tsp salt
- ½ tsp garam masala
- 4 cups ground lamb
- 1 green chili
- fresh cilantro leaves

1 Rinse the tomatoes, cut off the tops, and scoop out the flesh. Grease an ovenproof dish, using all of the butter. Place the tomatoes in the dish.

2 Heat the oil in a heavy-based pan. Add the onion and cook over medium heat, stirring frequently, until golden.

3 Lower the heat and add the ginger, garlic, pepper, salt, and garam masala. Cook the mixture, stirring occasionally,for 3–5 minutes.

4 Add the ground lamb to the pan and cook, stirring frequently to break up the meat, for 10–15 minutes until it has lost its pink color.

5 Add the green chili and fresh cilantro leaves and continue cooking the mixture for 3–5 minutes.

6 Spoon the lamb mixture into the tomatoes and replace the tops. Bake the tomatoes in a preheated oven, 350°F/180°C, for 15–20 minutes.

7 Transfer the tomatoes to serving plates and serve hot.

VARIATION

You could use the same recipe to stuff red or green bell peppers, if desired.

Pasta-stuffed Tomatoes

This unusual and inexpensive dish would make a good appetizer for eight people or a delicious lunch for four.

NUTRITIONAL INFORMATION

Calories	298	Sugars	4g
Protein	10g	Fat	20g
Carbohydrate	20g	Saturates	5g

15 mins — 35 mins

SERVES 8

INGREDIENTS

- 5 tbsp extra virgin olive oil, plus extra for greasing
- 8 beefsteak tomatoes or large round tomatoes
- 1 cup dried ditalini or other very small pasta shapes
- 8 black olives, pitted and finely chopped
- 2 tbsp finely chopped fresh basil
- 1 tbsp finely chopped fresh parsley
- ⅔ cup freshly grated Parmesan cheese
- salt and pepper
- fresh basil sprigs, to garnish

3

5

6

1 Brush a cookie sheet with olive oil and set aside until required.

2 Slice the tops off the tomatoes and reserve to make "lids." If the tomatoes will not stand up, cut a thin slice off the bottom of each of them.

3 Using a teaspoon, scoop out the tomato pulp into a strainer, but do not pierce the tomato shells. Invert the tomato shells onto paper towels, pat dry, and let drain.

4 Bring a large pan of lightly salted water to a boil. Add the pasta and 1 tablespoon of the remaining olive oil, bring back to a boil, and cook for 8–10 minutes or until tender, but still firm to the bite. Drain and set aside.

5 Put the olives, basil, parsley, and Parmesan cheese into a large mixing bowl and stir in the drained tomato pulp. Add the pasta to the bowl. Stir in the remaining olive oil, mix together well, and season to taste with salt and pepper.

6 Spoon the pasta mixture into the tomato shells, dividing it among them equally, and replace the lids. Arrange the tomatoes on the prepared cookie sheet and bake in a preheated oven, 375°F/190°C, for 15–20 minutes.

7 Remove the tomatoes from the oven and let cool until just warm.

8 Arrange the pasta-stuffed tomatoes on a serving dish, garnish with the basil sprigs and serve.

Mexican-Style Pizzas

Ready-made individual pizza doughs are covered with a chili-tomato sauce and topped with kidney beans, cheese, and jalapeño chilies.

NUTRITIONAL INFORMATION

Calories	350	Sugars	8g
Protein	18g	Fat	10g
Carbohydrate	49g	Saturates	3g

10 mins

20 mins

SERVES 4

INGREDIENTS

- 4 ready-made, pre-cooked individual pizza doughs
- 1 tbsp olive oil
- 7 oz/200 g canned chopped tomatoes with garlic and herbs
- 2 tbsp tomato paste
- 7 oz/200 g canned kidney beans, drained and rinsed
- ⅔ cup corn kernels, thawed if frozen
- 1–2 tsp chili sauce
- 1 large red onion, shredded
- 1 cup grated reduced-fat sharp Cheddar cheese
- 1 large green chili, seeded and sliced into rings
- salt and pepper

1 Arrange the pizza doughs on a cookie sheet and brush them lightly with the oil.

2 Combine the chopped tomatoes, tomato paste, kidney beans, and corn in a large bowl and add chili sauce to taste. Season to taste with salt and pepper.

3 Spread the tomato and kidney bean mixture evenly over each pizza dough to cover.

4 Top each pizza with shredded onion and sprinkle with some grated cheese and a few slices of fresh green chili to taste.

5 Bake in a preheated oven, 425°F/220°C, for about 20 minutes until the vegetables are tender, the cheese has melted, and the dough is crisp and golden.

6 Remove the pizzas from the cookie sheet and transfer to serving plates. Serve immediately.

1

3

4

COOK'S TIP

Serve a Mexican-style salad with this pizza. Arrange sliced tomatoes, fresh cilantro leaves, and a few slices of a small, ripe avocado on a platter. Sprinkle with fresh lime juice and coarse sea salt.

Cheese & Onion Pies

These crisp pies are filled with a tasty onion, garlic, and parsley mixture, making them ideal for school and office lunches.

NUTRITIONAL INFORMATION

Calories	544	Sugars	9g
Protein	11g	Fat	36g
Carbohydrate	47g	Saturates	18g

15 mins   35 mins

SERVES 4

INGREDIENTS

- 3 tbsp vegetable oil
- 4 onions, peeled and thinly sliced
- 4 garlic cloves, crushed
- 4 tbsp finely chopped fresh parsley
- ¾ cup grated sharp cheese
- salt and pepper

PIE DOUGH

- 1¼ cups all-purpose flour
- ½ tsp salt
- ⅓ cup butter, cut into small pieces
- 3–4 tbsp water

1 Heat the oil in a large pan. Add the onions and garlic and cook over low heat for 10–15 minutes or until the onions are soft. Remove the pan from the heat, stir in the parsley and cheese and season to taste with salt and pepper.

2 To make the pie dough, strain the flour and salt into a mixing bowl. Add the butter and rub it in with your fingertips until the mixture resembles bread crumbs. Stir in the water and mix to form a dough.

3 On a lightly floured counter, roll out the dough and divide it into 8 portions.

4 Roll out each portion into a circle 4 inches/10 cm across and use half of the circles to line 4 individual tart pans.

5 Fill each round with a quarter of the onion cheese mixture. Cover with the remaining 4 pie dough circles. Make a slit in the top of each pie with the point of a knife to allow steam to escape during cooking and seal the edges with the back of a teaspoon.

6 Bake in a preheated oven, 425°F/ 220°C, for 20 minutes. Transfer the pies to warm individual serving plates, if serving hot, or to a wire rack to cool, if serving cold.

1

1

5

COOK'S TIP

You can prepare the onion filling in advance and store it in the refrigerator until required.

Garlic & Pine Nut Tarts

A crisp lining of bread is filled with garlic butter and pine nuts to make an unusual and delightful light meal.

NUTRITIONAL INFORMATION

Calories	435	Sugars	1g
Protein	6g	Fat	39g
Carbohydrate	17g	Saturates	20g

20 mins — 15 mins

SERVES 4

INGREDIENTS

- 4 slices whole-wheat or Granary bread
- ½ cup pine nuts
- ¾ cup butter
- 5 garlic cloves, peeled and halved
- 2 tbsp chopped fresh oregano
- 4 pitted black olives, halved
- oregano leaves, to garnish

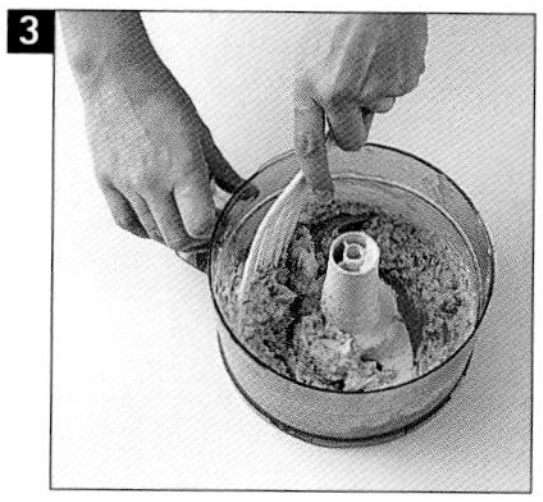

1 Using a rolling pin, flatten the bread slightly. Using a cookie cutter, cut out 4 circles of bread to fit your individual tart pans—they should measure about 4 inches/10 cm across. Reserve the offcuts of bread and leave them in the refrigerator for 10 minutes or until required.

2 Meanwhile, place the pine nuts on a cookie sheet. Toast the pine nuts under a preheated broiler for 2–3 minutes or until golden.

3 Put the bread offcuts, pine nuts, butter, garlic, and oregano into a food processor and blend for about 20 seconds. Alternatively, pound the ingredients by hand in a mortar with a pestle. The mixture should have a rough texture.

4 Spoon the pine nut and butter mixture into the lined pans and top with the olive halves. Bake in a preheated oven, 400°F/200°C, for 10–15 minutes or until golden.

5 Transfer the tarts to serving plates and serve warm, garnished with the fresh oregano leaves.

VARIATION

Puff pie dough can be used for the tarts. Use 7oz/200 g dough to line 4 tart pans. Chill it for 20 minutes. Line the pans with the dough and then with foil, and bake blind for 10 minutes. Remove the foil and bake for 3–4 minutes or until the dough is set. Cool, then continue from step 2, adding 2 tablespoons of bread crumbs to the mixture.

Eggplants & Yogurt

This is an unusual dish from India, in that the eggplants are first baked in the oven, then cooked in a pan.

NUTRITIONAL INFORMATION

Calories	147	Sugars	6g
Protein	3g	Fat	11g
Carbohydrate	8g	Saturates	1g

5 mins 1 hr 5 mins

SERVES 4

INGREDIENTS

- 2 medium eggplants
- 4 tbsp vegetable oil
- 1 onion, sliced
- 1 tsp white cumin seeds
- 1 tsp chili powder
- 1 tsp salt
- 3 tbsp plain yogurt
- ½ tsp mint sauce
- fresh mint leaves, to garnish

1 Rinse the eggplants and pat dry with paper towels.

2 Place the eggplants in an ovenproof dish. Bake in a preheated oven, 425°F/160°C, for 45 minutes. Remove the baked eggplants from the oven and let cool.

3 Using a spoon, scoop out the eggplant flesh and reserve.

4 Heat the oil in a heavy-based pan. Add the onions and cumin seeds and cook over low heat, stirring occasionally, for 1–2 minutes.

5 Add the chili powder, salt, yogurt, and mint sauce to the pan, and stir thoroughly to mix.

6 Add the eggplant flesh to the onion and yogurt mixture and cook over low heat for 5–7 minutes or until all of the liquid has been absorbed and the mixture has become quite dry.

7 Transfer the eggplant and yogurt mixture to a serving dish and garnish with fresh mint leaves.

3

4

5

COOK'S TIP

Rich in protein and calcium, yogurt plays an important part in Indian cooking. Thick unsweetened yogurt most closely resembles the yogurt made in many Indian homes.

Spinach & Ricotta Shells

This is a classic combination in which the smooth, creamy cheese balances the sharper taste of the spinach.

NUTRITIONAL INFORMATION

Calories	672	Sugars	10g
Protein	23g	Fat	26g
Carbohydrate	93g	Saturates	8g

5 mins   40 mins

SERVES 4

INGREDIENTS

- 14 oz/400 g dried lumache rigate grande pasta
- 5 tbsp olive oil
- 1 cup fresh white bread crumbs
- ½ cup milk
- 10½ oz/300 g frozen spinach, thawed and drained
- 1 cup ricotta cheese
- pinch of freshly grated nutmeg
- 14 oz/400 g canned chopped tomatoes, drained
- 1 garlic clove, crushed
- salt and pepper

1 Bring a large pan of lightly salted water to a boil. Add the lumache and 1 tablespoon of the olive oil, bring back to a boil, and cook for 8–10 minutes until just tender, but still firm to the bite. Drain the pasta, refresh under cold water and set aside until required.

2 Put the bread crumbs, milk, and 3 tablespoons of the remaining olive oil in a food processor and process to combine.

3 Add the spinach and ricotta cheese to the food processor and process to a smooth mixture. Transfer the mixture to a bowl, stir in the nutmeg, and season with salt and pepper to taste.

4 Combine the tomatoes, garlic, and the remaining oil and spoon the mixture into the bottom of a large ovenproof dish.

5 Using a teaspoon, fill the lumache with the spinach and ricotta mixture and arrange on top of the tomato mixture in the dish.

6 Cover and bake in a preheated oven, 350°F/180°C, for 20 minutes. Serve hot.

2

3

5

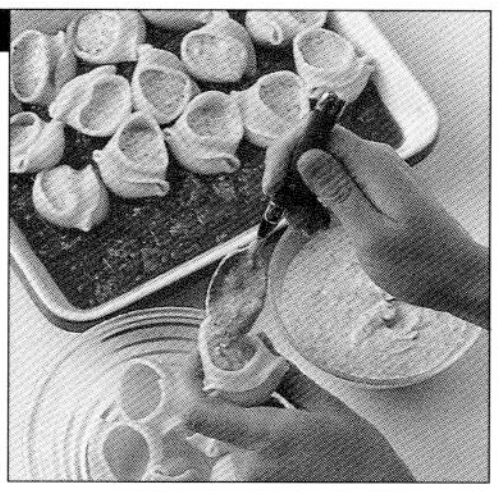

COOK'S TIP

Ricotta is a creamy Italian cheese traditionally made from sheeps' milk whey. It is soft and white, with a smooth texture and a slightly sweet flavor. It should be used within 2–3 days of purchase.

Tricolor Timballini

An unusual way of serving pasta, these delightful, little cheese molds are excellent with a crunchy salad for a light lunch.

NUTRITIONAL INFORMATION

Calories	529	Sugars	7g
Protein	18g	Fat	29g
Carbohydrate	46g	Saturates	12g

30 mins — 1 hr

SERVES 4

INGREDIENTS

- 1 tbsp butter, softened
- 1 cup dried white bread crumbs
- 6 oz/175 g dried tricolor spaghetti, broken into 2-inch/5-cm lengths
- 3 tbsp olive oil
- 1 egg yolk
- 1 cup grated Swiss cheese
- 1¼ cups Béchamel Sauce (see page 92)
- 1 onion, finely chopped
- 1 bay leaf
- ⅔ cup dry white wine
- ⅔ cup passata (strained tomatoes)
- 1 tbsp tomato paste
- salt and pepper
- fresh basil leaves, to garnish

1

3

6

1 Grease four ¾-cup molds or ramekins with the butter. Evenly coat the insides with half of the bread crumbs.

2 Bring a pan of lightly salted water to a boil. Add the spaghetti and 1 tablespoon of the oil, bring back to a boil, and cook for 8–10 minutes or until just tender. Drain and transfer to a mixing bowl. Add the egg yolk and cheese to the pasta and season to taste with salt and pepper.

3 Pour the Béchamel Sauce into the bowl containing the pasta and mix. Spoon the mixture into the ramekins and sprinkle over the remaining bread crumbs.

4 Stand the ramekins on a cookie sheet and bake in a preheated oven, 425°F/220°C, for 20 minutes. Set aside for 10 minutes.

5 Meanwhile, make the sauce. Heat the remaining oil in a pan and gently cook the onion and bay leaf for 2–3 minutes.

6 Stir in the wine, passata, and tomato paste, and season with salt and pepper to taste. Simmer gently for 20 minutes, until thickened. Remove and discard the bay leaf.

7 Turn the timballini out onto serving plates, garnish with the basil leaves, and serve with the tomato sauce.

Gnocchi Romana

This is a traditional Italian recipe but, if you prefer a less rich version, you can simply omit the eggs.

NUTRITIONAL INFORMATION			
Calories	709	Sugars	9g
Protein	32g	Fat	41g
Carbohydrate	58g	Saturates	25g

1¼ hrs 45 mins

SERVES 4

INGREDIENTS

- scant 4 cups milk
- pinch of freshly grated nutmeg
- 6 tbsp butter, plus extra for greasing
- 1¼ cups semolina
- generous 1 cup freshly grated Parmesan cheese
- 2 eggs, beaten
- ½ cup grated Swiss cheese
- salt and pepper
- fresh basil sprigs, to garnish

1 Pour the milk into a pan and bring to a boil. Remove the pan from the heat and stir in the nutmeg and 2 tablespoons of the butter. Season to taste with salt and pepper.

2 Gradually stir the semolina into the milk, whisking to prevent lumps forming, and return the pan to low heat. Simmer, stirring constantly, for about 10 minutes or until very thick.

3 Beat ⅔ cup of Parmesan cheese into the semolina mixture, then beat in the eggs. Continue beating the mixture until smooth. Let the mixture cool slightly.

4 Spread out the cooled semolina mixture in an even layer on a sheet of baking parchment or in a large, oiled baking pan, smoothing the surface with a damp spatula—it should be about ½ inch/1 cm thick. Let cool completely, then chill in the refrigerator for 1 hour.

5 Once chilled, cut out circles of gnocchi, measuring about 1½ inches/4 cm in diameter, using a plain, greased dough cutter.

6 Grease a shallow ovenproof dish or 4 individual ovenproof dishes. Lay the gnocchi trimmings in the base of the dish or dishes and arrange the circles of gnocchi on top, slightly overlapping each other.

7 Melt the remaining butter and drizzle it over the gnocchi. Sprinkle over the remaining grated Parmesan cheese, then sprinkle over the Swiss cheese.

8 Bake the gnocchi in a preheated oven, 400°F/200°C, for 25–30 minutes, until the top is crisp, golden brown and bubbling. Serve at once, garnished with the basil leaves.

2

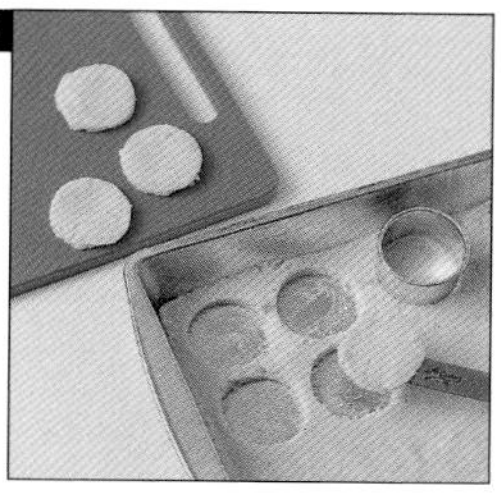
5

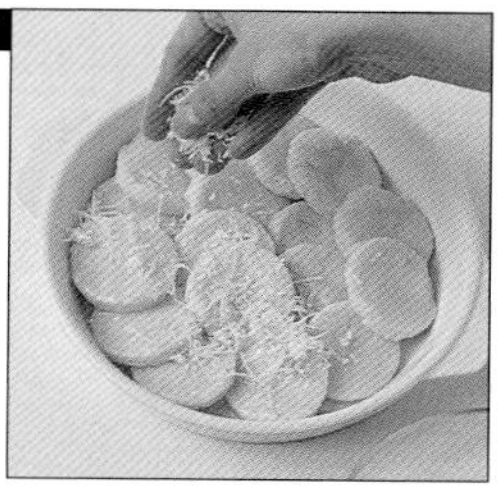
7

Three Cheese Bake

Serve this dish while the cheese is still hot and melted, as cooked cheese turns very rubbery if it is allowed to cool down.

NUTRITIONAL INFORMATION

Calories	710	Sugars	6g
Protein	34g	Fat	30g
Carbohydrate	80g	Saturates	16g

5 mins 1 hr

SERVES 4

INGREDIENTS

- butter, for greasing
- 14 oz/400 g dried penne pasta
- 1 tbsp olive oil
- 2 eggs, beaten
- 1½ cups ricotta cheese
- 4 sprigs fresh basil
- 1 cup grated mozzarella or halloumi cheese
- ⅔ cup freshly grated Parmesan cheese
- salt and pepper
- fresh basil leaves, to garnish (optional)

1 Lightly grease a large ovenproof dish with butter.

2 Bring a large pan of lightly salted water to a boil. Add the penne and olive oil, bring back to a boil, and cook for 8–10 minutes until just tender, but still firm to the bite. Drain the pasta, set aside, and keep warm.

3 Beat the eggs into the ricotta and season to taste with salt and pepper.

4 Spoon half of the penne into the bottom of the prepared dish and cover with half of the basil leaves.

5 Spoon half of the ricotta cheese mixture over the pasta. Sprinkle over the grated mozzarella or halloumi cheese and top with the remaining basil leaves. Cover with the remaining penne and then spoon over the remaining ricotta cheese mixture. Lightly sprinkle over the freshly grated Parmesan cheese.

6 Bake in a preheated oven, 375°F/190°C, for 30–40 minutes until golden brown and the cheese topping is hot and bubbling. Garnish the bake with fresh basil leaves, if liked, and serve hot straight from the dish.

3

4

5

VARIATION

Try substituting smoked Bavarian cheese for the mozzarella or halloumi and grated Cheddar cheese for the Parmesan, for a slightly different, but just as delicious flavor.

Mini Cheese & Onion Tarts

Serve these delicious little savory tarts as irresistible finger food at buffets or drinks parties or take them on a picnic.

NUTRITIONAL INFORMATION

Calories 114	Sugars 1g
Protein 3g	Fat 9g
Carbohydrate 7g	Saturates 5g

45 mins

25 mins

SERVES 12

INGREDIENTS

DOUGH

¾ cup all-purpose flour

¼ tsp salt

6 tbsp butter, cut into small pieces

1–2 tbsp water

FILLING

1 egg, beaten

generous ⅓ cup light cream

½ cup grated Dry Jack or Cheddar cheese

3 scallions, finely chopped

salt

cayenne pepper

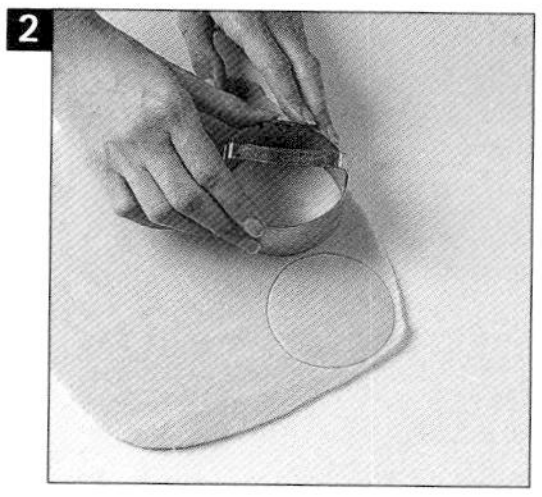

1 To make the dough, strain the flour and salt into a mixing bowl. Add the butter and rub it in with your fingertips until the mixture resembles bread crumbs. Stir in the water and mix to form a dough. Form into a ball, cover, and chill in the refrigerator for 30 minutes.

2 Roll out the dough on a lightly floured counter. Using a 3-inch/7.5-cm cookie cutter, stamp out 12 circles from the dough and line a shallow muffin pan.

3 To make the filling, whisk together the beaten egg, light cream, grated cheese, and chopped scallions in a pitcher. Season to taste with salt and cayenne.

4 Pour the filling mixture into the tart shells and bake in a preheated oven, 350°F/180°C, for about 20–25 minutes or until the filling is just set.

4 Serve at once, if serving warm, or transfer to a wire rack to cool.

COOK'S TIP

If you use 6 oz/175 g of ready-made pie dough instead of making it yourself, these tarts can be made in minutes.

Mini Pizzas

Pizette, as they are known in Italy, are tiny pizzas. This quantity will make 8 individual pizzas, or 16 cocktail pizzas to go with drinks.

NUTRITIONAL INFORMATION

Calories	139	Sugars	1g
Protein	4g	Fat	6g
Carbohydrate	18g	Saturates	1g

1¼ hrs — 15 mins

SERVES 8

INGREDIENTS

BASIC PIZZA DOUGH

- 2 tsp dried yeast
- 1 tsp sugar
- 1 cup warm water
- 2½ cups white bread flour
- 1 tsp salt
- 1 tbsp olive oil

TOPPING

- 2 zucchini
- generous ⅓ cup passata (strained tomatoes)
- ½ cup diced pancetta
- ½ cup pitted black olives, chopped
- 1 tbsp mixed dried herbs
- 2 tbsp olive oil
- salt and pepper

1 Place the yeast and sugar in a pitcher and mix with 4 tablespoons of the water. Set the yeast mixture aside in a warm place for 15 minutes or until frothy.

2 Mix the flour with the salt and make a well in the center. Add the oil, the yeast mixture, and the remaining water. Using a wooden spoon, mix to form a smooth dough.

3 Turn the dough out onto a floured counter and knead for 4–5 minutes or until smooth. Return the dough to the bowl, cover with an oiled sheet of plastic wrap, and let rise for 30 minutes or until the dough has doubled in size.

4 Knead the dough for 2 minutes and divide it into 8 balls. Roll out each portion thinly to form circles, then carefully transfer them to an oiled cookie sheet, pushing out the edges until even. The dough should be no more than ¼ inch/5 mm thick because it will rise during cooking.

5 To make the topping, grate the zucchini finely. Cover with paper towels and let stand for 10 minutes to absorb some of the juices.

6 Spread 2–3 teaspoons of the passata over the pizza doughs and top each with the grated zucchini, pancetta, and olives. Season with pepper, add mixed dried herbs to taste, and drizzle with oil.

7 Bake in a preheated oven, 400°F/200°C, for 15 minutes or until crispy. Season with salt and pepper to taste and serve hot.

4

5

6

Vegetable Pasta Nests

These large pasta nests look impressive when presented filled with broiled mixed vegetables and they taste simply delicious.

NUTRITIONAL INFORMATION

Calories	392	Sugars	1g
Protein	6g	Fat	28g
Carbohydrate	32g	Saturates	9g

25 mins — 40 mins

SERVES 4

INGREDIENTS

- 6 oz/175 g dried spaghetti
- 1 eggplant, halved and sliced
- 1 zucchini, diced
- 1 red bell pepper, seeded and chopped diagonally
- 6 tbsp olive oil
- 2 garlic cloves, crushed
- butter, for greasing
- 4 tbsp butter or margarine, melted
- 1 tbsp dry white bread crumbs
- salt and pepper
- fresh parsley sprigs, to garnish

3

5

6

1 Bring a large pan of water to a boil. Add the spaghetti, bring back to a boil, and cook for 8–10 minutes until tender, but still firm to the bite. Drain the spaghetti in a strainer and set aside until required.

2 Place the eggplant, zucchini, and bell pepper on a cookie sheet.

3 Combine the oil and garlic and pour over the vegetables, tossing them to coat all over.

4 Cook the vegetables under a preheated hot broiler for about 10 minutes, turning, until tender and lightly charred. Set aside and keep warm.

5 Lightly grease 4 large, shallow muffin pans and divide the spaghetti among them. Using 2 forks, curl the spaghetti to form nests.

6 Brush the pasta nests with melted butter or margarine and sprinkle with the bread crumbs. Bake in a preheated oven, 400°F/200°C, for 15 minutes or until lightly golden. Remove the pasta nests from the pans and transfer to warm individual serving plates. Divide the broiled vegetables among the pasta nests, season, and garnish.

COOK'S TIP

The Italian term, *al dente* means "to the bite" and describes cooked pasta that is not too soft, but still has a bite to it.

Macaroni Bake

This warming and satisfying dish would make an excellent supper for a mid-week family meal on a cold winter evening.

NUTRITIONAL INFORMATION

Calories	728	Sugars	11g
Protein	17g	Fat	42g
Carbohydrate	75g	Saturates	23g

15 mins   45 mins

SERVES 4

INGREDIENTS

- 4 cups dried short-cut macaroni
- 1 tbsp olive oil
- 4 tbsp beef drippings
- 1 lb/450 g potatoes, thinly sliced
- 1 lb/450 g onions, sliced
- 2 cups grated mozzarella cheese
- ⅔ cup heavy cream
- salt and pepper
- crusty brown bread and butter, to serve

3

3

3

1 Bring a large pan of lightly salted water to a boil. Add the macaroni and olive oil, bring back to a boil, and cook for about 12 minutes or until tender but still firm to the bite. Drain the macaroni thoroughly and set aside.

2 Melt the drippings in a large flame-proof casserole, then remove the pan from the heat.

3 Make alternate layers of potatoes, onions, macaroni, and grated mozzarella in the dish, seasoning well with salt and pepper between each layer and finishing with a layer of cheese on top. Finally, pour the cream over the top layer of cheese.

4 Bake in a preheated oven, 400°F/200°C, for 25 minutes. Remove the dish from the oven and carefully brown the top of the bake under a preheated hot broiler.

5 Serve the bake straight from the dish with crusty brown bread and butter as a main course. Alternatively, serve as a vegetable accompaniment with your favorite main course.

VARIATION

For a stronger flavor, use *mozzarella affumicata*, a smoked version of this cheese, or Swiss cheese, instead of the normal mozzarella.

Pancetta & Romano Cakes

This makes an excellent light meal when served with a topping of pesto or anchovy sauce and crisp salad greens.

NUTRITIONAL INFORMATION

Calories	619	Sugars	4g
Protein	22g	Fat	29g
Carbohydrate	71g	Saturates	8g

20 mins 25 mins

SERVES 4

INGREDIENTS

- 2 tbsp butter, plus extra for greasing
- 3½ oz/100 g pancetta, rind removed
- 2 cups self-rising flour
- ¾ cup grated romano cheese
- ⅔ cup milk, plus extra for glazing
- 1 tbsp tomato catsup
- 1 tsp Worcestershire sauce
- 14 oz/400 g dried farfalle pasta
- 1 tbsp olive oil
- salt

TO SERVE

- 3 tbsp Pesto Sauce (see page 15) or anchovy sauce, optional
- salad greens, to serve

1 Grease a cookie sheet with butter. Cook the pancetta under a preheated broiler until it is cooked. Let the pancetta cool, then chop it finely.

2 Sift together the flour and a pinch of salt into a mixing bowl. Add the butter and rub in with your fingertips. When the butter and flour have been thoroughly incorporated, add the pancetta and ¼ cup of the grated cheese.

3 Mix together the milk, tomato catsup, and Worcestershire sauce and add to the dry ingredients, mixing well to make a soft dough.

4 Roll out the dough on a lightly floured counter to make a 7-inch/18-cm circle. Brush with a little milk to glaze and cut into 8 wedges.

5 Arrange the dough wedges on the prepared cookie sheet and sprinkle over the remaining cheese. Bake in a preheated oven, 400°F/200°C, for 20 minutes.

6 Meanwhile, bring a pan of lightly salted water to a boil. Add the farfalle and the oil, bring back to a boil, and cook for 8–10 minutes until just tender, but still firm to the bite. Drain and transfer to a large serving dish. Top with the pancetta and romano cakes. Serve with the sauce of your choice and salad greens.

2

4

5

Fresh Tomato Tarts

These tomato-flavored tarts should be eaten as fresh as possible to enjoy the flaky and crisp buttery puff pastry.

NUTRITIONAL INFORMATION

Calories	217	Sugars	3g
Protein	5g	Fat	14g
Carbohydrate	18g	Saturates	1g

35 mins

20 mins

SERVES 6

INGREDIENTS

- 9 oz/250 g ready-made puff pie dough, thawed if frozen
- 1 egg, beaten
- 2 tbsp Pesto (see page 15)
- 6 plum tomatoes, sliced
- salt and pepper
- fresh thyme leaves, to garnish (optional)

1 On a lightly floured counter, roll out the pie dough to a rectangle measuring 12 x 10 inches/30 x 25 cm.

2 Cut the rectangle in half and divide each half into 3 pieces to make 6 even-size rectangles. Chill in the refrigerator for 20 minutes.

3 Lightly score the edges of the pie dough rectangles and brush with the beaten egg.

4 Spread the Pesto over the rectangles, dividing it equally among them, leaving a 1-inch/2.5-cm border around each one.

5 Arrange the tomato slices along the center of each rectangle on top of the Pesto.

3

4

5

6 Season well with salt and pepper to taste and lightly sprinkle with fresh thyme leaves, if using.

7 Bake in a preheated oven, 400°F/200°C, for 15–20 minutes, until well risen and golden brown.

8 Transfer the tomato tarts to warm serving plates straight from the oven and serve while they are still piping hot.

VARIATION

Instead of individual tarts, roll the dough out to form 1 large rectangle. Spoon over the Pesto and arrange the tomatoes over the top.

Provençal Tart

This tart is full of color and flavor from the zucchini and red and green bell peppers. It makes a great change from a quiche Lorraine.

NUTRITIONAL INFORMATION

Calories	355	Sugars	5g
Protein	5g	Fat	29g
Carbohydrate	21g	Saturates	9g

10–15 mins 55 mins

SERVES 6

INGREDIENTS

- 9 oz/250 g ready-made puff pie dough, thawed if frozen
- 3 tbsp olive oil
- 2 red bell peppers, seeded and diced
- 2 green bell peppers, seeded and diced
- ⅔ cup heavy cream
- 1 egg
- 2 zucchini, sliced
- salt and pepper

1 Roll out the pie dough on a lightly floured counter and line an 8-inch/20-cm loose-bottomed tart pan. Chill in the refrigerator for 20 minutes.

2 Meanwhile, heat 2 tablespoons of the olive oil in a skillet. Add the red and green bell peppers and cook over low heat, stirring frequently, for about 8 minutes until softened.

3 Whisk the heavy cream and egg together in a bowl and season to taste with salt and pepper. Stir in the cooked bell peppers.

4 Heat the remaining oil in a pan and cook the zucchini slices for 4–5 minutes until lightly browned.

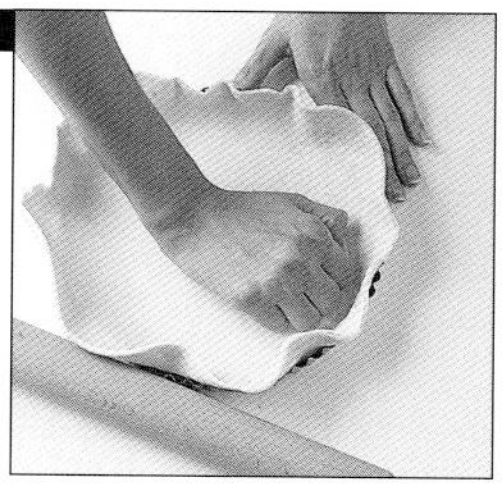

1

2

6

5 Pour the egg and bell pepper mixture into the tart shell.

6 Arrange the zucchini slices around the edge of the tart.

7 Bake in a preheated oven, 350°F/180°C, for 35–40 minutes or until just set and golden brown. Serve at once or let cool and serve cold.

COOK'S TIP

This recipe could be used to make 6 individual tarts—use 6 x 4-inch/15 x 10-cm pans and bake them for 20 minutes.

Baked Tuna & Ricotta Rigatoni

Ribbed tubes of pasta are filled with the classic combination of tuna and ricotta cheese and then baked in a creamy sauce.

NUTRITIONAL INFORMATION

Calories	949	Sugars	5g
Protein	51g	Fat	48g
Carbohydrate	85g	Saturates	26g

10 mins 45 mins

SERVES 4

INGREDIENTS

- butter, for greasing
- 1 lb/450 g dried rigatoni
- 1 tbsp olive oil
- 7 oz/200 g canned flaked tuna, drained
- 1 cup ricotta cheese
- ½ cup heavy cream
- 2 cups grated Parmesan cheese
- 4 oz/125 g sun-dried tomatoes in oil, drained and sliced
- salt and pepper

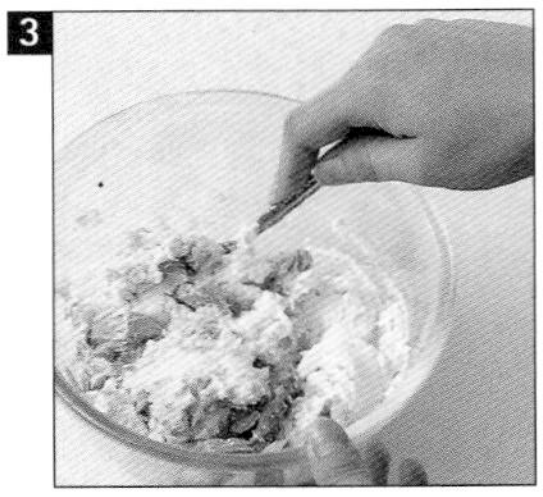

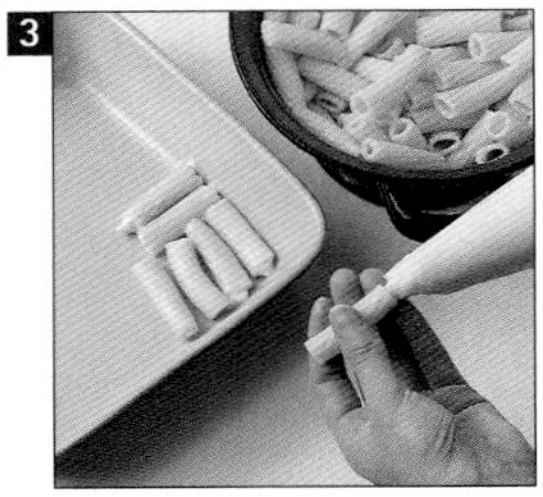

1 Lightly grease a large ovenproof dish with butter.

2 Bring a large pan of lightly salted water to a boil. Add the rigatoni and olive oil, bring back to a boil, and cook for 8–10 minutes until just tender, but still firm to the bite. Drain the pasta and set aside until cool enough to handle.

3 Meanwhile, in a bowl, combine the tuna and ricotta cheese to form a soft paste. Spoon the mixture into a pastry bag and use to fill the rigatoni. Arrange the filled pasta tubes side by side in a single layer in the prepared ovenproof dish.

4 To make the sauce, mix the cream and Parmesan cheese and season with salt and pepper to taste. Spoon the sauce over the rigatoni and top with the sun-dried tomatoes, arranged in a criss-cross pattern.

5 Bake in a preheated oven, 400°F/ 200°C, for 20 minutes. Serve hot straight from the dish.

VARIATION

For a vegetarian alternative to this recipe, simply substitute a mixture of pitted and chopped black olives and chopped walnuts for the tuna. Follow exactly the same cooking method.

Tuna Stuffed Tomatoes

Deliciously sweet roasted tomatoes are filled with tangy homemade lemon mayonnaise and tuna.

NUTRITIONAL INFORMATION

Calories	196	Sugars	2g
Protein	9g	Fat	17g
Carbohydrate	2g	Saturates	3g

5–10 mins 25 mins

SERVES 4

INGREDIENTS

- 4 plum tomatoes
- 2 tbsp sun-dried tomato paste
- 2 egg yolks
- 2 tsp lemon juice
- finely grated zest of 1 lemon
- 4 tbsp olive oil
- 4 oz/115 g canned tuna, drained
- 2 tbsp capers, rinsed
- salt and pepper

TO GARNISH

- 2 sun-dried tomatoes in oil, drained and cut into strips
- fresh basil leaves

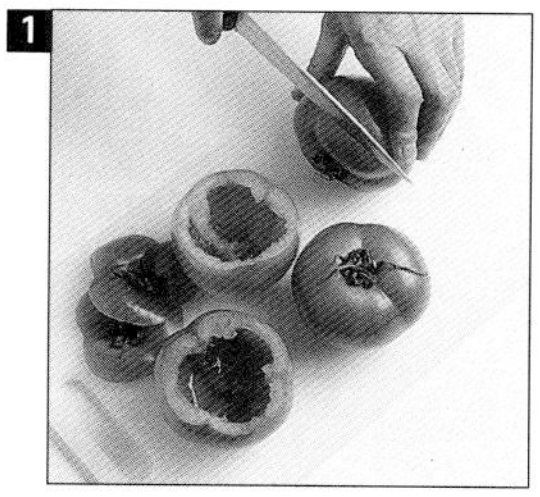

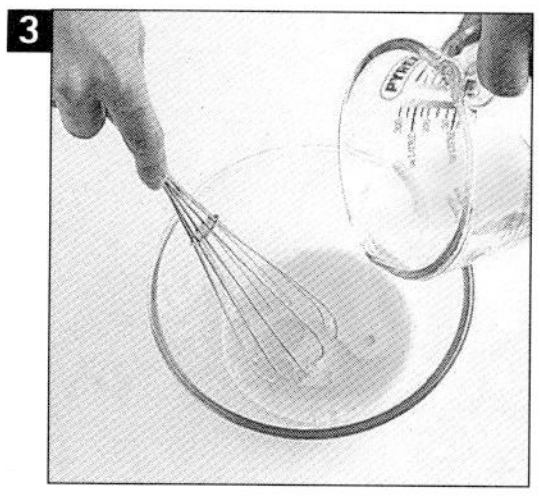

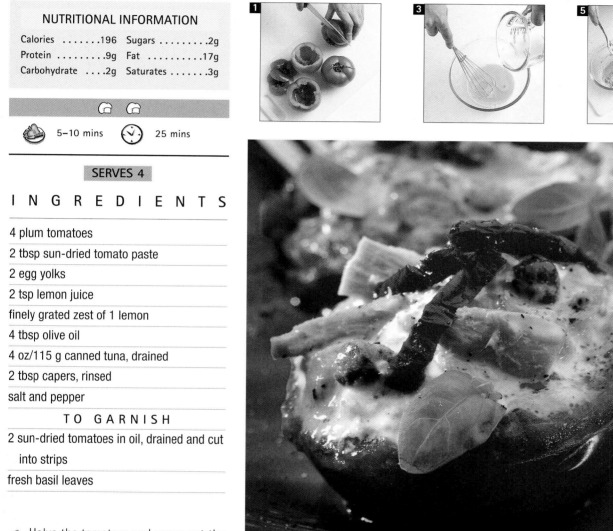

1 Halve the tomatoes and scoop out the seeds. Divide the sun-dried tomato paste among the tomato halves and spread around the inside of the skin.

2 Place on a cookie sheet and roast in a preheated oven, 400°F/200°C, for 12–15 minutes. Let cool slightly.

3 To make the mayonnaise. In a food processor, blend the egg yolks and lemon juice with the lemon zest until smooth. With the motor running slowly, add the olive oil. Stop the processor as soon as the mayonnaise has thickened. Alternatively, use a hand whisk, beating the mixture continuously until it thickens.

4 Add the tuna and capers to the mayonnaise and season to taste.

5 Spoon the tuna mixture into the tomato shells and garnish with sun-dried tomato strips and basil leaves. Return to the oven for a few minutes or serve chilled.

COOK'S TIP

For a picnic, do not roast the tomatoes, just scoop out the seeds, drain them, cut side down, on paper towels for 1 hour, and fill them with the mayonnaise mixture. They are firmer and easier to handle this way. If you prefer, store-bought mayonnaise may be used instead—just stir in the lemon zest.

Roasted Seafood

Vegetables become deliciously sweet and juicy when they are roasted, and they go particularly well with fish and seafood.

NUTRITIONAL INFORMATION

Calories	280	Sugars	5g
Protein	15g	Fat	12g
Carbohydrate	28g	Saturates	2g

15 mins

50 mins

SERVES 4

INGREDIENTS

- 1 lb 5 oz/600 g new potatoes
- 3 red onions, cut into wedges
- 2 zucchini, sliced into chunks
- 8 garlic cloves, peeled
- 2 lemons, cut into wedges
- 4 sprigs rosemary
- 4 tbsp olive oil
- 12 oz/350 g shell-on shrimp
- 2 small prepared squid, chopped into rings
- 4 tomatoes, quartered

1 Scrub the potatoes to remove any dirt. Cut any large potatoes in half. Place the potatoes in a large roasting pan, together with the onions, zucchini, garlic, lemon, and rosemary sprigs.

2 Pour over the olive oil and toss well to coat all of the vegetables. Cook in a preheated oven, 400°F/200°C, for about 40 minutes, turning occasionally, until the potatoes are tender.

3 Once the potatoes are tender, add the shrimp, squid, and tomatoes, tossing to coat them in the oil, and roast for a further 10 minutes. All of the vegetables should be cooked through and slightly charred for full flavor.

4 Transfer the roasted seafood and vegetables to warm serving plates and serve hot.

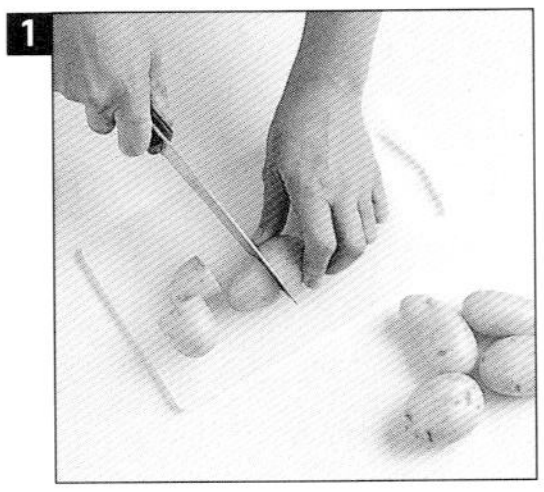

VARIATION

Most vegetables are suitable for roasting in the oven. Try adding 1 lb/450 g pumpkin, squash, or eggplant, if you prefer.

Pissaladière

This is a French variation of the classic Italian pizza but is made with ready-made puff pie dough. It is perfect for outdoor eating.

NUTRITIONAL INFORMATION

Calories	290	Sugars	7g
Protein	7g	Fat	19g
Carbohydrate	259g	Saturates	1g

10 mins | 55 mins

SERVES 8

INGREDIENTS

- butter, for greasing
- 4 tbsp olive oil
- 1 lb 9 oz/700 g red onions, thinly sliced
- 2 garlic cloves, crushed
- 2 tsp superfine sugar
- 2 tbsp red wine vinegar
- 12 oz/350 g ready-made puff pie dough, thawed if frozen
- salt and pepper

TOPPING

- 3½ oz/100 g canned anchovy fillets
- 12 green pitted olives
- 1 tsp dried marjoram

2

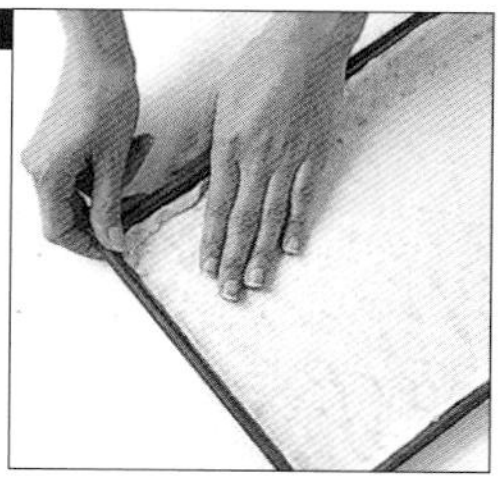
3

5

1 Lightly grease an edged cookie sheet. Heat the oil in a large pan. Cook the onions and garlic over low heat for about 30 minutes, stirring occasionally.

2 Add the sugar and red wine vinegar to the pan and season with plenty of salt and pepper.

3 On a lightly floured counter, roll out the pie dough to a rectangle measuring about 13 x 9 inches/33 x 23 cm. Carefully transfer the dough rectangle to the prepared cookie sheet, pushing the dough well into the corners.

4 Spread the onion mixture evenly over the dough.

5 Arrange the anchovy fillets in a criss-cross pattern on top, dot with the green olives, then sprinkle with the dried marjoram.

6 Bake in a preheated oven, 425°F/220°C, for about 20–25 minutes until the pissaladière is lightly golden. Serve piping hot, straight from the oven.

VARIATION

Cut the pissaladière into squares or triangles for easy finger food at a party or barbecue grill.

Creamy Ham Pizzas

This traditional recipe uses tart shells and Béchamel Sauce to make a type of savory flan. Grating the pie dough gives it a lovely nutty texture.

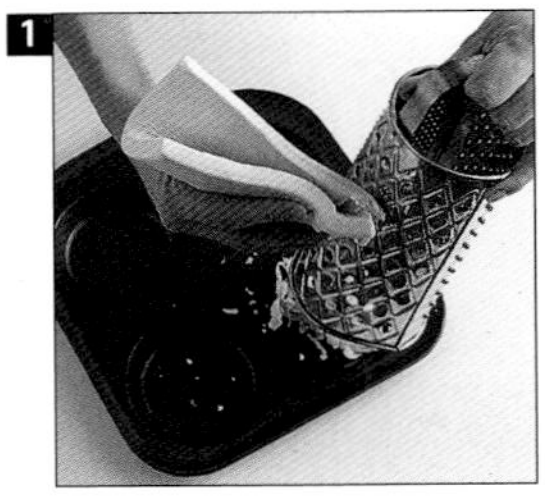

NUTRITIONAL INFORMATION

Calories	628	Sugars	5g
Protein	19g	Fat	47g
Carbohydrate	35g	Saturates	16g

20 mins

40 mins

SERVES 4

INGREDIENTS

- 9 oz/250 g flaky pie dough, well chilled
- 3 tbsp butter
- 1 red onion, chopped
- 1 garlic clove, chopped
- ⅓ cup white bread flour
- 1¼ cups milk
- scant ⅔ cup finely grated Parmesan cheese, plus extra for sprinkling
- 2 eggs, hard-cooked, cut into quarters
- 3½ oz/100 g Italian pork sausage, such as feline salame, cut into strips
- salt and pepper
- fresh thyme sprigs, to garnish

1 Fold the pie dough in half and grate it into 4 individual tart pans, each measuring 4 inches/10 cm across. Using a floured fork, gently press the dough flakes down so they are even and there are no holes, and so that it comes up the sides of the pans.

2 Line with foil and bake blind in a preheated oven, 425°F/220°C, for 10 minutes. Reduce the heat to 400°F/200°C, remove the foil, and cook for 15 minutes or until golden and set.

3 Heat the butter in a skillet. Add the onion and garlic and cook for 5–6 minutes or until softened.

4 Add the flour, stirring well to coat the onions. Gradually stir in the milk to make a thick sauce.

5 Season the sauce with salt and pepper to taste and then stir in the Parmesan cheese. Do not reheat once the cheese has been added or the sauce will become too stringy.

6 Spread the sauce evenly over the tart shells. Decorate with the egg and strips of sausage.

7 Sprinkle with a little extra Parmesan cheese, return to the oven, and bake for 5 minutes just to heat through.

8 Serve immediately, garnished with sprigs of fresh thyme.

COOK'S TIP

This pizza is just as good cold, but do not prepare it too far in advance as the tart shells will turn soggy.

Ham & Cheese Lattice Pies

These pretty lattice pies are equally delicious served hot or cold. They make a good picnic food served with salad.

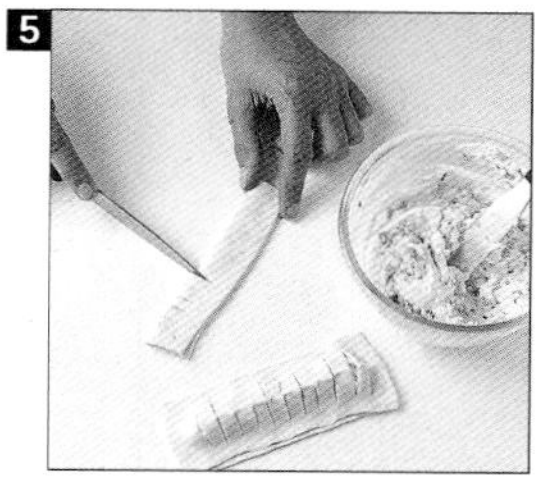

NUTRITIONAL INFORMATION

Calories	257	Sugars	1g
Protein	8g	Fat	19g
Carbohydrate	16g	Saturates	5g

45 mins

20 mins

SERVES 6

INGREDIENTS

- butter, for greasing
- 9 oz/250 g ready-made puff pie dough, thawed if frozen
- generous ⅓ cup finely chopped ham
- 4½ oz/125 g full fat soft cheese
- 2 tbsp chopped fresh chives
- 1 egg, beaten
- scant ½ cup freshly grated Parmesan cheese
- pepper

1 Lightly grease 2 cookie sheets with butter. Roll out the pie dough thinly on a lightly floured counter. Cut out 12 rectangles measuring 6 x 2 inches/ 15 x 5 cm.

2 Place the rectangles on the prepared cookie sheets and chill in the refrigerator for 30 minutes.

3 Meanwhile, combine the ham, cheese, and chives in a small bowl. Season with pepper to taste.

4 Divide the ham, cheese, and chives mixture between 6 of the rectangles. Spread the mixture along the center of each, leaving a 1-inch/2.5-cm border around each one. Brush the border with the beaten egg.

5 To make the lattice pattern, fold the remaining rectangles lengthwise. Leaving a 1-inch/2.5-cm border, cut vertical lines across the folded edge.

6 Unfold the latticed rectangles and place them over the rectangles topped with the ham and cheese mixture on the cookie sheets. Seal the dough edges well and lightly sprinkle with the grated Parmesan cheese.

7 Bake in a preheated oven, 350°F/ 180°C, for 15–20 minutes. Serve at once or let cool and serve cold.

COOK'S TIP

These pies can be made in advance, frozen uncooked and baked fresh when required.

Savory Meals

This chapter presents a mouthwatering array of savory dishes to tempt any palate, including pies, pastries, tarts, and flans, as well as a variety of delicious savory bakes.

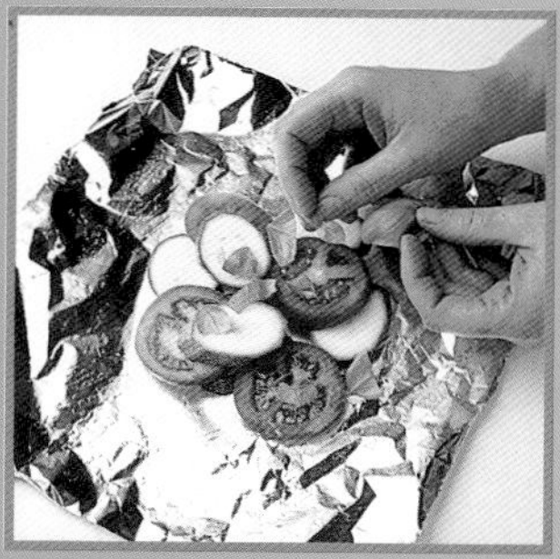

The choice is wide, including Cheese Pudding, Red Onion Tart Tatin, and Asparagus & Cheese Tart. Fish fans can choose from a wide menu, including Smoky Fish Pie, Baked Scallops & Pasta, and Fillets of Snapper & Pasta. Meat and poultry dishes include Creamed Strips of Sirloin, Layered Meat Loaf, and Italian Chicken Parcels.

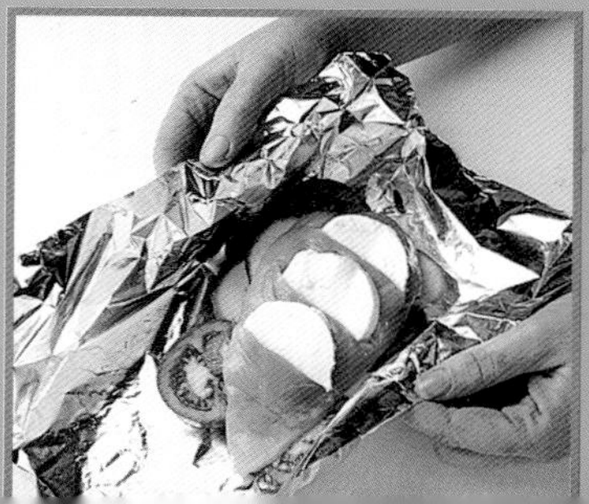

Cheese Pudding

This savory cheese pudding is very like a soufflé in texture, but it does not rise like a traditional soufflé.

NUTRITIONAL INFORMATION

Calories 483	Sugars 3g
Protein 15g	Fat 39g
Carbohydrate ...20g	Saturates 24g

10 mins   45 mins

SERVES 4

INGREDIENTS

- butter, for greasing
- 2½ cups fresh white bread crumbs
- 1 cup grated Swiss cheese
- ⅔ cup lukewarm milk
- ½ cup butter, melted
- 2 eggs, separated
- salt and pepper
- 2 tbsp chopped fresh parsley
- salad greens, to serve (optional)

1 Grease a 4-cup/1-litre ovenproof dish with a little butter.

2 Place the bread crumbs and cheese in a bowl and mix.

3 Pour the milk over the cheese and bread crumb mixture and stir to mix. Add the melted butter, egg yolks, salt and pepper to taste, and parsley. Mix well.

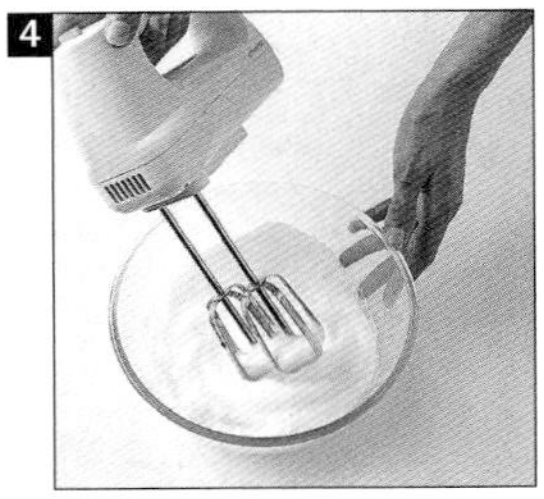

4 Whisk the egg whites until they form soft peaks. Gently fold the cheese mixture into the egg whites, using a figure-eight movement.

5 Transfer the mixture to the prepared ovenproof dish and bake the pudding in a preheated oven, 375°F/190°C, for about 45 minutes or until golden and slightly risen, and a toothpick inserted into the middle of the pudding comes out clean.

6 Serve the cheese pudding at once, straight from the dish, with salad greens, if desired.

COOK'S TIP

For a slightly healthier alternative, make the cheese pudding with fresh whole-wheat bread crumbs instead of white bread crumbs.

Red Onion Tart Tatin

Ready-made puff pie dough works extremely well in this recipe and means you create a tasty savory tart in very little time.

NUTRITIONAL INFORMATION

Calories	398	Sugars	14g
Protein	5g	Fat	25g
Carbohydrate	40g	Saturates	7g

15 mins 50 mins

SERVES 4

INGREDIENTS

- 4 tbsp butter
- 2 tbsp sugar
- 1 lb 2 oz/500 g red onions, peeled and quartered
- 3 tbsp red wine vinegar
- 2 tbsp fresh thyme leaves
- 8 oz/250 g ready-made puff pie dough, thawed if frozen
- salt and pepper

1 Place the butter and sugar in a 9-inch/23-cm ovenproof skillet and cook over medium heat until the butter has melted and the sugar has dissolved.

2 Add the red onion quarters and sweat them over low heat for 10–15 minutes until golden, stirring occasionally.

3 Add the red wine vinegar and thyme leaves to the skillet and increase the heat. Season with salt and pepper to taste, then simmer over medium heat until the liquid has reduced and the red onion pieces are coated in the buttery sauce and are beginning to caramelize.

4 On a lightly floured counter, roll out the pie dough into a circle slightly larger than the skillet.

2

3

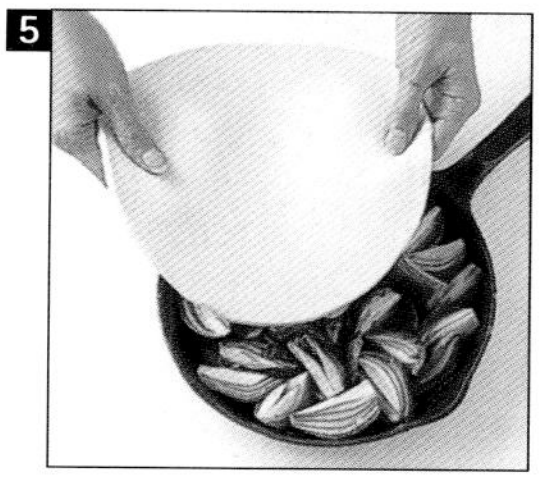

5

5 Place the pie dough over the onion mixture in the skillet and gently press down, carefully tucking in the edges to seal the dough.

6 Bake in a preheated oven, 350°F/180°C, for 20–25 minutes. Remove the skillet from the oven and let the tart stand for 10 minutes.

7 To turn out, place a serving plate over the skillet and, holding them together, carefully invert them both so that the pie dough becomes the base of the tart. Serve the tart warm.

VARIATION

Replace the red onions with shallots, leaving them whole, if you prefer.

Asparagus & Cheese Tart

Fresh asparagus is now readily available all year round, so you can make this tasty and attractive supper dish at any time.

NUTRITIONAL INFORMATION

Calories	360	Sugars	4g
Protein	11g	Fat	25g
Carbohydrate	23g	Saturates	10g

5–10 mins   50 mins

SERVES 6

INGREDIENTS

- 9 oz/250 g ready-made shortcrust pie dough, thawed if frozen
- 9 oz/250 g asparagus
- 1 tbsp vegetable oil
- 1 red onion, finely chopped
- 2 tbsp chopped hazelnuts
- 7 oz/200 g goat cheese
- 2 eggs, beaten
- 4 tbsp light cream
- salt and pepper

1 On a lightly floured counter, roll out the pie dough and line a 9½-inch/24-cm loose-bottomed tart pan. Prick the bottom of the tart shell with a fork and chill in the refrigerator for 30 minutes.

2

4

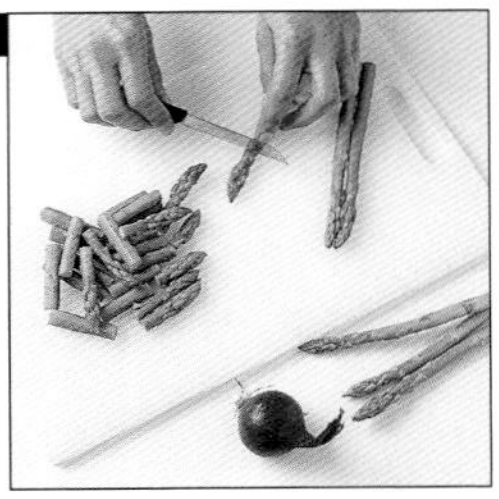

6

2 Line the tart shell with foil and baking beans and bake in a preheated oven, 375°F/190°C, for about 15 minutes.

3 Remove the foil and baking beans and cook for a further 15 minutes.

4 Cook the asparagus in boiling water for 2–3 minutes, drain, and cut into bite-size pieces.

5 Heat the oil in a small skillet. Add the onion and cook over low heat, stirring occasionally for about 5 minutes until soft and lightly golden. Spoon the asparagus, onion, and hazelnuts into the prepared tart shell, spreading them out evenly.

6 Beat together the cheese, eggs, and cream until smooth, or process in a blender until smooth. Season well with salt and pepper, then pour the mixture over the asparagus, onion, and hazelnuts.

7 Bake the tart for 15–20 minutes or until the cheese filling is just set. Serve warm or cold.

VARIATION

Omit the hazelnuts and sprinkle Parmesan cheese over the top of the tart just before cooking in the oven, if you prefer.

Celery & Onion Pies

These savoury celery and onion pies are quite irresistible, so it is probably a good idea to bake a double batch!

NUTRITIONAL INFORMATION

Calories	102	Sugars	1g
Protein	2g	Fat	6g
Carbohydrate	10g	Saturates	4g

1¼ hrs

15–20 mins

MAKES 12

INGREDIENTS

PIE DOUGH

- 1 cup all-purpose flour
- ½ tsp salt
- 2 tbsp butter, cut into small pieces
- ¼ cup grated sharp cheese
- 3-4 tbsp water

FILLING

- 2 tbsp butter
- 1 cup finely chopped celery
- 2 garlic cloves, crushed
- 1 small onion, finely chopped
- 1 tbsp all-purpose flour
- ¼ cup milk
- salt
- pinch of cayenne pepper

2

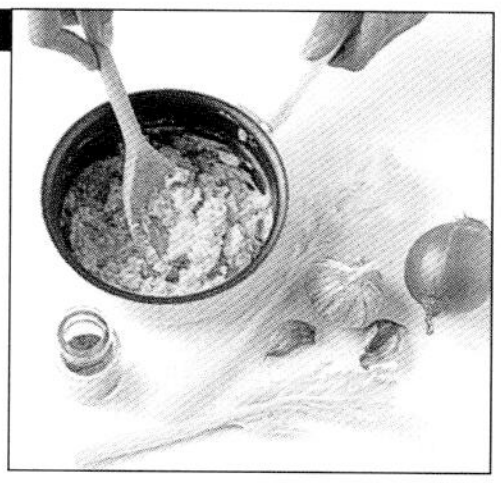

5

5

1 To make the filling, melt the butter in a heavy-based pan. Add the celery, garlic, and onion and fry over low heat, stirring occasionally, for about 5 minutes or until softened.

2 Reduce the heat and stir in the flour, then the milk. Bring back to a simmer, then heat gently until the mixture is thick, stirring frequently. Season with salt and cayenne pepper to taste and let cool.

3 To make the pie dough, strain the flour and salt into a mixing bowl and rub in the butter with your fingertips. Stir the cheese into the mixture, together with the water, and mix to form a dough.

4 Roll out three-quarters of the dough on a lightly floured kitchen counter. Using a 2½-inch/6-cm cookie cutter, cut out 12 circles. Line a patty pan with the dough circles.

5 Divide the filling among the dough circles. Roll out the remaining dough and, using a 2-inch/5-cm cutter, cut out 12 circles. Place the smaller circles on top of the pie filling and seal well. Make a slit in each pie and chill for 30 minutes.

6 Bake in a preheated oven, 425°F/220°C, for 15-20 minutes. Let cool in the pan for about 10 minutes before turning out. Serve warm.

Onion Tart

This crisp tart shell is filled with succulent, caramelized onions and cheese and baked until it melts in the mouth.

NUTRITIONAL INFORMATION

Calories	394	Sugars	7g
Protein	11g	Fat	27g
Carbohydrate	29g	Saturates	12g

5 mins

55 mins

SERVES 4

INGREDIENTS

- 9 oz/250 g ready-made shortcrust pie dough, thawed if frozen
- 3 tbsp butter
- generous ⅓ cup chopped bacon
- 1lb 9 oz/700 g onions, peeled and thinly sliced
- 2 eggs, beaten
- scant ⅔ cup freshly grated Parmesan cheese
- 1 tsp dried sage
- salt and pepper

1 Roll out the pie dough on a lightly floured counter and line a 9½-inch/24-cm loose-bottomed tart pan.

2 Prick the base of the tart shell with a fork and chill in the refrigerator for 30 minutes.

3 Meanwhile, heat the butter in a heavy-based pan, add the chopped bacon and sliced onions, and sweat them over low heat for about 25 minutes until tender. If the onion slices start to brown, add 1 tablespoon of water to the pan.

4 Add the beaten eggs to the onion mixture and stir in the grated cheese and sage. Season with salt and pepper to taste.

5 Spoon the onion mixture into the prepared tart shell, spreading it out evenly over the base.

6 Bake in a preheated oven, 350°F/180°C, for 20–30 minutes or until the filling has just set and the pastry is golden brown.

7 Let the tart cool slightly in the pan, then serve it warm or cold.

2

3

5

VARIATION

For a vegetarian version of this tart, replace the bacon with the same amount of chopped mushrooms.

Pizza Margherita

Pizza means "pie" in Italian. The fresh bread dough is not difficult to make but it does take a little time.

NUTRITIONAL INFORMATION

Calories	456	Sugars	7g
Protein	16g	Fat	13g
Carbohydrate	74g	Saturates	5g

1 hr

45 mins

SERVES 4

INGREDIENTS

½ oz/15 g fresh yeast
½ tsp sugar
6 tbsp lukewarm water
1 tbsp olive oil
1½ cups all-purpose flour
1 tsp salt

TOPPING

14 oz/400 g canned tomatoes, chopped
2 garlic cloves, crushed
2 tsp dried basil
1 tbsp olive oil
2 tbsp tomato paste
3½ oz/100 g mozzarella cheese, chopped
scant ½ cup freshly grated Parmesan cheese
salt and pepper

1 Combine the yeast, sugar, and 4 tablespoons of the water. Stand in a warm place for 15 minutes until frothy.

2 Mix the flour with the salt and make a well in the center. Add the oil, the yeast mixture, and the remaining water. Using a wooden spoon, mix to form a smooth dough.

1
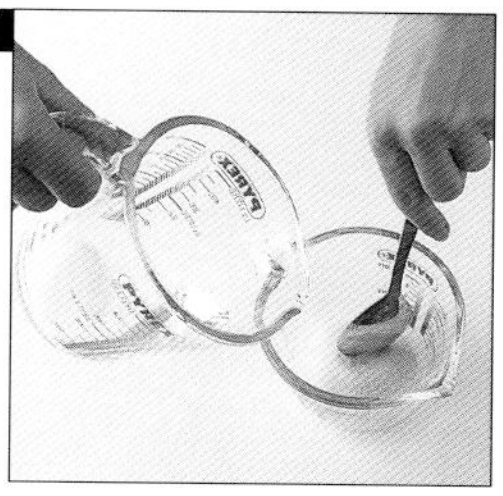

2

3
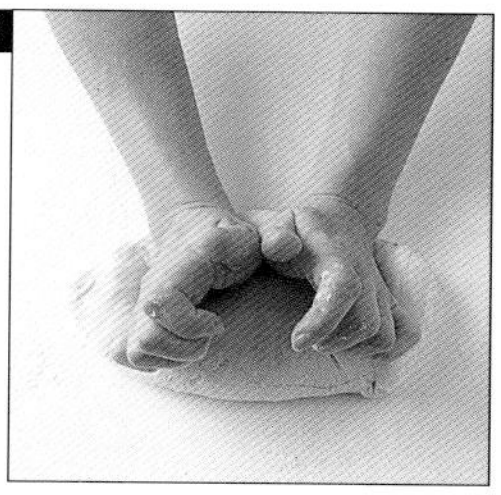

3 Turn the dough out onto a floured surface and knead for 4–5 minutes or until smooth.

4 Return the dough to the bowl, cover with an oiled sheet of plastic wrap, and let rise for 30 minutes or until doubled in size.

5 Knead the dough for 2 minutes. Stretch it with your hands, then place it on an oiled cookie sheet, pushing out the edges until even. The dough should be no more than ¼ inch/5 mm thick because it will rise during cooking.

6 To make the topping, place the tomatoes, garlic, dried basil, olive oil, and salt and pepper to taste in a large skillet and simmer over low heat for about 20 minutes or until the sauce has thickened. Stir in the tomato paste and let cool slightly.

7 Spread the topping evenly over the pizza dough almost to the edge. Top with the chopped mozzarella and grated Parmesan cheese and bake in a preheated oven, 400°F/200°C, for 20–25 minutes until the topping is golden and bubbling. Serve hot.

Gorgonzola & Pumpkin Pizza

Blue Gorgonzola cheese and juicy pears combine to give a colorful pizza. The whole-wheat base adds a nutty flavor and texture.

NUTRITIONAL INFORMATION

Calories	470	Sugars	5g
Protein	17g	Fat	15g
Carbohydrate	72g	Saturates	6g

1¼ hrs — 35 mins

SERVES 4

INGREDIENTS

PIZZA DOUGH

- ¼ oz/7 g dried yeast
- 1 tsp sugar
- 1 cup lukewarm water
- 1¼ cups whole-wheat all-purpose flour
- 1¼ cups white bread flour
- 1 tsp salt
- 1 tbsp olive oil

TOPPING

- 14 oz/400 g pumpkin or squash, peeled and cubed
- 1 tbsp olive oil
- 1 pear, cored, peeled, and sliced
- 3½ oz/100 g Gorgonzola cheese
- 1 sprig fresh rosemary, to garnish

1 Place the yeast and sugar in a pitcher and mix with 4 tablespoons of the lukewarm water. Let the yeast mixture stand in a warm place for 15 minutes or until frothy.

2 Combine both of the flours with the salt and make a well in the center. Add the oil, the yeast mixture, and the remaining water. Using a wooden spoon, mix to form a dough.

3 Turn the dough out onto a floured counter and knead for 4–5 minutes or until smooth.

4 Return the dough to the bowl, cover with an oiled sheet of plastic wrap, and let rise for 30 minutes or until doubled in size.

5 Remove the dough from the bowl. Knead the dough for 2 minutes. Using a rolling pin, roll out the dough to form a long oval shape, then place it on an oiled cookie sheet, pushing out the edges until even. The dough should be no more than ¼ inch/5 mm thick because it will rise during cooking.

6 To make the topping, place the pumpkin in a shallow roasting pan. Drizzle with the olive oil and cook under a preheated broiler for 20 minutes or until soft and lightly golden.

7 Top the dough with the pear and the pumpkin, brushing with the oil from the pan. Crumble over the Gorgonzola. Bake in a preheated oven, 400°F/200°C, for 15 minutes or until the base is golden. Garnish with rosemary.

5

7

7

Tomato & Ricotta Pizza

This is a traditional dish from the Calabrian Mountains in southern Italy, where it is made with naturally sun-dried tomatoes and ricotta cheese.

NUTRITIONAL INFORMATION

Calories	274	Sugars	4g
Protein	8g	Fat	11g
Carbohydrate	38g	Saturates	4g

1¼ hrs — 30 mins

SERVES 4

INGREDIENTS

1 quantity Basic Pizza Dough (see page 14)

TOPPING

4 tbsp sun-dried tomato paste

⅔ cup ricotta cheese

10 sun-dried tomatoes in oil, drained

1 tbsp fresh thyme

salt and pepper

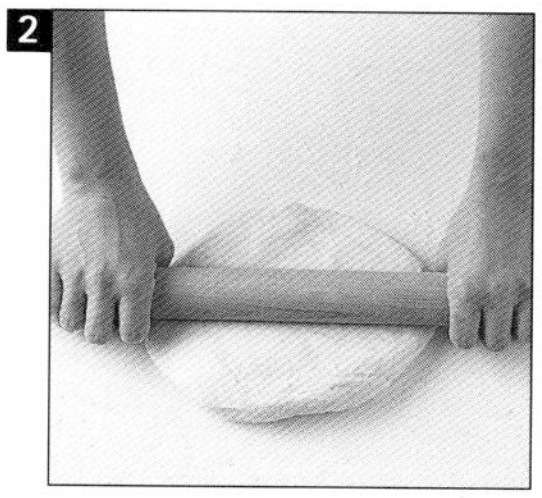

1 Knead the Basic Pizza Dough on a lightly floured counter for 2 minutes.

2 Using a rolling pin, roll out the dough to form a circle, then carefully transfer it to an oiled cookie sheet, pushing out the edges until even. The dough should be no more than about ¼ inch/5 mm thick because it will rise during cooking.

3 Spread the sun-dried tomato paste evenly over the dough, then add spoonfuls of ricotta cheese, dotting them over the pizza.

8 Cut the sun-dried tomatoes into strips and arrange these on top of the pizza.

9 Sprinkle the thyme over the top of the pizza and season with salt and pepper to taste. Bake in a preheated oven, 400°F/200°C, for 30 minutes or until piping hot and the crust is golden. Serve the pizza at once.

COOK'S TIP

Sun-dried tomatoes are also available in packets. Soak them in a small bowl of hot water until softened before using. You can use the tomato-flavored water for stocks and soups.

Mushroom Pizza

Juicy mushrooms and stringy mozzarella top this tomato-based pizza. Use exotic mushrooms or a combination of exotic and cultivated mushrooms.

NUTRITIONAL INFORMATION

Calories	302	Sugars	7g
Protein	10g	Fat	12g
Carbohydrate	41g	Saturates	4g

1¼ hrs — 45 mins

SERVES 4

INGREDIENTS

1 quantity Basic Pizza Dough (see page 14)

TOPPING

- 7 oz/200 g mushrooms
- 14 oz/400 g canned chopped tomatoes
- 2 garlic cloves, crushed
- 1 tsp dried basil
- 1 tbsp olive oil
- 2 tbsp tomato paste
- 1½ cups grated mozzarella cheese
- salt and pepper
- basil leaves, to garnish

3

4

4

1 Knead the Basic Pizza Dough on a lightly floured counter for 2 minutes.

2 Roll out the dough to form an oval or a circular shape, then place it on an oiled cookie sheet, pushing out the edges until even. The dough should be no more than ¼ inch/5 mm thick because it will rise during cooking.

3 Using a sharp knife, cut the mushrooms into slices.

4 To make the topping, place the tomatoes, garlic, dried basil, olive oil, and salt and pepper in a large pan and simmer for 20 minutes or until the sauce has thickened. Stir in the tomato paste and let cool slightly.

5 Spread the sauce over the pizza dough, top with the mushrooms, and scatter over the mozzarella. Bake in a preheated oven, 400°F/200°C, for 25 minutes. Garnish with basil leaves.

COOK'S TIP

To intensify the mushroom flavor, you could add a few dried porcini mushrooms, as they have a very concentrated flavour. Soak them in hot water before use. They are expensive, but you will need only a few.

Onion, Ham, & Cheese Pizza

This pizza is a favorite of the Romans. It is slightly unusual because the topping is made without a tomato sauce base.

NUTRITIONAL INFORMATION

Calories	333	Sugars	8g
Protein	12g	Fat	14g
Carbohydrate	43g	Saturates	4g

1 hr — 40 mins

SERVES 4

INGREDIENTS

1 quantity Basic Pizza Dough (see page 14)

TOPPING

- 2 tbsp olive oil
- 9 oz/250 g onions, sliced into rings
- 2 garlic cloves, crushed
- 1 red bell pepper, diced
- 3½ oz/100 g prosciutto, cut into strips
- 3½ oz/100 g mozzarella cheese, sliced
- 2 tbsp fresh rosemary, stalks removed, and coarsely chopped

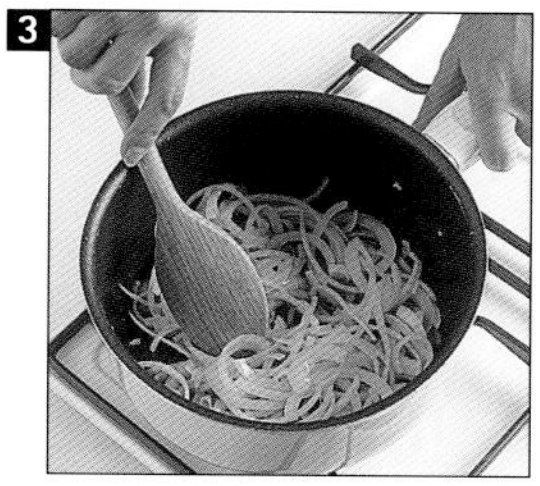

1 Knead the Basic Pizza Dough on a lightly floured counter for 2 minutes.

2 Roll out the dough to form a square shape, then carefully transfer it to an oiled cookie sheet, pushing out the edges until even. The dough should be no more than ¼ inch/5 mm thick because it will rise during cooking.

3 To make the topping, heat the oil in a pan. Add the onions and garlic and cook for 3 minutes. Add the bell pepper and cook for 2 minutes.

4 Cover the pan and cook the vegetables over low heat for about 10 minutes, stirring occasionally, until the onions are slightly caramelized. Remove the pan from the heat and let cool slightly.

5 Spread the topping evenly over the pizza dough almost to the edge. Arrange the strips of prosciutto, mozzarella slices, and rosemary over the top.

6 Bake in a preheated oven, 400°F/200°C, for 20–25 minutes. Serve hot.

COOK'S TIP

Prosciutto is an Italian, dry-cured, raw ham, said by many to be the best in the world. Other famous varieties of prosciutto include San Daniele and Veneto. This pizza would also be delicious made with Virginian Smithfield ham.

Tomato Sauce & Bell Peppers

This pizza is made with a dough base flavored with cheese and topped with a delicious tomato sauce and roasted bell peppers.

NUTRITIONAL INFORMATION

Calories	611	Sugars	8g
Protein	14g	Fat	38g
Carbohydrate	56g	Saturates	21g

1½ hrs

55 mins

SERVES 4

INGREDIENTS

- generous 1½ cups all-purpose flour
- 1 cup butter, diced
- ½ tsp salt
- scant ½ cup dried Parmesan cheese
- 1 egg, beaten
- 2 tbsp water
- 2 tbsp olive oil
- 1 large onion, finely chopped
- 1 garlic clove, chopped
- 14 oz/400 g canned chopped tomatoes
- 4 tbsp concentrated tomato paste
- 1 red bell pepper, halved
- 5 sprigs fresh thyme, stalks removed
- 6 black olives, pitted, and halved
- ⅓ cup freshly grated Parmesan cheese

1

1

3

1 Strain the flour into a bowl. Rub in the butter with your fingertips until the mixture resembles bread crumbs. Stir in the salt and dried Parmesan. Mix in the egg and 1 tablespoon of the water with a round-bladed knife. Add more water if necessary to make a soft dough. Cover with plastic wrap and chill for 30 minutes.

2 Meanwhile, heat the oil in a skillet and cook the onions and garlic for about 5 minutes or until golden. Add the tomatoes and cook for 8–10 minutes. Stir in the tomato paste.

3 Place the bell pepper, skin side up, on a cookie sheet and cook under a preheated broiler for 15 minutes until charred. Place in a plastic bag and let sweat for 10 minutes. Peel off the skin and slice the flesh into thin strips.

4 Roll out the dough to fit a 9-inch/23-cm loose-bottomed fluted tart pan. Line with foil and bake in a preheated oven, 400°F/200°C, for 10 minutes or until just set. Remove the foil and bake for a further 5 minutes until lightly golden. Let cool slightly.

5 Spoon the tomato sauce evenly over the dough and top with the bell pepper strips, thyme, olives, and fresh Parmesan. Return to the oven for 15 minutes or until the dough is crisp. Serve warm or cold.

Green Easter Pie

This traditional Easter risotto pie is from Piedmont in northern Italy. Serve it warm or chilled in slices.

NUTRITIONAL INFORMATION

Calories	392	Sugars	3g
Protein	17g	Fat	17g
Carbohydrate	41g	Saturates	5g

25 mins — 50 mins

SERVES 4

INGREDIENTS

- butter for greasing
- 3 oz/85 g arugula (about 1½ bunches)
- 2 tbsp olive oil
- 1 onion, chopped
- 2 garlic cloves, chopped
- 7 oz/200 g risotto rice
- scant 3 cups hot chicken or vegetable bouillon
- scant ½ cup white wine
- scant ⅔ cup freshly grated Parmesan cheese
- 1 cup frozen peas, thawed
- 2 tomatoes, diced
- 4 eggs, beaten
- 3 tbsp chopped fresh marjoram
- 1 cup fresh bread crumbs
- salt and pepper

1 Lightly grease a 9-inch/23-cm deep cake pan with butter and line the base with baking parchment. Using a sharp knife, coarsely chop the arugula, then set aside.

2 Heat the oil in a large skillet. Add the onion and garlic and cook over low heat for 4–5 minutes or until softened.

3 Add the rice to the mixture in the skillet, mix well to combine, then begin adding the bouillon, a ladleful at a time. Wait until all of the bouillon has been absorbed before adding another ladleful of liquid.

4 Continue to cook the mixture, adding the wine, until the rice is tender. This will take at least 15 minutes.

5 Stir in the grated Parmesan cheese, peas, arugula, tomatoes, eggs, and 2 tablespoons of the marjoram. Season to taste with salt and pepper.

6 Spoon the risotto into the prepared pan and level the surface by pressing down with the back of a wooden spoon.

7 Top with the bread crumbs and the remaining marjoram.

8 Bake in a preheated oven, 350°F/180°C, for 30 minutes or until set. Cut into slices and serve immediately.

2

6

7

Spinach & Ricotta Pie

This puff pastry pie looks extremely impressive, but it is actually fairly easy to make. Serve it hot or cold.

NUTRITIONAL INFORMATION

Calories	545	Sugars	3g
Protein	19g	Fat	42g
Carbohydrate	25g	Saturates	13g

25 mins 50 mins

SERVES 4

INGREDIENTS

- 8 oz/225 g spinach
- ¼ cup pine nuts
- ½ cup ricotta cheese
- 2 large eggs, beaten
- scant ½ cup ground almonds
- ½ cup freshly grated Parmesan cheese
- 9 oz puff pie dough, thawed if frozen
- 1 small egg, beaten

1 Rinse the spinach, place in a large pan with just the water clinging to the leaves after washing. Cook over a low heat for 4–5 minutes until wilted. Drain thoroughly. When the spinach is cool enough to handle, squeeze out the excess liquid with your hands.

2 Place the pine nuts on a cookie sheet and lightly toast under a preheated broiler for 2–3 minutes or until golden.

3 Place the ricotta, spinach, and eggs in a bowl and mix together. Add the pine nuts, beat well, then stir in the ground almonds and Parmesan cheese.

4 Roll out the puff pie dough on a lightly floured counter and make 2 squares 8 inches/20 cm wide. Trim the edges, reserving the pastry trimmings.

3

4
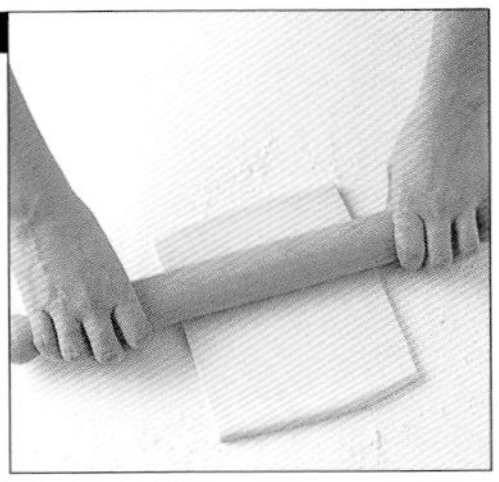

6
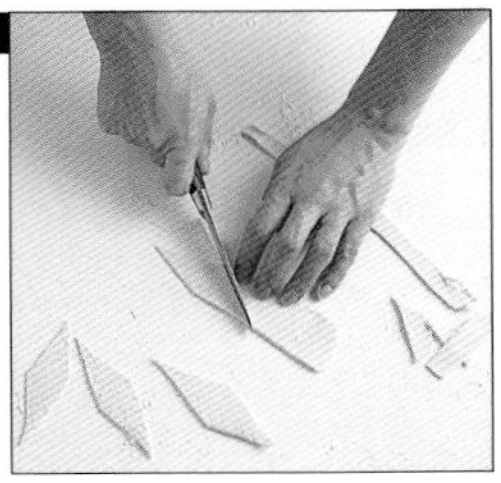

5 Place 1 dough square on a cookie sheet. Spoon the spinach mixture on top, keeping within ½ inch/1 cm of the edge of the square. Brush the edges with beaten egg and place the second square over the top.

6 Using a round-bladed knife, press the edges together by tapping along the sealed edge. Use the pie dough trimmings to make a few leaves to decorate the pie.

7 Brush the pie with the beaten egg and bake in a preheated oven, 425°F/220°C, for 10 minutes. Reduce the oven temperature to 375°F/190°C and bake for a further 25–30 minutes. Serve hot.

COOK'S TIP

Spinach must be washed very thoroughly in several changes of water to get rid of the grit and soil that can be trapped in it. Cut off any thick central ribs.

Spinach & Mushroom Lasagna

Always check the seasoning of vegetables—you can always add a little more to a recipe, but you cannot take it out once it has been added.

NUTRITIONAL INFORMATION

Calories	720	Sugars	9g
Protein	31g	Fat	52g
Carbohydrate	36g	Saturates	32g

20 mins — 40 mins

SERVES 4

INGREDIENTS

- ½ cup butter, plus extra for greasing
- 2 garlic cloves, finely chopped
- 4 oz/115 g shallots
- 8 oz/225 g exotic mushrooms, such as chanterelles
- 1 lb/450 g spinach, cooked, drained, and finely chopped
- 2 cups grated Cheddar cheese
- ¼ tsp freshly grated nutmeg
- 1 tsp chopped fresh basil
- scant ½ cup all-purpose flour
- 2½ cups hot milk
- ⅔ cup grated mellow hard cheese
- 8 sheets pre-cooked lasagna
- salt and pepper

1 Lightly grease a large ovenproof dish with a little butter and set aside until required.

2 Melt 4 tablespoons of the butter in a skillet. Add the garlic, shallots, and exotic mushrooms and fry over low heat, stirring frequently, for 3 minutes. Stir in the spinach, Cheddar cheese, nutmeg, and basil. Season with salt and pepper to taste and set aside.

3 Melt the remaining butter in another skillet over low heat. Add the flour and cook, stirring constantly, for 1 minute. Gradually stir in the hot milk, whisking constantly until smooth. Stir in ¼ cup/25 g of the mellow hard cheese and season to taste with salt and pepper.

4 Spread half of the mushroom and spinach mixture over the bottom of the prepared dish. Cover with a layer of lasagna and then with half of the cheese sauce. Repeat the layering process and sprinkle over the remaining mellow hard cheese.

5 Bake in a preheated oven, at 400°F/200°C, for about 30 minutes or until the topping is golden brown and bubbling. Serve hot straight from the dish.

2

2

4

VARIATION

You could substitute 4 bell peppers for the spinach. Roast in a preheated oven, at 400°F/200°C, for 20 minutes. Rub off the skins under cold water, seed, and chop before using.

Vegetable Ravioli

It is important not to overcook the vegetable filling or it will become sloppy and unexciting, instead of firm to the bite and delicious.

Calories 622	Sugars 10g
Protein 12g	Fat 40g
Carbohydrate ...58g	Saturates 6g

1½ hrs — 55 mins

SERVES 4

INGREDIENTS

- 1 lb/450 g Basic Pasta Dough (see page 14)
- 1 tbsp olive oil
- 6 tbsp butter
- ⅔ cup light cream
- ¾ cup freshly grated Parmesan cheese
- fresh basil sprigs, to garnish

STUFFING

- 2 large eggplants
- 3 large zucchini
- 6 large tomatoes
- 1 large green bell pepper
- 1 large red bell pepper
- 3 garlic cloves
- 1 large onion
- ½ cup olive oil
- 2 tbsp tomato paste
- ½ tsp chopped fresh basil
- salt and pepper

1 First, make the stuffing, cut the eggplants and zucchini into 1-inch/2.5 cm chunks. Put the eggplant pieces in a strainer, sprinkle liberally with salt and set aside for 20 minutes. Rinse and drain.

2 Blanch the tomatoes in boiling water for 2 minutes. Drain, peel, and chop the flesh. Core and seed the bell peppers and cut into 1-inch/2.5-cm dice. Chop the garlic and onion.

3 Heat the oil in a pan. Add the garlic and onion and fry over low heat, stirring occasionally, for 3 minutes.

4 Stir in the eggplants, zucchini, tomatoes, bell peppers, tomato paste, and basil. Season with salt and pepper to taste, cover and simmer for 20 minutes, stirring frequently.

5 Roll out the pasta dough and cut out 3-inch/7.5-cm circles with a plain cutter. Put a spoonful of the vegetable stuffing on each circle. Dampen the edges slightly and fold the pasta circles over, pressing together to seal.

6 Bring a pan of salted water to a boil. Add the ravioli and the oil, bring back to a boil, and cook for 3–4 minutes. Drain and transfer to an ovenproof dish, dotting each layer with butter. Pour over the cream and sprinkle over the Parmesan cheese. Bake in a preheated oven, 400°F/200°C, for 20 minutes. Garnish with basil and serve.

1

2

4

Vegetable Lasagna

This rich, baked pasta dish is packed full of flavorsome vegetables, tomatoes, and Italian mozzarella cheese.

NUTRITIONAL INFORMATION

Calories	510	Sugars	14g
Protein	17g	Fat	38g
Carbohydrate	28g	Saturates	14g

50 mins | 50 mins

SERVES 6

INGREDIENTS

- 2 large or 3 medium eggplants, about 1 kg/2 lb 4 oz total weight
- ½ cup olive oil
- 2 tbsp garlic and herb butter
- 1 lb/450 g zucchini, sliced
- 2 cups grated mozzarella cheese
- 2½ cups passata (strained tomatoes)
- 6 sheets pre-cooked green lasagna
- 2½ cups Béchamel Sauce (see page 92)
- ⅔ cup freshly grated Parmesan cheese
- 1 tsp dried oregano
- salt and pepper

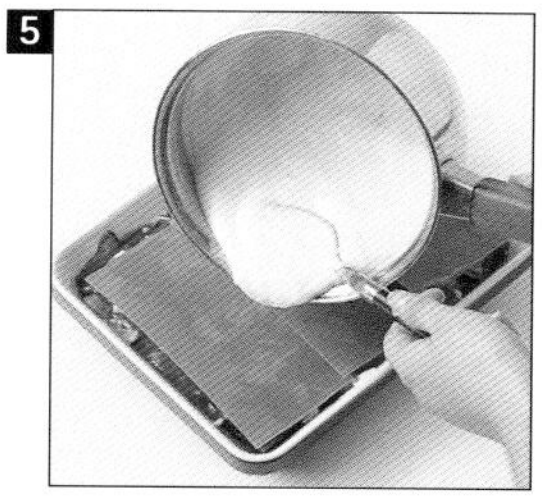

1 Thinly slice the eggplants and place in a strainer. Sprinkle with salt and set aside for 20 minutes. Rinse under cold running water and pat dry with absorbent paper towels.

2 Heat 4 tablespoons of the oil in a large skillet. Cook half of the eggplant slices over low heat for 6–7 minutes, or until golden. Drain thoroughly on paper towels. Repeat with the remaining oil and eggplant slices.

3 Melt the garlic and herb butter in the skillet. Add the zucchini and fry over medium heat, stirring frequently, for 5–6 minutes until golden brown all over. Drain thoroughly on paper towels.

4 Place half of the eggplant and half of the zucchini slices in a large ovenproof dish. Season with pepper to taste and sprinkle over half of the mozzarella cheese. Spoon over half of the passata and top with 3 sheets of lasagna. Repeat the layering process, ending with a layer of lasagna.

5 Spoon over the Béchamel Sauce and sprinkle over the grated Parmesan cheese and oregano. Put the dish on a cookie sheet and bake in a preheated oven, 425°F/220°C, for 30–35 minutes, or until golden brown. Serve immediately straight from the dish.

Vermicelli & Vegetable Tart

Lightly cooked vermicelli is pressed into a tart pan and baked with a creamy mushroom filling to create this spectacular dish.

NUTRITIONAL INFORMATION

Calories	528	Sugars	6g
Protein	15g	Fat	32g
Carbohydrate	47g	Saturates	17g

15 mins — 1 hr

SERVES 4

INGREDIENTS

- 6 tbsp butter, plus extra for greasing
- 8 oz/225 g dried vermicelli or spaghetti
- 1 tbsp olive oil
- 1 onion, chopped
- 5 oz/140 g white mushrooms
- 1 green bell pepper, cored, seeded, and sliced into thin rings
- ⅔ cup milk
- 3 eggs, lightly beaten
- 2 tbsp heavy cream
- 1 tsp dried oregano
- freshly grated nutmeg
- ¼ cup freshly grated Parmesan cheese
- salt and pepper
- tomato and basil salad, to serve (optional)

1 Generously grease an 8-inch/20-cm loose-bottomed tart pan with butter.

2 Bring a large pan of lightly salted water to a boil. Add the vermicelli and olive oil, bring back to a boil, and cook for 8–10 minutes until tender, but still firm to the bite. Drain, return to the pan, add 2 tablespoons of the butter and shake the pan to coat the pasta.

3 Press the pasta onto the bottom and around the sides of the tart pan to make a tart shell.

4 Melt the remaining butter in a skillet over a medium heat. Add the onion and cook until it is translucent.

5 Add the mushrooms and bell pepper rings to the skillet and cook, stirring constantly, for 2–3 minutes. Spoon the onion, mushroom, and bell pepper mixture into the pasta tart shell and press it evenly into the bottom.

6 Beat together the milk, eggs, and cream, stir in the oregano, and season to taste with nutmeg and pepper. Carefully pour this mixture over the vegetables and then sprinkle with the Parmesan cheese.

7 Bake the tart in a preheated oven, 350°F/180°C, for 40–45 minutes or until the filling has set.

8 Slide the tart out of the pan onto a serving platter and serve warm with a tomato and basil salad, if wished.

3

5

5

Filled Eggplants

Combined with tomatoes and mozzarella cheese, pasta makes a tasty filling for baked eggplant shells.

NUTRITIONAL INFORMATION

Calories	342	Sugars	6g
Protein	11g	Fat	16g
Carbohydrate	40g	Saturates	4g

25 mins | 55 mins

SERVES 4

INGREDIENTS

- 8 oz/225 g dried penne or other short pasta shapes
- 4 tbsp olive oil, plus extra for brushing
- 2 eggplants
- 1 large onion, chopped
- 2 garlic cloves, crushed
- 14 oz/400 g canned chopped tomatoes
- 2 tsp dried oregano
- 2 oz/55 g mozzarella cheese, thinly sliced
- ⅓ cup freshly grated Parmesan cheese
- 2 tbsp dry bread crumbs
- salt and pepper
- salad greens, to serve

1 Bring a pan of lightly salted water to a boil. Add the pasta and 1 tablespoon of the olive oil, bring back to a boil, and cook for 8–10 minutes or until tender, but still firm to the bite. Drain, return to the pan, cover, and keep warm.

2 Cut the eggplants in half lengthwise and score around the inside with a sharp knife, being careful not to pierce the shells. Scoop out the flesh with a spoon. Brush the insides of the shells with olive oil. Chop the flesh and set aside.

3 Heat the remaining oil in a skillet. Cook the onion until translucent. Add the garlic and cook for 1 minute. Add the chopped eggplant flesh and fry, stirring frequently, for 5 minutes. Add the tomatoes and oregano and season to taste with salt and pepper. Bring to a boil and simmer for 10 minutes or until thickened. Remove the skillet from the heat and stir in the pasta.

4 Brush a cookie sheet with oil and arrange the eggplant shells in a single layer. Divide half of the tomato and pasta mixture among them. Sprinkle over the mozzarella, then pile the remaining tomato and pasta mixture on top.

5 Mix the Parmesan cheese and bread crumbs and sprinkle over the top, patting it lightly into the mixture.

6 Bake in a preheated oven, 400°C/200°C, for about 25 minutes or until the topping is golden brown. Serve hot with a selection of salad greens.

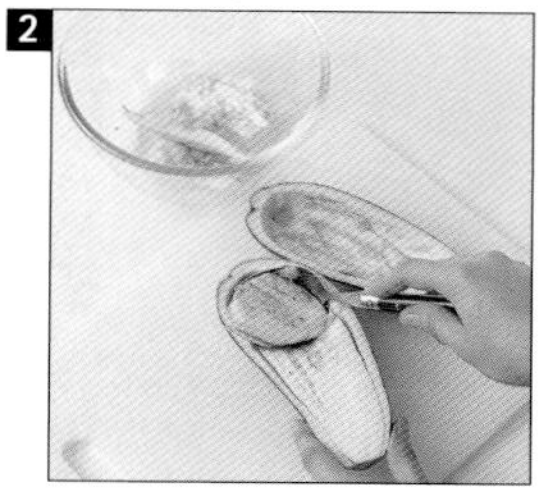
2

3

4

Macaroni & Shrimp Bake

This adaptation of an 18th-century Italian dish is baked until it is golden brown and sizzling, then cut into wedges, like a cake.

NUTRITIONAL INFORMATION

Calories	576	Sugars	6g
Protein	25g	Fat	35g
Carbohydrate	42g	Saturates	19g

20 mins — 1 hr 5 mins

SERVES 4

INGREDIENTS

- 12 oz/350 g short pasta, such as short-cut macaroni
- 1 tbsp olive oil, plus extra for brushing
- 6 tbsp butter, plus extra for greasing
- 2 small fennel bulbs, thinly sliced, leaves reserved
- 2½ cups thinly sliced mushrooms
- 6 oz/175 g shelled shrimp
- ⅔ cup freshly grated Parmesan cheese
- 2 large tomatoes, sliced
- 1 tsp dried oregano
- salt and pepper
- Béchamel Sauce (see page 92)
- cayenne pepper

1 Bring a large pan of lightly salted water to a boil. Add the pasta with 1 tablespoon of olive oil, bring back to a boil and cook for 8–10 minutes or until tender, but still firm to the bite. Drain the pasta in a strainer, return to the pan, and dot with 2 tablespoons of the butter. Shake the pan well, cover, and keep warm.

2 Melt the remaining butter in a pan over a medium heat and cook the fennel for 3–4 minutes, until it begins to soften. Stir in the mushrooms and cook, stirring constantly, for 2 minutes. Stir in the shrimp, remove the pan from the heat, and set aside until required.

3 Make the Béchamel Sauce and season with a pinch of cayenne pepper. Remove the pan from the heat and stir in the reserved vegetables and shrimp and the pasta.

4 Grease a round, shallow ovenproof dish. Pour in the pasta mixture and spread evenly. Sprinkle with the Parmesan and arrange the tomato slices in a ring around the edge of the dish. Brush the tomato with olive oil and sprinkle with the dried oregano.

5 Bake in a preheated oven, 350°F/180°C, for 25 minutes, or until golden brown. Serve hot.

Pasta & Shrimp Parcels

This is the ideal dish when you have unexpected guests because the parcels can be prepared in advance, then put in the oven when you are ready to eat.

NUTRITIONAL INFORMATION

Calories	640	Sugars	1g
Protein	50g	Fat	29g
Carbohydrate	42g	Saturates	4g

15 mins 30 mins

SERVES 4

INGREDIENTS

- 1 lb/450 g dried fettuccine pasta
- ⅔ cup Pesto Sauce (see page 15)
- 4 tsp extra virgin olive oil
- lb 10 oz/750 g jumbo shrimp, peeled and deveined
- 2 garlic cloves, crushed
- ½ cup dry white wine
- salt and pepper

1 Cut 4 squares, 12 inches/30 cm wide, out of waxed paper.

2 Bring a large pan of lightly salted water to a boil. Add the fettuccine, bring back to a boil, and cook for 2–3 minutes, until the pasta is just softened. Drain thoroughly.

3 Combine the fettuccine and half of the Pesto Sauce. Spread out the paper squares and put 1 teaspoon of olive oil in the middle of each. Divide the fettuccine between the squares, then divide the shrimp, and place on top of the fettuccine.

4 Mix together the remaining Pesto Sauce and the garlic and spoon it over the shrimp. Season each parcel with salt and black pepper and sprinkle with the white wine.

5 Dampen the edges of the waxed paper and wrap the parcels loosely, twisting the edges to seal.

6 Place the parcels on a cookie sheet and bake in a preheated oven, 400°F/200°C, for 10–15 minutes.

7 Transfer the parcels to 4 individual serving plates and serve.

COOK'S TIP

Traditionally, these parcels are designed to look like money bags. The resemblance is more effective with waxed paper rather than with foil.

Seafood Lasagna

You can use any fish and any sauce you like in this recipe: try smoked finnan haddock and whisky sauce or cod with cheese sauce.

NUTRITIONAL INFORMATION

Calories	790	Sugars	23g
Protein	55g	Fat	32g
Carbohydrate	74g	Saturates	19g

30 mins | 45 mins

SERVES 4

INGREDIENTS

- 1 lb/450 g finnan haddock, filleted, skin removed and flesh flaked
- 4 oz/115 g shrimp
- 4 oz/114 g sole fillet, skin removed and flesh sliced
- juice of 1 lemon
- 4 tbsp butter
- 3 leeks, very thinly sliced
- scant ½ cup all-purpose flour
- 2⅓ cups milk
- 2 tbsp clear honey
- 2 cups grated mozzarella cheese
- 1 lb/450 g pre-cooked lasagna
- ⅔ cup freshly grated Parmesan cheese
- pepper

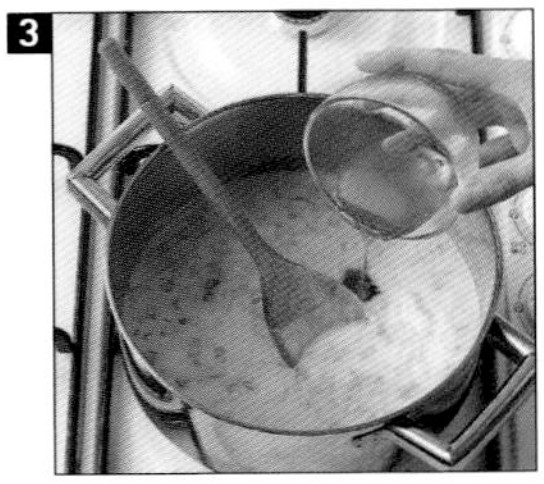

1 Put the haddock fillet, shrimp, and sole fillet into a large bowl and season with pepper and lemon juice according to taste. Set aside while you make the sauce.

2 Melt the butter in a large pan. Add the leeks and cook over low heat, stirring occasionally, for about 8 minutes until softened. Add the flour and cook, stirring constantly, for 1 minute. Gradually stir in enough milk to make a thick, creamy sauce.

3 Blend in the honey and mozzarella cheese and cook for a further 3 minutes. Remove the pan from the heat and mix in the fish and shrimp.

4 Make alternate layers of fish sauce and lasagna in an ovenproof dish, finishing with a layer of fish sauce on top. Generously sprinkle over the grated Parmesan cheese and bake in a preheated oven, 350°F/180°C, for 30 minutes. Serve immediately.

VARIATION

For a hard cider sauce, substitute 1 finely chopped shallot for the leeks, 1½ cups cider and 1½ cups heavy cream for the milk, and 1 teaspoon of mustard for the honey. For a Tuscan sauce, substitute 1 chopped fennel bulb for the leeks; omit the honey.

Seafood Pizza

Make a change from the standard pizza toppings—this dish is piled high with seafood baked with a red bell pepper and tomato sauce.

NUTRITIONAL INFORMATION

Calories	248	Sugars	7g
Protein	27g	Fat	6g
Carbohydrate	22g	Saturates	2g

25 mins

55 mins

SERVES 4

INGREDIENTS

5 oz/145 g standard pizza dough mix

4 tbsp chopped fresh dill or 2 tbsp dried dill

fresh dill, to garnish

SAUCE

1 large red bell pepper

14 oz/400 g canned chopped tomatoes with onion and herbs

3 tbsp tomato paste

salt and pepper

TOPPING

12 oz/350 g assorted cooked seafood, thawed if frozen

1 tbsp capers in brine, drained

1 oz/25 g pitted black olives in brine, drained

¼ cup grated low-fat mozzarella cheese

¼ cup freshly grated Parmesan cheese

2

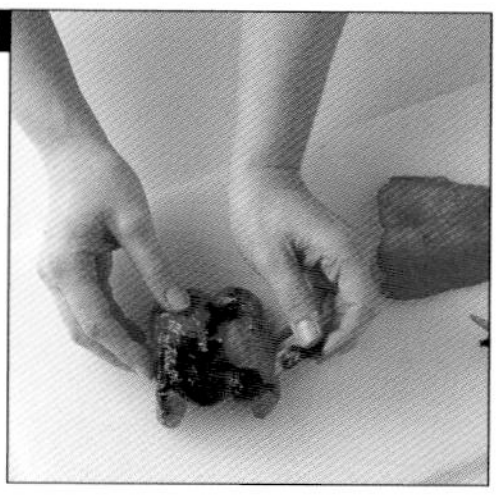

3

5

1 Place the pizza dough mix in a bowl and stir in the chopped or dried dill. Make the dough according to the instructions on the packet.

2 Press the dough into a circle measuring about 10 inches/25 cm across on a cookie sheet lined with baking parchment. Cover with a dish cloth and set aside to rise.

3 To make the sauce, halve and seed the bell pepper and arrange on a broiler rack. Cook under a preheated broiler for 8–10 minutes until softened and charred. Let cool slightly, peel off the skin, and chop the flesh.

4 Place the tomatoes and bell pepper in a heavy-based pan. Bring to a boil and simmer over low heat for 10 minutes. Stir in the tomato paste and season to taste with salt and pepper.

5 Spread the sauce evenly over the pizza dough and top with the seafood. Sprinkle over the capers and olives, top with the grated cheeses and bake in a preheated oven, 400°F/200°C, for 25–30 minutes. Garnish with sprigs of fresh dill and serve hot.

Smoky Fish Pie

This flavorsome, colorful fish pie is perfect for a light supper. The addition of smoked salmon gives it a touch of luxury.

NUTRITIONAL INFORMATION

Calories	523	Sugars	15g
Protein	58g	Fat	6g
Carbohydrate	63g	Saturates	2g

15 mins 1 hr

SERVES 4

INGREDIENTS

- 2 lb/900 g smoked haddock or cod fillets
- 2½ cups skim milk
- 2 bay leaves
- 4 oz/115 g white mushrooms, quartered
- 1 cup frozen peas
- ⅔ cup frozen corn kernels
- 4 cups diced potatoes
- 5 tbsp low-fat plain yogurt
- 4 tbsp chopped fresh parsley
- 2 oz/60 g smoked salmon, sliced into thin strips
- 3 tbsp cornstarch
- ¼ cup grated smoked cheese
- salt and pepper

COOK'S TIP

If possible, use smoked haddock or cod that has not been dyed bright yellow or artificially flavored to give the illusion of having been smoked.

1 Place the fish in a large pan and add the milk and bay leaves. Bring to a boil, cover, and then simmer gently for 5 minutes.

2 Add the mushrooms, peas, and corn, bring back to a simmer, cover, and cook for 5–7 minutes. Let cool.

3 Place the potatoes in a pan, cover with water, bring to a boil, and cook for 8 minutes. Drain well and mash with a fork or a potato masher. Stir in the yogurt and parsley and season to taste with salt and pepper. Set aside.

4 Using a perforated spoon, remove the fish from the pan. Flake the cooked fish away from the skin and place in an ovenproof gratin dish. Reserve the cooking liquid.

5 Drain the vegetables, reserving the cooking liquid, and gently stir into the fish with the salmon strips.

6 Blend a little cooking liquid into the cornstarch to make a paste. Transfer the rest of the liquid to a pan and add the paste. Heat through, stirring, until thickened. Discard the bay leaves and season to taste. Pour the sauce over the fish and vegetables and mix. Spoon over the mashed potato so that the fish is covered, sprinkle with cheese, and bake in a preheated oven, 400°F/200°C, for 25–30 minutes.

1

3

6

Shrimp Pasta Bake

This dish is ideal for a substantial supper. You can use whatever pasta you like, but the tricolor varieties will give the most colorful results.

NUTRITIONAL INFORMATION

Calories	723	Sugars	9g
Protein	56g	Fat	8g
Carbohydrate	114g	Saturates	2g

10 mins 50 mins

SERVES 4

INGREDIENTS

- 8 oz/225 g dried tricolor pasta shapes
- 1 tbsp vegetable oil
- 2½ cups sliced white mushrooms
- 1 bunch scallions, trimmed and chopped
- 14 oz/400 g canned tuna in brine, drained and flaked
- 6 oz/175 g peeled shrimp, thawed if frozen
- 2 tbsp cornstarch
- 1¾ cups skim milk
- 4 tomatoes, thinly sliced
- ½ cup fresh bread crumbs
- ¼ cup grated reduced-fat Cheddar cheese
- salt and pepper

TO SERVE

- whole-wheat bread
- fresh salad

2

3

5

1 Bring a large pan of lightly salted water to a boil. Add the pasta, bring back to a boil, and cook for 8–10 minutes until tender, but still firm to the bite. Drain well.

2 Meanwhile, heat the vegetable oil in a skillet and cook the mushrooms and all but a handful of the scallions over low heat, stirring frequently, for 4–5 minutes until softened.

3 Place the cooked pasta in a bowl and mix in the mushroom and scallion mixture, tuna, and shrimp.

4 Blend the cornstarch with a little milk to make a smooth paste. Pour the remaining milk into a pan and stir in the paste. Heat, stirring constantly, until the sauce begins to thicken. Season well with salt and pepper. Add the sauce to the pasta mixture and mix thoroughly. Transfer to an ovenproof gratin dish and place on a cookie sheet.

5 Arrange the tomato slices over the pasta and sprinkle with the bread crumbs and cheese. Bake in a preheated oven, 375°F/190°C, for 25–30 minutes until golden.

6 Serve garnished with the reserved scallions, with bread and salad.

Baked Scallops & Pasta

This is another wonderfully tempting seafood dish where the eye is delighted as much as the tastebuds.

NUTRITIONAL INFORMATION	
Calories 725	Sugars 2g
Protein 38g	Fat 48g
Carbohydrate ...38g	Saturates 25g

20 mins 30 mins

SERVES 4

INGREDIENTS

- 12 scallops
- 3 tbsp olive oil
- 3 cups small, dried whole-wheat pasta shells
- ⅔ cup fish bouillon
- 1 onion, chopped
- juice and finely grated zest of 2 lemons
- ⅔ cup heavy cream
- generous 2 cups grated Cheddar cheese
- salt and pepper
- crusty brown bread, to serve

1 Remove the scallops from their shells. Scrape off the skirt and the black intestinal thread. Reserve the white part (the flesh) and the orange part (the coral or roe). Very carefully ease the flesh and coral from the shell with a short, but very strong knife.

2 Wash the shells thoroughly and dry them well. Put the shells on a cookie sheet, sprinkle lightly with two-thirds of the olive oil, and set aside.

3 Meanwhile, bring a large pan of lightly salted water to a boil. Add the pasta shells and remaining olive oil, bring back to a boil, and cook for 8–10 minutes or until tender, but still firm to the bite. Drain well and spoon about 1 oz/25 g of pasta into each scallop shell.

4

5

5

4 Put the scallops, fish bouillon, lemon zest, and onion in an ovenproof dish and season to taste with pepper. Cover with foil and bake in a preheated oven, 350°F/180°C, for 8 minutes.

5 Remove the dish from the oven. Discard the foil and, using a perforated spoon, transfer the scallops to the prepared shells. Add 1 tablespoon of the cooking liquid to each scallop shell, together with a drizzle of lemon juice and a little heavy cream, and top with the grated cheese.

6 Increase the oven temperature to 450°F/230°C and return the scallops to the oven for a further 4 minutes.

7 Serve the scallops in their shells with crusty brown bread and butter.

Fresh Baked Sardines

Here, fresh sardines are baked with eggs, herbs, and vegetables to form a dish similar to an omelet.

NUTRITIONAL INFORMATION

Calories	690	Sugars	12g
Protein	63g	Fat	42g
Carbohydrate	17g	Saturates	15g

35 mins   20–25 mins

SERVES 4

INGREDIENTS

- 2 tbsp olive oil
- 2 large onions, sliced into rings
- 3 garlic cloves, chopped
- 2 large zucchini, cut into sticks
- 3 tbsp fresh thyme, stalks removed
- 8 sardine fillets or about 2¼ lb sardines, filleted
- 1 cup grated Parmesan cheese
- 4 eggs, beaten
- ⅔ cup milk
- salt and pepper

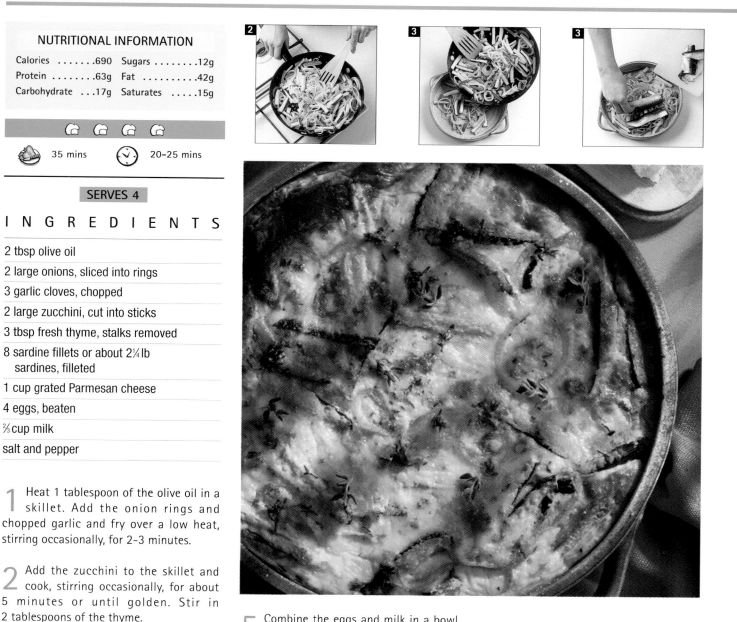

1 Heat 1 tablespoon of the olive oil in a skillet. Add the onion rings and chopped garlic and fry over a low heat, stirring occasionally, for 2-3 minutes.

2 Add the zucchini to the skillet and cook, stirring occasionally, for about 5 minutes or until golden. Stir in 2 tablespoons of the thyme.

3 Place half the onions and zucchini in the base of a large ovenproof dish. Top with the sardine fillets and half the grated Parmesan cheese.

4 Place the remaining onions and zucchini on top and sprinkle with the remaining thyme.

2

3

3

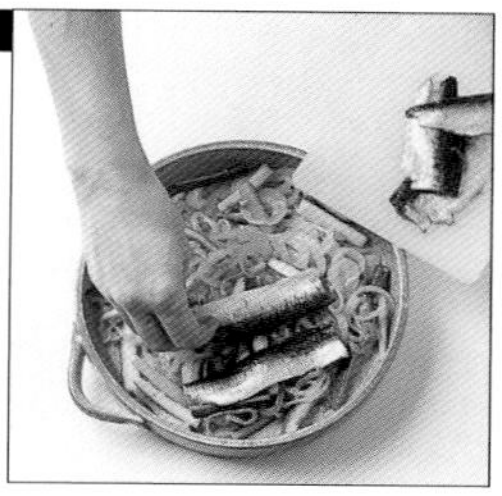

5 Combine the eggs and milk in a bowl and season to taste with salt and pepper. Pour the mixture over the vegetables and sardines in the dish. Sprinkle the remaining Parmesan cheese over the top.

6 Bake in a preheated oven, 350°F/180°C, for 20-25 minutes or until golden and set. Serve immediately.

VARIATION

If you cannot find sardines that are large enough to fillet, use small mackerel instead.

Baked Trout Mexican-Style

Make this dish as hot or as mild as you like by adjusting the amount of green chili. The red chilies are milder and add a pungency to the dish.

NUTRITIONAL INFORMATION

Calories	329	Sugars	5g
Protein	53g	Fat	10g
Carbohydrate	6g	Saturates	2g

10 mins   30 mins

SERVES 4

INGREDIENTS

- 4 trout, 8 oz/225 g each
- 1 small bunch fresh cilantro
- 4 shallots, finely shredded
- 1 small yellow bell pepper, seeded and very finely chopped
- 1 small red bell pepper, seeded and very finely chopped
- 2 green chilies, seeded and finely chopped
- 1–2 red chilies, seeded and finely chopped
- 1 tbsp lemon juice
- 1 tbsp white wine vinegar
- 2 tsp superfine sugar
- salt and pepper
- fresh cilantro, to garnish
- salad greens, to serve

COOK'S TIP

Seeding chilies reduces the degree of heat. However, this is not because the hot factor—capsaicin—is in the seeds, but because it is most concentrated in the flesh surrounding them. Removing the seeds removes most of the fiery flesh at the same time.

1 Wash the trout inside and out with cold running water and pat dry with paper towels. Season with salt and pepper and stuff with cilantro leaves.

2 Place the fish side by side in a shallow ovenproof dish. Sprinkle over the shallots, bell peppers, and chilies.

3 Combine the lemon juice, vinegar, and sugar in a bowl. Spoon the mixture over the trout and season with salt and pepper to taste. Cover the dish and bake in a preheated oven, 350°C/180°F for about 30 minutes or until the fish is tender and the flesh is opaque.

4 Remove the the fish and drain. Transfer to warm serving plates and spoon the cooking juices over the fish. Garnish with fresh cilantro and serve with salad greens.

1

2

3

Smoked Cod Cornmeal

Using cornmeal as a crust for a gratin dish gives a lovely crispy outer texture and a smooth inside. It works well with smoked fish and chicken.

NUTRITIONAL INFORMATION

Calories 616	Sugars 3g
Protein 41g	Fat 24g
Carbohydrate . . .58g	Saturates 12g

30 mins | 1¼ hrs

SERVES 4

INGREDIENTS

- 6½ cups water
- generous 2⅓ cups instant cornmeal
- 7 oz/200 g chopped frozen spinach, thawed
- 3 tbsp butter
- ½ cup grated romano cheese
- generous ¾ cup milk
- 1 lb/450 g smoked cod fillet, skinned and boned
- 4 eggs, beaten
- salt and pepper

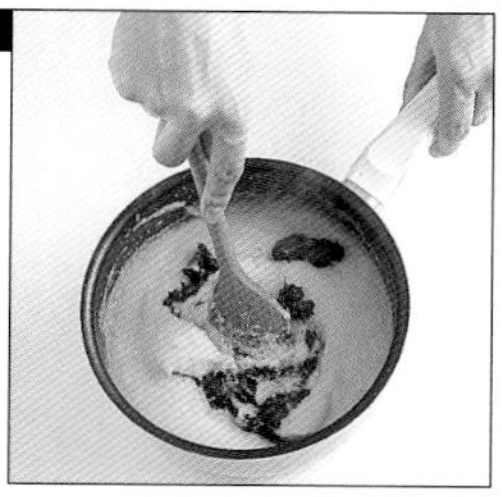
2

4

5

1 Bring the water to a boil in a large pan. Add the cornmeal and cook, stirring constantly, for 30–35 minutes.

2 Stir the spinach, butter, and half of the romano cheese into the cornmeal. Season to taste with salt and pepper.

3 Divide the cornmeal mixture among 4 individual ovenproof dishes, spreading it evenly across the bottom and up the sides of the dishes.

4 In a skillet, bring the milk to a boil over a low heat. Add the fish and simmer gently, turning once, for 8–10 minutes until the flesh is tender and flakes easily when tested with a fork. Remove the fish with a perforated spoon.

5 Remove the pan from the heat. Pour the eggs into the milk in the pan and mix well together.

6 Using a fork, flake the fish into smaller pieces and place it in the center of the dishes.

7 Pour the milk and egg mixture over the fish.

8 Sprinkle with the remaining cheese and bake in a preheated oven, 375°F/190°C, for 25–30 minutes or until set and golden. Serve hot.

VARIATION

Try using 12 oz/350 g cooked chicken breast with 2 tablespoons of chopped tarragon, instead of the smoked cod, if you prefer.

Italian Cod

Cod roasted with herbs and topped with a lemon and rosemary crust is a delicious main course for a warm summer evening.

NUTRITIONAL INFORMATION

Calories	313	Sugars	0.4g
Protein	29g	Fat	20g
Carbohydrate	6g	Saturates	5g

10 mins   35 mins

SERVES 4

INGREDIENTS

- 2 tbsp butter
- 1 cup fresh whole-wheat bread crumbs
- 2 tbsp chopped walnuts
- grated zest and juice of 2 lemons
- 2 sprigs fresh rosemary, stems removed
- 2 tbsp chopped fresh parsley
- 4 cod fillets, 5½ oz/150 g each
- 1 garlic clove, crushed
- 1 small red chili, seeded and diced
- 3 tbsp walnut oil
- salad greens, to serve

VARIATION

If preferred, the walnuts may be omitted from the crust. In addition, extra virgin olive oil can be used instead of walnut oil, if desired.

1 Melt the butter in a large pan, stirring over low heat.

2 Remove the pan from the heat and add the bread crumbs, walnuts, the zest and juice of 1 lemon, half of the rosemary, and half of the parsley.

3 Gently press the bread crumb mixture over the top of the cod fillets. Place the cod fillets in a shallow, foil-lined roasting pan.

4 Bake in a preheated oven, 400°F/200°C, for 25–30 minutes.

5 Mix the garlic, the remaining lemon zest and juice, rosemary, parsley, and the chili in a bowl. Beat in the walnut oil and mix well to combine. Drizzle the dressing over the cod steaks as soon as they are cooked.

6 Transfer the fish to serving plates and serve immediately with salad greens.

2

2

3

Orange Mackerel

Mackerel can be quite rich, but when it is stuffed with oranges and toasted ground almonds it is tangy and light.

NUTRITIONAL INFORMATION

Calories	623	Sugars	7g
Protein	42g	Fat	47g
Carbohydrate	8g	Saturates	8g

15 mins   35 mins

SERVES 4

INGREDIENTS

- 2 tbsp oil
- 4 scallions, chopped
- 2 oranges
- scant ½ cup ground almonds
- 1 tbsp oats
- ½ cup mixed pitted green and black olives, chopped
- 8 mackerel fillets
- salt and pepper
- salad greens, to serve

1 Heat the oil in a skillet. Add the scallions and cook over a low heat, stirring frequently, for 2 minutes.

2 Finely grate the zest of the oranges, then, using a sharp knife, cut away the remaining skin and white pith.

3 Using a sharp knife, segment the oranges by cutting down either side of the membranes to loosen each segment. Do this over a plate so that you can reserve any juices. Cut each orange segment in half.

4 Lightly toast the almonds, under a preheated broiler, for 2–3 minutes or until golden; watch them carefully as they brown very quickly.

1

5

6

5 Combine the scallions, orange segments, ground almonds, oats, and olives in a bowl and season to taste with salt and pepper.

6 Spoon the orange mixture along the center of each fillet. Roll up each fillet, securing it in place with a toothpick or small skewer.

7 Bake in a preheated oven, 375°F/190°C, for 25 minutes until the fish is tender and cooked through.

8 Using a perforated spoon, transfer the mackerel to warm individual serving plates and remove and discard the toothpicks or skewers. Serve warm with salad greens.

Cannelloni Filetti di Sogliola

This is a lighter dish than the better-known cannelloni stuffed with ground beef and would be a good choice for an informal dinner party.

NUTRITIONAL INFORMATION

Calories	555	Sugars	4g
Protein	53g	Fat	21g
Carbohydrate	36g	Saturates	12g

20 mins   45 mins

SERVES 6

INGREDIENTS

- 12 small fillets of sole, 4 oz/115 g each
- ⅔ cup red wine
- 6 tbsp butter
- 1⅔ cups sliced white mushrooms
- 4 shallots, finely chopped
- 4 oz/115 g tomatoes, chopped
- 2 tbsp tomato paste
- scant ½ cup all-purpose flour, strained
- ⅔ cup warm milk
- 2 tbsp heavy cream
- 6 dried cannelloni tubes
- 6 oz/175 g cooked, peeled shrimp, preferably freshwater
- salt and pepper
- 1 sprig fresh fennel, to garnish

1 Brush the fillets with a little wine, season with salt and pepper and roll them up, skin side inward. Secure with a skewer or toothpick.

2 Arrange the fish rolls in a single layer in a large skillet, add the remaining red wine, and poach for 4 minutes. Remove the fish from the pan and reserve the liquid.

3 Melt the butter in another pan over low heat. Cook the mushrooms and shallots for 2 minutes, then add the tomatoes and tomato paste.

4 Season the flour and stir it into the pan. Stir in the reserved cooking liquid and half the milk. Cook over low heat, stirring, for 4 minutes. Remove from the heat and stir in the cream.

5 Bring a large pan of lightly salted water to a boil. Add the cannelloni, bring back to a boil, and cook for about 8 minutes, until tender but still firm to the bite. Drain and let cool.

6 Remove the skewers or toothpicks from the fish rolls. Put 2 sole fillets into each cannelloni tube with 2–3 shrimp and a little red wine sauce. Arrange the cannelloni in an ovenproof dish, pour over the sauce and bake in a preheated oven, 400°F/200°C, for 20 minutes.

7 Serve the cannelloni with the red wine sauce, garnished with the remaining shrimp and the fennel.

1
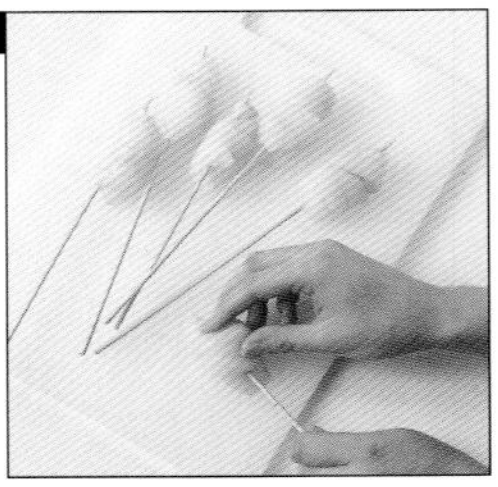

2

4

Spaghetti alla Bucaniera

Brill was once known as poor man's turbot, an unfair description as it is a delicately flavored and delicious fish in its own right.

NUTRITIONAL INFORMATION

Calories	588	Sugars	5g
Protein	36g	Fat	18g
Carbohydrate	68g	Saturates	9g

25 mins 50 mins

SERVES 4

INGREDIENTS

- ¾ cup all-purpose flour
- 1 lb/450 g brill or sole fillets, skinned and chopped
- 1 lb/450 g hake fillets, skinned and chopped
- 6 tbsp butter
- 4 shallots, finely chopped
- 2 garlic cloves, crushed
- 1 carrot, diced
- 1 leek, finely chopped
- 1¼ cups hard cider
- 1¼ cups medium sweet cider
- 2 tsp anchovy paste
- 1 tbsp tarragon vinegar
- 1 lb/450 g dried spaghetti
- 1 tbsp olive oil
- salt and pepper
- chopped fresh parsley, to garnish
- crusty brown bread, to serve

1 Season the flour with salt and pepper. Sprinkle ¼ cup of the seasoned flour onto a shallow plate. Press the fish pieces into the seasoned flour to coat thoroughly.

2 Melt the butter in a flameproof casserole. Add the fish fillets, shallots, garlic, carrot, and leek and cook over a low heat, stirring frequently, for about 10 minutes.

3 Sprinkle over the remaining seasoned flour and cook, stirring constantly, for 2 minutes. Gradually stir in the cider, anchovy paste, and tarragon vinegar. Bring to a boil and transfer to a preheated oven, 350°F/180°C. Bake for 30 minutes.

4 About 15 minutes before the end of the cooking time, bring a large pan of lightly salted water to a boil. Add the spaghetti and olive oil, bring back to a boil, and cook for about 12 minutes until tender, but still firm to the bite. Drain the pasta thoroughly and transfer to a large, warm serving dish.

5 Arrange the fish on top of the spaghetti and pour the sauce over it. Garnish with chopped parsley and serve immediately with warm, crusty brown bread.

2

3

3

Fillets of Snapper & Pasta

This simple recipe perfectly complements the exceptionally sweet flavor and delicate texture of the fish.

NUTRITIONAL INFORMATION

Calories	457	Sugars	3g
Protein	39g	Fat	12g
Carbohydrate	44g	Saturates	5g

15 mins · 1 hr

SERVES 4

INGREDIENTS

- 2 lb 4 oz/1 kg red snapper fillets
- 1¼ cups dry white wine
- 4 shallots, finely chopped
- 1 garlic clove, crushed
- 3 tbsp finely chopped mixed fresh herbs
- finely grated zest and juice of 1 lemon
- pinch of freshly grated nutmeg
- 3 anchovy fillets, coarsely chopped
- 2 tbsp heavy cream
- 1 tsp cornstarch
- 1 lb/450 g dried vermicelli
- 1 tbsp olive oil
- salt and pepper

TO GARNISH

- 1 sprig fresh mint
- lemon slices
- lemon zest

1

2

3

1 Put the red snapper fillets in a large casserole. Pour over the wine and add the shallots, garlic, herbs, lemon zest and juice, nutmeg, and anchovies. Season to taste. Cover and bake in a preheated oven, 350°F/180°C, for 35 minutes.

2 Transfer the snapper to a warm dish. Set aside and keep warm.

3 Pour the cooking liquid into a pan and bring to a boil. Simmer gently for 25 minutes, until reduced by half. Combine the cream and cornstarch and stir into the sauce to thicken.

4 Meanwhile, bring a pan of lightly salted water to a boil. Add the vermicelli and oil, bring back to a boil and cook for 8–10 minutes until tender, but still firm to the bite. Drain the pasta and transfer to a warm serving dish.

5 Arrange the red snapper fillets on top of the vermicelli and pour the sauce over them. Garnish with a fresh mint sprig, slices of lemon, and strips of lemon zest, and serve immediately.

Trout with Smoked Bacon

Most trout available nowadays is farmed rainbow trout, however, if you can, buy the marvelous-tasting wild brown trout for this recipe.

NUTRITIONAL INFORMATION

Calories	802	Sugars	8g
Protein	68g	Fat	36g
Carbohydrate	54g	Saturates	10g

35 mins 25 mins

SERVES 4

INGREDIENTS

- butter, for greasing
- 4 whole trout, 9½ oz/275 g each, gutted and cleaned
- 12 anchovies in oil, drained and chopped
- 2 apples, peeled, cored, and sliced
- 4 sprigs fresh mint
- juice of 1 lemon
- 12 slices smoked fatty bacon
- 1 lb/450 g dried tagliatelle
- 1 tbsp olive oil
- salt and pepper

TO GARNISH

- 2 apples, cored and sliced
- 4 sprigs fresh mint

1 Grease a deep cookie sheet with butter.

2 Open up the cavities of each trout and rinse with warm salt water. Season each cavity with salt and pepper. Divide the anchovies, sliced apples, and mint sprigs among the cavities. Sprinkle the lemon juice into each cavity.

3 Carefully cover the whole of each trout, except the head and tail, with three slices of smoked bacon in a spiral.

4 Arrange the trout on the cookie sheet with the loose ends of bacon tucked underneath. Season with pepper and bake in a preheated oven, 400°F/200°C, for 20 minutes, turning the trout over halfway through cooking.

5 Meanwhile, bring a large pan of lightly salted water to a boil. Add the tagliatelle and olive oil, bring back to a boil and cook for about 12 minutes until tender, but still firm to the bite. Drain and transfer to a large, warm serving dish.

6 Remove the trout from the oven and arrange on the tagliatelle. Garnish with sliced apples and fresh mint sprigs and serve immediately.

2

2

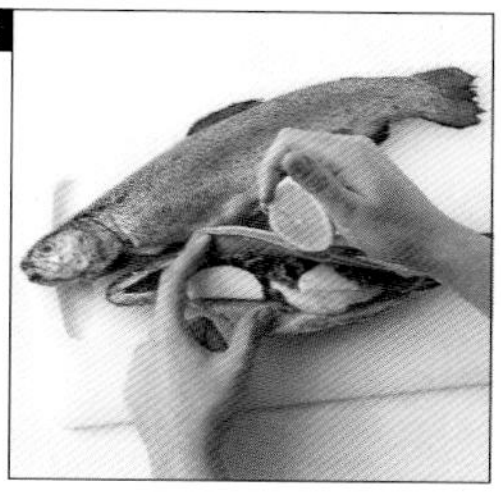

3

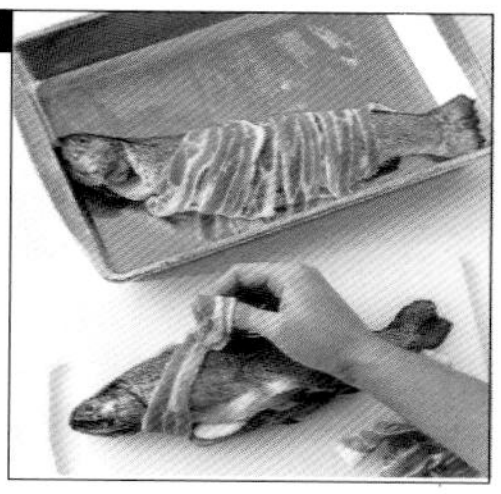

Smoked Haddock Casserole

This quick, easy, and inexpensive dish would be ideal for a mid-week family supper and will quickly become a firm favorite.

Calories 525	Sugars 8g
Protein 41g	Fat 18g
Carbohydrate ...53g	Saturates 10g

20 mins | 45 mins

SERVES 4

INGREDIENTS

- 2 tbsp butter, plus extra for greasing
- 1 lb/450 g smoked haddock fillets, cut into 4 slices
- 2½ cups milk
- scant ¼ cup all-purpose flour
- pinch of freshly grated nutmeg
- 3 tbsp heavy cream
- 1 tbsp chopped fresh parsley
- 2 eggs, hard-cooked and mashed to a pulp
- 4 cups/450 g dried fusilli pasta
- 1 tbsp lemon juice
- salt and pepper
- boiled new potatoes and beets, to serve

1 Thoroughly grease a casserole with butter. Put the haddock in the casserole and pour over the milk. Bake in a preheated oven, 400°F/200°C, for about 15 minutes until tender and the flesh flakes easily. Carefully pour the cooking liquid into a pitcher without breaking up the fish.

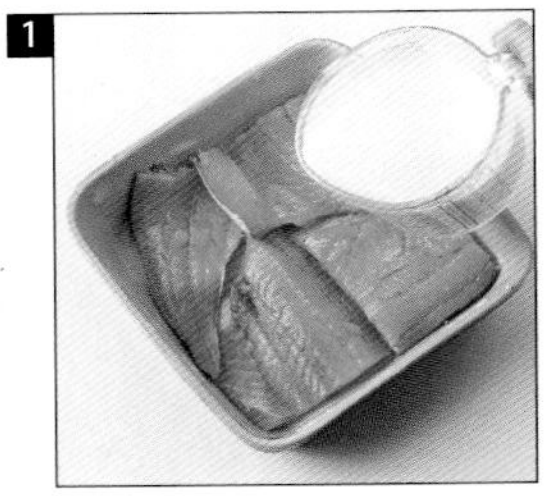

2 Melt the butter in a pan and stir in the flour. Gradually whisk in the reserved cooking liquid. Season to taste with salt, pepper, and nutmeg. Stir in the cream, parsley, and mashed egg and cook, stirring constantly, for 2 minutes.

3 Meanwhile, bring a large pan of lightly salted water to a boil. Add the fusilli and the lemon juice, bring back to a boil, and cook for 8–10 minutes until tender, but still firm to the bite.

4 Drain the pasta and spoon or tip it over the fish. Top with the egg sauce and return the casserole to the oven for 10 minutes.

5 Serve the haddock casserole piping hot with boiled new potatoes and beets.

VARIATION

You can use any type of dried pasta for this casserole. Try penne, conchiglie, or rigatoni.

Quick Chicken Bake

This recipe is a type of cottage pie and is just as versatile. Add vegetables and herbs of your choice, depending on what you have at hand.

NUTRITIONAL INFORMATION

Calories	530	Sugars	8g
Protein	37g	Fat	23g
Carbohydrate	48g	Saturates	12g

1¾ hrs

40 mins

SERVES 4

INGREDIENTS

- 1 lb 2 oz/500 g ground chicken
- 1 large onion, finely chopped
- 2 carrots, finely diced
- ¼ cup all-purpose flour
- 1 tbsp tomato paste
- 1¼ cups chicken bouillon
- pinch of fresh thyme
- 2 lb/900 g boiled potatoes, creamed with butter and milk and highly seasoned
- ¾ cup grated Lancashire or Cheddar cheese
- salt and pepper
- peas, to serve

1 Dry-fry the ground chicken, onion, and carrots in a non-stick saucepan for 5 minutes, stirring frequently.

2 Sprinkle the chicken with the flour and simmer for a further 2 minutes.

3 Gradually blend in the tomato paste and bouillon, then simmer gently for 15 minutes. Season to taste with salt and pepper and add the thyme.

4 Transfer the chicken and vegetable mixture to a casserole and let cool.

5 Spoon the mashed potato over the chicken mixture and sprinkle with the grated cheese.

6 Bake in a preheated oven, 400°F/200°C, for 20 minutes or until the cheese topping is bubbling and golden, then serve with the peas.

VARIATION

Instead of Lancashire or Cheddar cheese, you could sprinkle Fresh Jack, Plymouth cheese, or even Toscana over the top, if available.

Italian Chicken Parcels

This cooking method makes the chicken aromatic and succulent, and reduces the oil needed as the chicken and vegetables cook in their own juices.

NUTRITIONAL INFORMATION

Calories	234	Sugars	5g
Protein	28g	Fat	12g
Carbohydrate	5g	Saturates	5g

25 mins

30 mins

SERVES 6

INGREDIENTS

- 1 tbsp olive oil
- 6 skinless chicken breast fillets
- 9 oz/250 g mozzarella cheese
- 3½ cups sliced zucchini
- 6 large tomatoes, sliced
- 1 small bunch fresh basil or oregano
- pepper
- rice or pasta, to serve

1 Cut 6 pieces of foil, each measuring about 10-inches/25-cm square. Brush the foil squares lightly with oil and set aside until required.

2 With a sharp knife, slash each chicken breast at regular intervals. Slice the mozzarella cheese and place between the cuts in the chicken.

COOK'S TIP

To aid cooking, place the vegetables and chicken on the shiny side of the foil so that when the parcel is wrapped up the dull surface of the foil is facing outward. This ensures that the heat is absorbed into the parcel and not reflected away from it.

3 Divide the zucchini and tomatoes between the pieces of foil and season with pepper to taste. Tear or roughly chop the basil or oregano and scatter over the vegetables in each parcel.

4 Place the chicken on top of each pile of vegetables, then wrap the foil to enclose the chicken and vegetables, tucking in the ends.

5 Place on a cookie sheet and bake in a preheated oven, 400°C/200°C, for about 30 minutes.

6 To serve, unwrap each foil parcel and serve with rice or pasta.

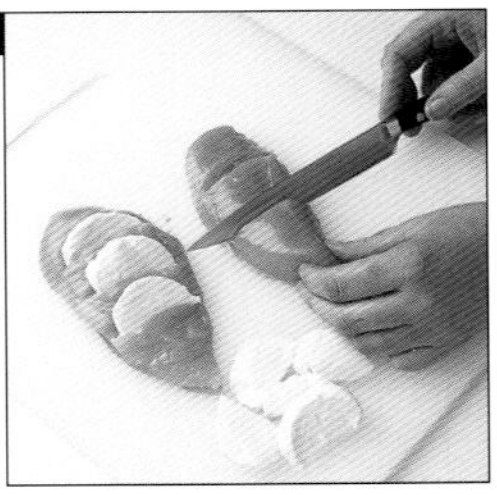

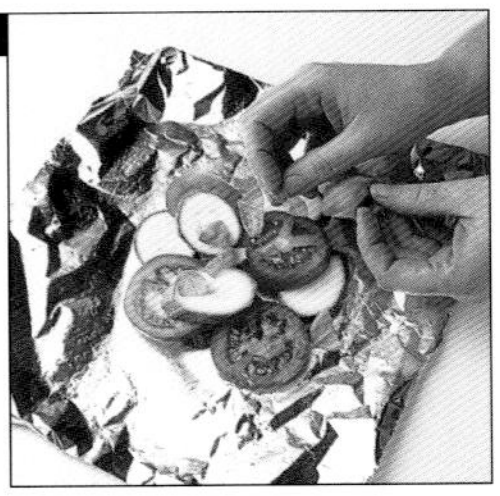

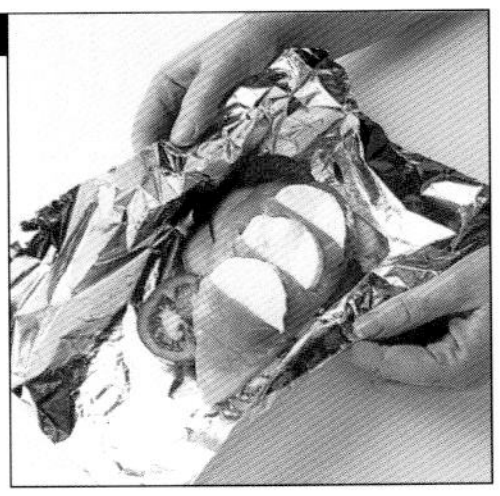

Garlicky Chicken Cushions

Stuffed with creamy ricotta, spinach, and garlic, then gently cooked in a rich tomato sauce, this is a suitable dish to make ahead of time.

NUTRITIONAL INFORMATION

Calories	316	Sugars	6g
Protein	40g	Fat	13g
Carbohydrate	6g	Saturates	5g

10 mins

40 mins

SERVES 4

INGREDIENTS

- 4 part-boned chicken breasts
- 4½ oz/125 g frozen spinach, thawed
- ¾ cup low-fat ricotta cheese
- 2 garlic cloves, crushed
- 1 tbsp olive oil
- 1 onion, chopped
- 1 red bell pepper, seeded and sliced
- 15 oz/425 g canned chopped tomatoes
- 6 tbsp wine or chicken bouillon
- 10 stuffed olives, sliced
- salt and pepper
- fresh flat leaf parsley sprigs, to garnish
- pasta, to serve

1 Make a slit between the skin and meat on one side of each chicken breast. Lift the skin to form a pocket, being careful to leave the skin attached to the other side.

2 Put the spinach into a strainer and press out the water with a spoon. Mix with the ricotta and half the garlic and season to taste with salt and pepper.

3 Spoon the spinach mixture under the skin of each chicken breast and secure the edge of the skin with toothpicks.

4 Heat the oil in a skillet, add the onion, and cook for 1 minute, stirring. Add the remaining garlic and red bell pepper and cook for 2 minutes. Stir in the tomatoes, wine or bouillon, olives, and seasoning. Set the sauce aside and chill the chicken if preparing in advance.

5 Bring the sauce to a boil, pour into an ovenproof dish, and arrange the chicken breasts on top in a single layer.

6 Cook, uncovered, in a preheated oven, 400°F/200°C, for 35 minutes until the chicken is golden and cooked through. Test by making a slit in one of the chicken breasts with a point of a sharp knife to make sure the juices run clear.

7 Spoon a little of the sauce over the chicken breasts, then transfer to serving plates, and garnish with parsley. Serve with pasta.

1

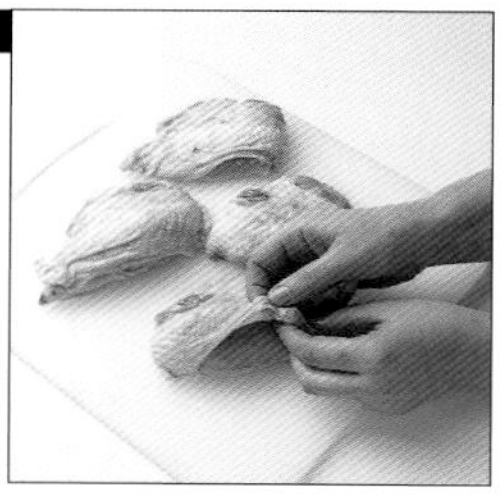

3

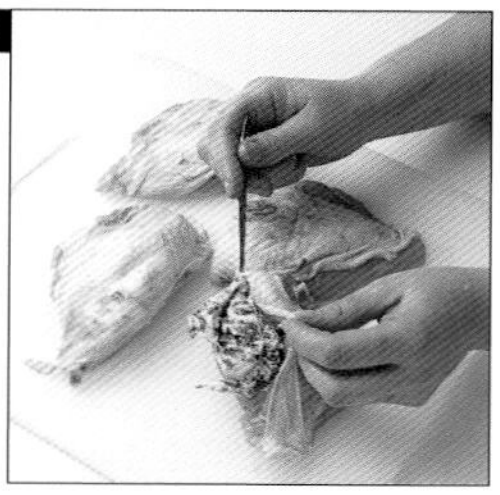

5

Parma Wraped Ham

Chicken is stuffed with ricotta, nutmeg, and spinach, then wrapped with wafer-thin slices of prosciutto, and gently cooked in white wine.

NUTRITIONAL INFORMATION

Calories	426	Sugars	4g
Protein	44g	Fat	21g
Carbohydrate	9g	Saturates	8g

30 mins | 45 mins

SERVES 4

INGREDIENTS

4½ oz/125 g frozen spinach, thawed
¾ cup ricotta cheese
pinch of grated nutmeg
4 skinless, boneless chicken breasts, 6 oz/175 g each
4 prosciutto slices
2 tbsp butter
1 tbsp olive oil
12 small onions or shallots
2 cups sliced white mushrooms
1 tbsp all-purpose flour
⅔ cup dry white or red wine
1¼ cups chicken bouillon
salt and pepper

TO SERVE

carrot purée
green beans

2
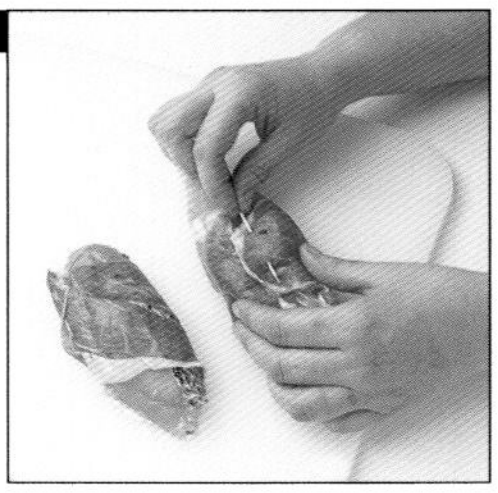

3

4

1 Put the spinach into a strainer and press out the water with a spoon. Mix with the ricotta and nutmeg and season with salt and pepper to taste.

2 Using a sharp knife, slit each chicken breast through the side and enlarge each cut to form a pocket. Fill the pockets with the spinach mixture, reshape the chicken breasts, wrap each breast in a slice of ham, and secure with toothpicks. Cover and chill in the refrigerator.

3 Heat the butter and oil in a skillet and brown the chicken breasts for 2 minutes on each side. Transfer the chicken to a large, shallow ovenproof dish and keep warm until required.

4 Cook the onions and mushrooms in the skillet for 2–3 minutes until lightly browned. Stir in the flour, then gradually add the wine and bouillon. Bring to a boil, stirring constantly. Season with salt and pepper to taste. Spoon the mixture around the chicken.

5 Cook the chicken, uncovered, in a preheated oven, 400°F/200°C, for about 20 minutes. Turn the breasts over and cook for a further 10 minutes. Remove the toothpicks and serve with the sauce, carrot purée, and green beans.

Chicken with Green Olives

Olives are a popular flavoring for poultry and game in the Apulia region of Italy, where this recipe originates.

NUTRITIONAL INFORMATION

Calories 614	Sugars 6g
Protein 34g	Fat 30g
Carbohydrate . . . 49g	Saturates 11g

15 mins

1½ hrs

SERVES 4

INGREDIENTS

- 3 tbsp olive oil
- 2 tbsp butter
- 4 chicken breasts, part boned
- 1 large onion, finely chopped
- 2 garlic cloves, crushed
- 2 red, yellow, or green bell peppers, seeded and cut into large pieces
- 9 oz/250 g white mushrooms, sliced or quartered
- 6 oz/175 g tomatoes, peeled and halved
- ⅔ cup dry white wine
- 1½ cups pitted green olives
- 4–6 tbsp heavy cream
- 14 oz/400 g dried pasta
- salt and pepper
- chopped fresh flat leaf parsley, to garnish

1

2

4

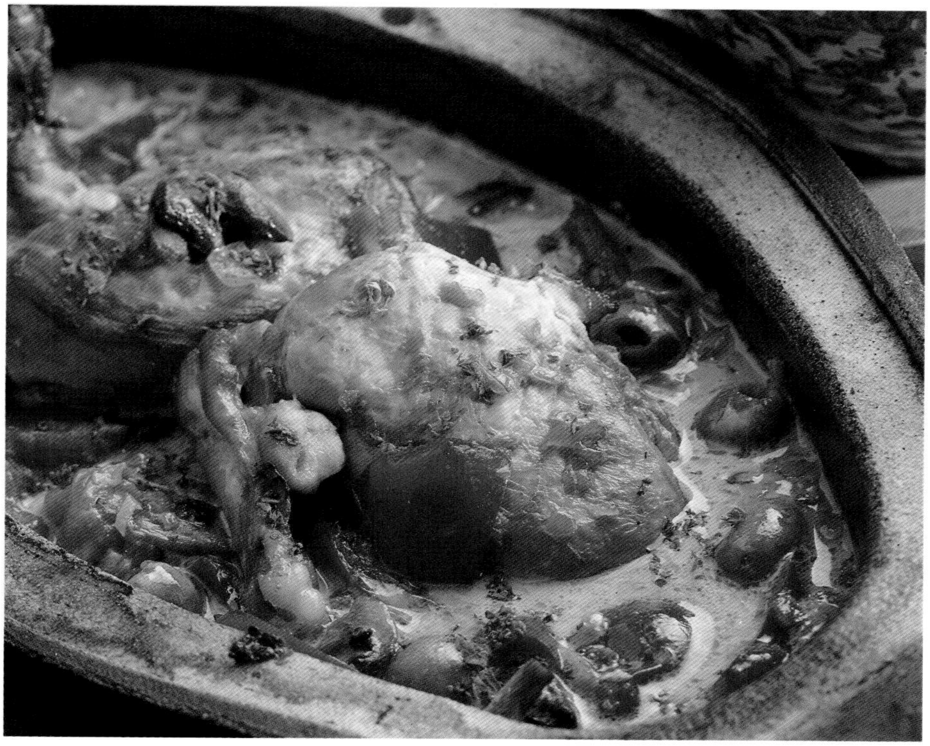

1 Heat 2 tablespoons of the oil and the butter in a skillet. Add the chicken breasts and cook until golden brown all over. Remove the chicken from the pan.

2 Add the onion and garlic to the pan and cook over medium heat until beginning to soften. Add the bell peppers and mushrooms and cook for 2–3 minutes.

3 Add the tomatoes and season to taste with salt and pepper. Transfer the vegetables to a casserole and arrange the chicken on top.

4 Add the wine to the skillet and bring to a boil. Pour the wine over the chicken. Cover and cook in a preheated oven, 350°F/180°C, for 50 minutes.

5 Add the olives to the casserole and stir well to mix in. Pour in the cream, cover, and return the casserole to the oven for 10–20 minutes.

6 Meanwhile, bring a large pan of lightly salted water to a boil. Add the pasta and the remaining oil, bring back to a boil, and cook for 8–10 minutes or until tender, but still firm to the bite.

7 Drain the pasta well and transfer to a warm serving dish. Arrange the chicken on top of the pasta, spoon over the sauce, garnish with the parsley, and serve immediately. Alternatively, place the pasta in a large serving bowl and serve separately. Serve the chicken straight from the casserole.

Chicken & Lobster on Penne

While this is certainly a wonderful treat to get the taste buds tingling, it is not actually as extravagant as it sounds.

NUTRITIONAL INFORMATION

Calories	696	Sugars	4g
Protein	59g	Fat	32g
Carbohydrate	45g	Saturates	9g

20 mins   30 mins

SERVES 6

INGREDIENTS

- butter, for greasing
- 6 chicken suprêmes (see Cook's Tip)
- 1 lb/450 g dried penne rigate pasta
- 6 tbsp extra virgin olive oil
- 1 cup freshly grated Parmesan cheese
- salt

FILLING

- 4 oz/115 g lobster meat, chopped
- 2 shallots, very finely chopped
- 2 figs, chopped
- 1 tbsp Marsala wine
- 2 tbsp bread crumbs
- 1 large egg, beaten
- salt and pepper

2

3

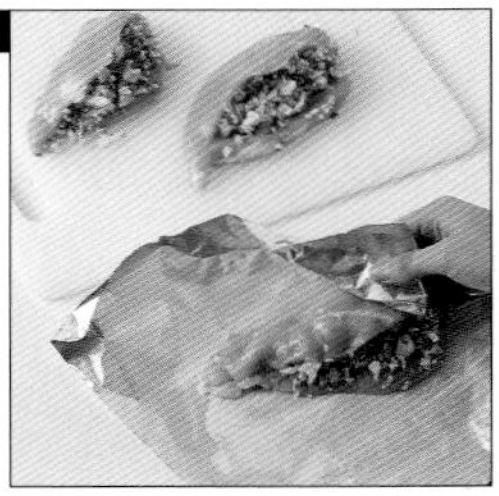

3

1 Grease 6 pieces of foil large enough to enclose each chicken suprême and lightly grease a cookie sheet.

2 Place all of the filling ingredients into a mixing bowl and blend together thoroughly with a spoon.

3 Cut a pocket in each chicken suprême with a sharp knife and fill with the lobster mixture. Wrap each chicken suprême in foil, place the parcels on the greased cookie sheet and bake in a preheated oven, 400°F/200°C, for 30 minutes.

4 Meanwhile, bring a large pan of lightly salted water to a boil. Add the pasta and 1 tablespoon of the olive oil, bring back to a boil, and cook for about 10 minutes or until tender, but still firm to the bite. Drain the pasta thoroughly and transfer to a large, warm serving plate. Sprinkle over the remaining olive oil and the grated Parmesan cheese, set aside, and keep warm.

5 Carefully remove the foil from around the chicken suprêmes. Slice the suprêmes very thinly, arrange over the pasta, and serve immediately.

COOK'S TIP

The cut of chicken known as suprême consists of the breast and wing. It is always skinned.

Italian Chicken Spirals

These little foil parcels retain all the natural juices of the chicken, making a truly superb and delicious sauce for the pasta.

NUTRITIONAL INFORMATION

Calories	367	Sugars	1g
Protein	33g	Fat	12g
Carbohydrate	35g	Saturates	2g

20 mins 25 mins

SERVES 4

INGREDIENTS

- 4 skinless, boneless chicken breasts
- 1 cup fresh basil leaves
- 1 tbsp hazelnuts
- 1 garlic clove, crushed
- 9 oz/250 g dried whole-wheat fusilli pasta
- 2 sun-dried tomatoes or fresh tomatoes
- 1 tbsp lemon juice
- 1 tbsp olive oil
- 1 tbsp capers
- ½ cup pitted black olives
- salt and pepper

1 Beat the chicken breasts with a rolling pin to flatten evenly.

2 Place the basil and hazelnuts in a food processor and process until finely chopped. Mix with the garlic and salt and pepper to taste.

3 Spread the basil mixture over the chicken breasts and roll up from one short end. Wrap the chicken rolls tightly in foil so that they hold their shape, then seal the ends well. Place on a cookie sheet and bake in a preheated oven 400°F/200°C, for 20–25 minutes

4 Meanwhile, bring a pan of lightly salted water to a boil. Add the pasta, bring back to a boil, and cook for 8–10 minutes or until tender, but firm to the bite.

5 Using a sharp knife, dice the tomatoes.

6 Drain the pasta and return to the pan with the lemon juice, olive oil, tomatoes, capers, and olives. Warm through over low heat.

7 Pierce the chicken with a skewer to make sure that the juices run clear. Slice the chicken, arrange over the pasta in a warm serving dish and serve.

2

3

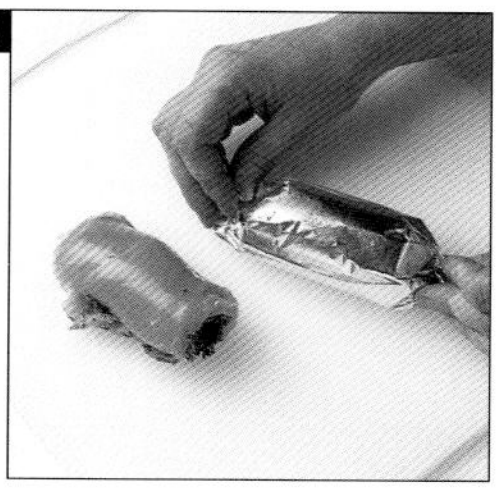

6

COOK'S TIP

Sun-dried tomatoes have a wonderful, rich flavor but if they are unavailable, use fresh tomatoes instead.

Mustard Baked Chicken

Chicken pieces are cooked in a succulent, mild mustard sauce, then coated in poppy seeds, and served on a bed of fresh pasta shells.

NUTRITIONAL INFORMATION

Calories	652	Sugars	5g
Protein	51g	Fat	31g
Carbohydrate	46g	Saturates	12g

10 mins · 35 mins

SERVES 4

INGREDIENTS

- 8 chicken pieces, 4 oz/115 g each
- 4 tbsp butter, melted
- 4 tbsp mild mustard (see Cook's Tip)
- 2 tbsp lemon juice
- 1 tbsp brown sugar
- 1 tsp paprika
- 3 tbsp poppy seeds
- 14 oz/400 g dried pasta shells
- 1 tbsp olive oil
- salt and pepper

1

3

3

1 Arrange the chicken pieces in a single layer in a large ovenproof dish.

2 Combine the butter, mustard, lemon juice, sugar, and paprika in a bowl and season with salt and pepper to taste. Brush the mixture over the upper surfaces of the chicken pieces and bake in a preheated oven, 400°F/200°C, for 15 minutes.

3 Remove the dish from the oven and carefully turn over the chicken pieces. Coat the upper surfaces of the chicken with the remaining mustard mixture, sprinkle the chicken pieces with poppy seeds, and return to the oven for a further 15 minutes.

4 Meanwhile, bring a large pan of lightly salted water to a boil. Add the pasta shells and olive oil, bring back to a boil, and cook for 8–10 minutes or until tender, but still firm to the bite.

5 Drain the pasta thoroughly and arrange on a warm serving dish. Top the pasta with the chicken pieces, pour the mustard sauce over them, and serve immediately.

COOK'S TIP

Dijon is the type of mustard most often used in cooking, as it has a clean and only mildly spicy flavor. German mustard has a sweet-sour taste, with Bavarian mustard being slightly sweeter. American mustard is mild and sweet.

Chicken Lasagna

You can use your favorite mushrooms, such as chanterelles or oyster mushrooms, for this delicately flavored dish.

NUTRITIONAL INFORMATION

Calories	708	Sugars	17g
Protein	35g	Fat	35g
Carbohydrate	57g	Saturates	14g

40 mins | $1\frac{3}{4}$ hrs

SERVES 4

INGREDIENTS

- butter, for greasing
- 14 sheets pre-cooked lasagna
- $3\frac{1}{2}$ cups Béchamel Sauce (see page 92)
- $\frac{3}{4}$ cup freshly grated Parmesan cheese

EXOTIC MUSHROOM SAUCE

- 2 tbsp olive oil
- 2 garlic cloves, crushed
- 1 large onion, finely chopped
- 8 oz/225 g exotic mushrooms, sliced
- $2\frac{1}{2}$ cups ground chicken
- 3 oz/80 g chicken livers, finely chopped
- $\frac{3}{4}$ cup diced prosciutto
- $\frac{2}{3}$ cup Marsala wine
- 10 oz/285 g canned chopped tomatoes
- 1 tbsp chopped fresh basil leaves
- 2 tbsp tomato paste
- salt and pepper

2

3

4

1 To make the chicken and exotic mushroom sauce, heat the olive oil in a large pan. Add the garlic, onion, and mushrooms, and cook, stirring frequently, for 6 minutes.

2 Add the ground chicken, chicken livers, and prosciutto, and cook over low heat, stirring frequently, for 12 minutes or until the meat has browned.

3 Stir the Marsala, tomatoes, basil, and tomato paste into the mixture and cook for 4 minutes. Season with salt and pepper to taste, cover, and simmer gently for 30 minutes, stirring occasionally. Uncover the pan, stir, and simmer for a further 15 minutes.

4 Lightly grease an ovenproof dish with butter. Arrange sheets of lasagna over the base of the dish, spoon over a layer of chicken and exotic mushroom sauce, then spoon over a layer of Béchamel Sauce. Place another layer of lasagna on top and repeat the process twice, finishing with a layer of Béchamel Sauce. Sprinkle over the grated Parmesan cheese and bake in a preheated oven, 375°F/190°C, for 35 minutes until golden brown and bubbling. Serve immediately.

Chicken & Tomato Lasagna

This variation of the traditional beef dish has layers of pasta and chicken or turkey baked in red wine, tomatoes, and a delicious cheese sauce.

NUTRITIONAL INFORMATION

Calories	550	Sugars	11g
Protein	35g	Fat	29g
Carbohydrate	34g	Saturates	12g

20 mins   1¼ hrs

SERVES 4

INGREDIENTS

- 9 sheets fresh or dried lasagna
- butter, for greasing
- 1 tbsp olive oil
- 1 red onion, finely chopped
- 1 garlic clove, crushed
- 1⅓ cups mushrooms
- 12 oz/350 g chicken or turkey breast, cut into chunks
- ⅔ cup red wine, diluted with generous ⅓ cup water
- generous 1 cup passata (strained tomatoes)
- 1 tsp sugar

BECHAMEL SAUCE

- 5 tbsp butter
- generous ⅓ cup all-purpose flour
- 2½ cups milk
- 1 egg, beaten
- ¾ cup freshly grated Parmesan cheese
- salt and pepper

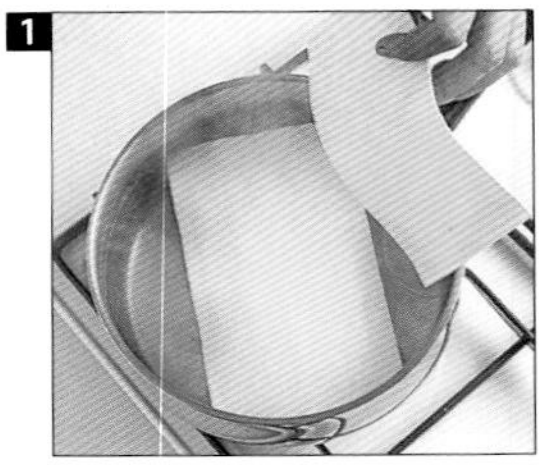

1 Cook the lasagna in a pan of boiling water according to the instructions on the packet. Lightly grease a deep ovenproof dish.

2 Heat the oil in a pan. Add the onion and garlic and cook over low heat, stirring occasionally, for 3–4 minutes. Add the mushrooms and chicken and cook for 4 minutes or until the meat browns.

3 Add the wine, bring to a boil, then simmer for 5 minutes. Stir in the passata and sugar and cook for 3–5 minutes until the meat is tender and cooked through. The sauce should have thickened, but still be quite runny.

4 To make the Béchamel Sauce, melt the butter in a pan, stir in the flour and cook for 2 minutes, stirring constantly. Remove the pan from the heat and gradually add the milk, mixing to form a smooth sauce. Return the pan to the heat and bring to a boil, stirring until thickened. Let cool slightly, then beat in the egg and half of the cheese. Season to taste with salt and pepper.

5 Place 3 sheets of lasagna in the base of the dish and spread with half of the chicken mixture. Repeat the layers. Top with the last 3 sheets of lasagna, pour over the Béchamel Sauce, and sprinkle with the Parmesan. Bake in a preheated oven, 375°F/190°C, for 30 minutes until golden and the pasta is cooked. Serve immediately.

Spicy Roast Chicken

This chicken dish, ideal for dinner parties, is cooked in the oven—which is very rare in Indian cooking. The chicken can be boned, if desired.

NUTRITIONAL INFORMATION

Calories	586	Sugars	6g
Protein	34g	Fat	47g
Carbohydrate	8g	Saturates	12g

5 mins

50 mins

SERVES 4

INGREDIENTS

- scant ½ cup ground almonds
- ½ cup shredded coconut
- ⅔ cup oil
- 1 onion, finely chopped
- 1 tsp chopped fresh ginger root
- 1 tsp crushed garlic
- 1 tsp chili powder
- 1½ tsp garam masala
- 1 tsp salt
- ⅔ cup plain yogurt
- 4 chicken quarters, skinned
- salad greens, to serve

TO GARNISH

- fresh cilantro leaves
- 1 lemon, cut into wedges

1 In a heavy-based pan, dry roast the ground almonds and coconut over low heat and set aside.

2 Heat the oil in a skillet. Add the onion and fry over low heat, stirring occasionally, until golden brown.

3 Place the ginger, garlic, chili powder, garam masala, and salt in a bowl and mix with the yogurt. Add the almonds and coconut and mix well.

4 Add the onions to the spice mixture, blend and set aside.

5 Arrange the chicken quarters in a single layer in the bottom of an ovenproof dish. Spoon the spice mixture over the chicken sparingly.

6 Cook in a preheated oven, 425°F/160°C, for 35–45 minutes. Check that the chicken is cooked thoroughly by piercing the thickest part of the meat with the point of a sharp knife or a fine skewer—the juices will run clear when the chicken is cooked through.

7 Garnish with the cilantro and lemon wedges and serve with a salad.

COOK'S TIP

If you want a spicier dish, simply add more chili powder and garam masala.

Chicken with a Yogurt Crust

A spicy, Indian-style coating is baked around lean chicken to give a full flavor. Serve with a tomato, cucumber, and cilantro relish.

NUTRITIONAL INFORMATION

Calories	176	Sugars	5g
Protein	30g	Fat	4g
Carbohydrate	5g	Saturates	1g

10 mins — 35 mins

SERVES 4

INGREDIENTS

- 1 garlic clove, crushed
- 2 tsp finely chopped fresh ginger root
- 1 fresh green chili, seeded and finely chopped
- 6 tbsp low-fat plain yogurt
- 1 tbsp tomato paste
- 1 tsp ground turmeric
- 1 tsp garam masala
- 1 tbsp lime juice
- 4 boneless, skinless chicken breasts, 4½ oz/125 g each
- salt and pepper
- wedges of lime or lemon, to serve

RELISH

- 4 tomatoes
- ¼ cucumber
- 1 small red onion
- 2 tbsp chopped fresh cilantro

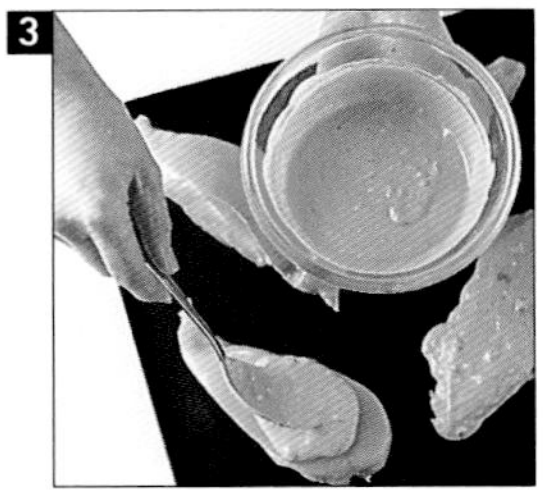

1 Place the garlic, ginger, chili, yogurt, tomato paste, spices, lime juice, and seasoning in a bowl and mix to combine all the ingredients.

2 Wash the chicken breasts, pat dry with paper towels and place them on a cookie sheet.

3 Brush or spread the spicy yogurt mixture over the chicken and bake in a preheated oven, 375°F/190°C, for 30–35 minutes until the meat is tender and cooked through.

4 Meanwhile, make the relish. Finely chop the tomatoes, cucumber, and onion, and mix together with the cilantro. Season with salt and pepper to taste, cover, and chill in the refrigerator.

5 Drain the cooked chicken on paper towels and serve hot with the relish and lemon or lime wedges. Alternatively, let cool, chill for at least 1 hour, and serve sliced as part of a salad.

Crispy Stuffed Chicken

An attractive main course of chicken breasts filled with mixed bell peppers and set on a sea of red bell pepper and tomato sauce.

NUTRITIONAL INFORMATION

Calories	196	Sugars	4g
Protein	29g	Fat	6g
Carbohydrate	6g	Saturates	2g

20 mins — 50 mins

SERVES 4

INGREDIENTS

- 4 boneless chicken breasts, 5½ oz/150 g each, skinned
- 4 sprigs fresh tarragon
- ½ small orange bell pepper, seeded and sliced
- ½ small green bell pepper, seeded and sliced
- ¼ cup fresh whole-wheat bread crumbs
- 1 tbsp sesame seeds
- 4 tbsp lemon juice
- 1 small red bell pepper, halved and seeded
- 7 oz/200 g canned chopped tomatoes
- 1 small red chili, seeded and chopped
- ¼ tsp celery salt
- salt and pepper
- fresh tarragon, to garnish

1

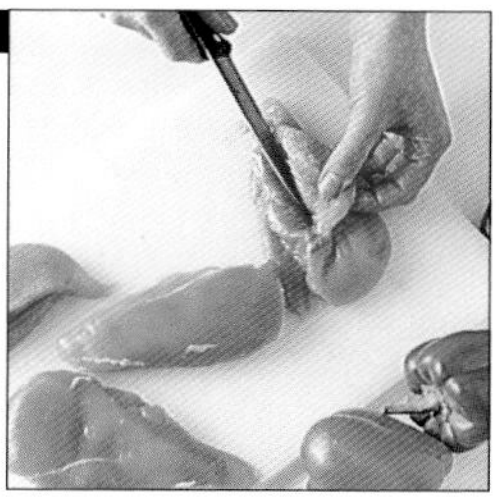

3

5

1 Slit the chicken breasts with a small, sharp knife to create a pocket in each. Season inside each pocket with salt and pepper to taste.

2 Place a sprig of tarragon and a few slices of orange and green bell pepper in each pocket. Place the chicken breasts in a single layer on a non-stick cookie sheet and sprinkle the bread crumbs and sesame seeds over them.

3 Spoon 1 tablespoon of lemon juice over each chicken breast and bake in a preheated oven, 400°F/200°C, for 35–40 minutes until the chicken is tender and cooked through.

4 Arrange the red bell pepper halves, skin side up, on a rack, and cook under a preheated broiler for 5–6 minutes until the skin blisters. Let cool for 10 minutes, then peel off the skins.

5 Put the red bell pepper in a blender, add the tomatoes, chili, and celery salt, and process for a few seconds. Season to taste. Alternatively, finely chop the red bell pepper and press through a strainer with the tomatoes and chili.

6 When the chicken is cooked, heat the sauce, spoon a little onto a warm plate and arrange a chicken breast in the center. Garnish with tarragon and serve.

Chicken Pasta Bake

Tender lean chicken is baked with pasta in a creamy low-fat sauce which contrasts well with the fennel and the sweetness of the raisins.

NUTRITIONAL INFORMATION

Calories	380	Sugars	15g
Protein	39g	Fat	14g
Carbohydrate	27g	Saturates	6g

15 mins · 45 mins

SERVES 4

INGREDIENTS

- 2 bulbs fennel
- 2 red onions, finely shredded
- 1 tbsp lemon juice
- 4½ oz/125 g white mushrooms
- 1 tbsp olive oil
- 8 oz/225 g dried penne pasta
- ⅓ cup raisins
- 8 oz/225 g lean, boneless cooked chicken, skinned and shredded
- 13 oz/375 g low-fat soft cheese with garlic and herbs
- 4½ oz/125 g low-fat mozzarella cheese, thinly sliced
- scant ½ cup freshly grated Parmesan cheese
- salt and pepper
- chopped fennel fronds, to garnish

1

5

6

1 Trim the fennel, reserving the green fronds, and slice the bulbs thinly.

2 Generously coat the onions in the lemon juice. Quarter the mushrooms.

3 Heat the oil in a large skillet and cook the fennel, onion, and mushrooms for 4–5 minutes, stirring, until just softened. Season well, transfer the mixture to a large bowl and set aside.

4 Bring a pan of lightly salted water to a boil. Add the pasta, bring back to a boil, and cook for 8–10 minutes until tender, but still firm to the bite. Drain and mix the pasta with the vegetables.

5 Stir the raisins and chicken into the pasta mixture. Soften the soft cheese by beating it, then mix into the pasta and chicken—the heat from the pasta should make the cheese melt slightly.

6 Put the mixture into an ovenproof dish and place on a cookie sheet. Arrange slices of mozzarella cheese over the top and sprinkle with the grated Parmesan cheese.

7 Bake in a preheated oven, 400°F/200°C, for 20–25 minutes until golden brown and the topping is bubbling. Garnish with chopped fennel fronds and serve hot.

Chicken & Spinach Lasagna

A delicious pasta bake with all the colors of the Italian flag—red tomatoes, green spinach and pasta, and white chicken and sauce.

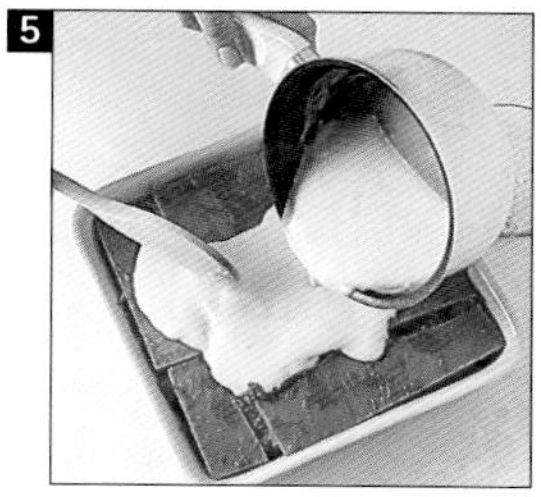

NUTRITIONAL INFORMATION

Calories	358	Sugars	12g
Protein	42g	Fat	9g
Carbohydrate	22g	Saturates	4g

25 mins   50 mins

SERVES 4

INGREDIENTS

- 12 oz/350 g frozen chopped spinach, thawed and drained
- ½ tsp ground nutmeg
- 1 lb/450 g lean, cooked chicken meat, skinned and diced
- 4 sheets pre-cooked lasagna verde
- 1½ tbsp cornstarch
- 1¾ cups skim milk
- scant ¾ cup freshly grated Parmesan cheese
- salt and pepper

TOMATO SAUCE

- 14 oz/400 g canned chopped tomatoes
- 1 onion, finely chopped
- 1 garlic clove, crushed
- ⅔ cup white wine
- 3 tbsp tomato paste
- 1 tsp dried oregano
- salad greens, to serve

1 For the tomato sauce, place the tomatoes in a pan and stir in the onion, garlic, wine, tomato paste, and oregano. Bring to a boil and simmer gently for 20 minutes until thick. Season well.

2 Drain the spinach again and spread it out on paper towels to make sure that as much water as possible is removed. Layer the spinach in the bottom of an ovenproof dish. Sprinkle with nutmeg and season with salt and pepper.

3 Arrange the diced chicken over the spinach and spoon over the tomato sauce. Arrange the sheets of lasagna over the tomato sauce.

4 Blend the cornstarch with a little of the milk to make a smooth paste. Pour the remaining milk into a pan and stir in the cornstarch paste. Heat gently for 2–3 minutes, stirring constantly, until the sauce thickens. Season to taste with salt and pepper.

5 Spoon the sauce over the lasagna and transfer the dish to a cookie sheet. Sprinkle the grated cheese over the sauce and bake in a preheated oven, 400°F/200°C, for 25 minutes until golden brown. Serve with fresh salad greens.

Turkey & Vegetable Loaf

This impressive-looking turkey loaf is flavored with herbs and a layer of juicy tomatoes, and covered with zucchini ribbons.

NUTRITIONAL INFORMATION

Calories	165	Sugars	1g
Protein	36g	Fat	2g
Carbohydrate	1g	Saturates	0.5g

10 mins — 1¼ hrs

SERVES 6

INGREDIENTS

- 1 onion, finely chopped
- 1 garlic clove, crushed
- 2 lb/900 g lean ground turkey
- 1 tbsp chopped fresh parsley
- 1 tbsp chopped fresh chives
- 1 tbsp chopped fresh tarragon
- 1 egg white, lightly beaten
- 2 zucchini
- 2 tomatoes
- salt and pepper
- tomato and herb sauce, to serve

2

3

4

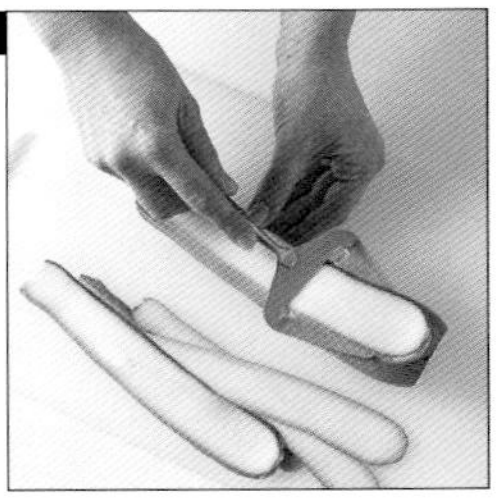

1 Line a non-stick loaf pan with baking parchment. Place the onion, garlic, and turkey in a bowl, add the herbs, and season well with salt and pepper. Mix together with your hands, then add the egg white to bind.

2 Press half of the turkey mixture into the bottom of the prepared loaf pan. Thinly slice 1 zucchini and both the tomatoes and arrange the slices over the meat. Top with the rest of the turkey and press down firmly.

3 Cover with a layer of foil and place in a roasting pan. Pour in enough boiling water to come halfway up the sides of the loaf pan. Bake in a preheated oven, 375°F.190°C, for 1–1¼ hours, removing the foil for the last 20 minutes of cooking. Test the loaf is cooked by inserting a toothpick into the center—the juices should run clear. The loaf will also shrink away from the sides of the pan.

4 Meanwhile, trim the other zucchini. Using a vegetable peeler or hand-held metal cheese slicer, cut the zucchini into thin slices. Bring a pan of water to the boil and blanch the zucchini ribbons for 1–2 minutes until just tender. Drain and keep warm.

5 Remove the turkey loaf from the pan and transfer to a warm serving plate. Drape the zucchini ribbons over the turkey loaf and serve immediately with a tomato and herb sauce.

Roast Duck with Apple

The richness of the duck meat contrasts well with the apricot sauce. If duckling portions are unavailable, use a whole bird cut into portions.

NUTRITIONAL INFORMATION

Calories	316	Sugars	38g
Protein	25g	Fat	6g
Carbohydrate	40g	Saturates	1g

10 mins   1½ hrs

SERVES 4

INGREDIENTS

- 4 duckling portions, 12 oz/350 g each
- 4 tbsp dark soy sauce
- 2 tbsp light brown sugar
- 2 red-skinned apples
- 2 green-skinned apples
- juice of 1 lemon
- 2 tbsp clear honey
- a few bay leaves
- salt and pepper
- assorted fresh vegetables, to serve

SAUCE

- 14 oz/400 g canned apricots, in natural juice
- 4 tbsp sweet sherry

1 Wash the duck and trim away any excess fat. Place on a wire rack over a roasting pan and prick all over with a fork or a large needle.

1

2 Brush the duck with the soy sauce. Sprinkle over the sugar and season with pepper. Cook in a preheated oven, 375°F/190°C, basting occasionally, for 50–60 minutes until the meat is cooked through—the juices should run clear when a skewer is inserted into the thickest part of the meat.

3 Meanwhile, core the apples and cut each into 6 wedges. Place in a small roasting pan and mix with the lemon juice and honey. Add a few bay leaves and season. Cook alongside the duck, basting occasionally, for 20–25 minutes until tender. Discard the bay leaves.

3

4 To make the sauce, place the apricots in a blender or food processor with the juice from the can and the sherry. Process for a few seconds until smooth. Alternatively, mash the apricots with a fork until smooth and mix with the juice and sherry.

4

5 Just before serving, heat the apricot paste in a small pan. Remove the skin from the duck and pat the flesh with paper towels to absorb any fat. Serve the duck with the apple wedges, apricot sauce, and fresh vegetables.

VARIATION

Fruit complements duck perfectly. Use canned pineapple in natural juice for a delicious alternative.

Honey-Glazed Duck

Chinese-style duck is incredibly easy to prepare, but makes an impressive main course for a dinner party.

NUTRITIONAL INFORMATION

Calories	230	Sugars	9g
Protein	23g	Fat	9g
Carbohydrate	14g	Saturates	3g

2¼ hrs — 30 mins

SERVES 4

INGREDIENTS

- 1 tsp dark soy sauce
- 2 tbsp clear honey
- 1 tsp garlic vinegar
- 2 garlic cloves, crushed
- 1 tsp ground star anise
- 2 tsp cornstarch
- 2 tsp water
- 2 large boneless duck breasts, about 8 oz/225 g each

TO GARNISH

- celery leaves
- cucumber wedges
- snipped chives

1 Mix the soy sauce, clear honey, garlic vinegar, garlic and star anise. Blend the cornstarch with the water to form a smooth paste and stir it into the mixture.

COOK'S TIP

If the duck begins to burn slightly while it is cooking in the oven, cover with foil. Check that the duck breasts are cooked through by inserting the point of a sharp knife into the thickest part of the flesh—the juices should run clear.

2

4

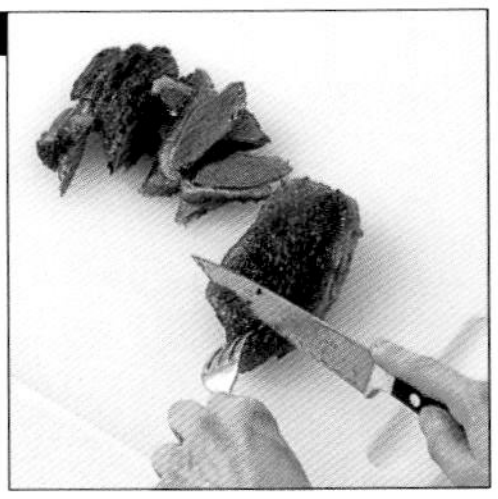

5

2 Place the duck breasts in a shallow ovenproof dish. Brush all over with the soy marinade, turning to coat them completely. Cover and set aside to marinate in the refrigerator for at least 2 hours or overnight.

3 Remove the duck from the marinade and cook in a preheated oven, 425°F/220°C, for 20–25 minutes, basting frequently with the glaze.

4 Remove the duck from the oven and arrange on a broiler rack. Broil under a preheated broiler for about 3–4 minutes to caramelize the top.

5 Remove the duck from the broiler pan and cut into fairly thin slices. Arrange the duck slices in a warm serving dish, garnish with celery leaves, cucumber wedges, and snipped chives, and serve immediately.

Pesto Baked Partridge

Partridge has a more delicate flavor than many game birds, and this subtle sauce perfectly complements it.

NUTRITIONAL INFORMATION

Calories	895	Sugars	5g
Protein	79g	Fat	45g
Carbohydrate	45g	Saturates	18g

15 mins

40 mins

SERVES 4

INGREDIENTS

- 8 partridge pieces, 115 g/4 oz each
- 4 tbsp butter, melted
- 4 tbsp Dijon mustard
- 2 tbsp lime juice
- 1 tbsp brown sugar
- 6 tbsp Pesto Sauce (see page 15)
- 1 lb/450 g dried rigatoni pasta
- 1 tbsp olive oil
- 1 cup freshly grated Parmesan cheese
- salt and pepper

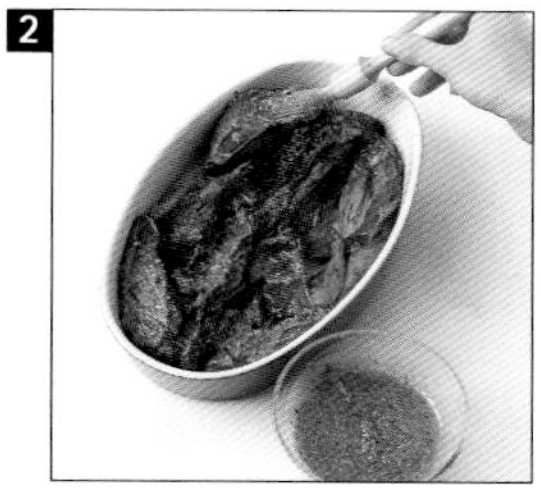

1 Arrange the partridge pieces, smooth side down, in a single layer in a large, ovenproof dish.

2 Mix together the butter, Dijon mustard, lime juice, and brown sugar in a bowl. Season to taste with salt and pepper. Brush this mixture over the partridge pieces and bake in a preheated oven, 400°F/200°C, for 15 minutes.

3 Remove the dish from the oven and coat the partridge pieces with 3 tablespoons of the Pesto Sauce. Return the dish to the oven and bake for a further 12 minutes.

4 Remove the dish from the oven and carefully turn over the partridge pieces. Coat the top of the partridge with the remaining mustard mixture and return to the oven for a further 10 minutes.

5 Meanwhile, bring a large pan of lightly salted water to a boil. Add the rigatoni and olive oil, bring back to a boil, and cook for 8–10 minutes until tender, but still firm to the bite. Drain and transfer to a serving dish. Toss the pasta with the remaining Pesto Sauce and the Parmesan cheese. Serve the partridge with the pasta, pouring over the cooking juices.

VARIATION

You could also prepare young pheasant in the same way.

Pheasant Lasagna

This scrumptious and unusual baked lasagna is virtually a meal in itself. It is served with pearl onions and green peas.

NUTRITIONAL INFORMATION

Calories	1038	Sugars	13g
Protein	65g	Fat	64g
Carbohydrate	54g	Saturates	27g

40 mins · 1¼ hrs

SERVES 4

INGREDIENTS

- butter, for greasing
- 14 sheets pre-cooked lasagna
- 3½ cups Béchamel Sauce (see page 92)
- ¾ cup grated mozzarella cheese

FILLING

- 8 oz/225 g pork fat, diced
- 2 tbsp butter
- 16 pearl onions
- 8 large pheasant breasts, thinly sliced
- scant ¼ cup all-purpose flour
- 2½ cups chicken bouillon
- 1 bouquet garni
- 1 lb/450 g fresh peas, shelled
- salt

1 To make the filling, put the pork fat into a pan of boiling, salted water and simmer gently for 3 minutes, then drain, and pat dry with paper towels.

2 Melt the butter in a large skillet. Add the pork fat and onions to the skillet and cook for about 3 minutes or until lightly browned.

3 Remove the pork fat and onions from the skillet and set aside. Add the slices of pheasant and cook over low heat for about 12 minutes until browned all over. Transfer to an ovenproof dish.

4 Stir the flour into the skillet and cook until just brown, then blend in the bouillon. Pour the mixture over the pheasant, add the bouquet garni, and cook in a preheated oven, 400°F/200°C, for 5 minutes. Remove the bouquet garni. Add the onions, pork fat, and peas, and return to the oven for 10 minutes.

5 Put the pheasant and pork fat in a food processor and grind finely.

6 Lower the oven temperature to 375°F/190°C. Grease an ovenproof dish with butter. Make layers of lasagna, pheasant sauce, and Béchamel Sauce in the dish, ending with Béchamel Sauce. Sprinkle over the cheese and bake for 30 minutes.

2

3

5

Red Roast Pork in Soy Sauce

In this traditional Chinese dish the pork turns "red" during cooking because it is basted in dark soy sauce.

NUTRITIONAL INFORMATION

Calories	268	Sugars	20g
Protein	26g	Fat	8g
Carbohydrate	22g	Saturates	3g

1¼ hrs

1¼ hrs

SERVES 4

INGREDIENTS

- 1 lb/450 g lean pork fillets
- 6 tbsp dark soy sauce
- 2 tbsp dry sherry
- 1 tsp Chinese five-spice powder
- 2 garlic cloves, crushed
- 2 tsp finely chopped fresh ginger root
- 1 large red bell pepper
- 1 large yellow bell pepper
- 1 large orange bell pepper
- 4 tbsp superfine sugar
- 2 tbsp red wine vinegar

TO GARNISH

- shredded scallions
- snipped fresh chives

2

4

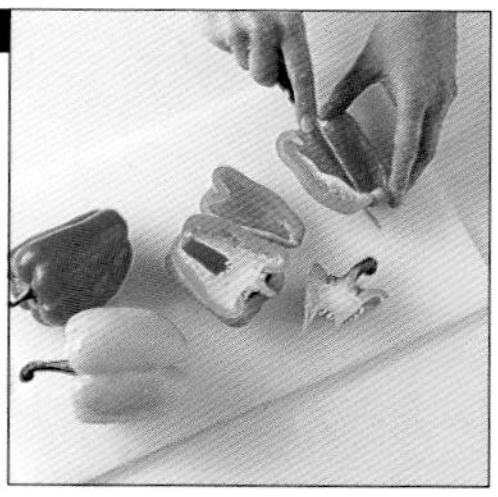

6

1 Trim away any excess fat and the silver skin from the pork and place in a shallow dish.

2 Mix together the soy sauce, sherry, five-spice powder, garlic, and ginger. Spoon the mixture over the pork, cover, and marinate in the refrigerator for at least 1 hour or until required.

3 Drain the pork, reserving the marinade. Place the pork on a roasting rack over a roasting pan. Cook in a preheated oven, 375°F/190°C, occasionally basting with the marinade, for 1 hour or until cooked through.

4 Meanwhile, halve and seed the bell peppers. Cut each bell pepper half into 3 equal portions. Arrange them on a cookie sheet and bake alongside the pork for the last 30 minutes of cooking time.

5 Place the superfine sugar and vinegar in a pan and heat gently until the sugar dissolves. Bring to a boil and simmer for 3–4 minutes until syrupy.

6 When the pork is cooked, remove it from the oven and brush with the sugar syrup. Let stand for about 5 minutes, then slice, and arrange on a warm serving plate.

7 Serve garnished with the scallions and freshly snipped chives.

Italian Calzone

A calzone is like a pizza in reverse—it resembles a large turnover with the dough on the outside and the filling on the inside.

NUTRITIONAL INFORMATION

Calories	405	Sugars	7g
Protein	19g	Fat	17g
Carbohydrate	48g	Saturates	5g

5 mins 20 mins

SERVES 4

I N G R E D I E N T S

1 quantity Basic Pizza Dough (see page 14)

1 egg, beaten

1 tbsp tomato paste

1 oz/25 g Italian salami, chopped

1 oz/25 g mortadella ham, chopped

1 tomato, peeled and chopped

2 tbsp ricotta cheese

2 scallions, trimmed and chopped

¼ tsp dried oregano

salt and pepper

1 Knead the Basic Pizza Dough and roll out on a lightly floured counter to form a 9-inch/23-cm circle.

2 Brush the edge of the dough with a little beaten egg.

3 Spread the tomato paste over the half of the circle nearest to you.

4 Scatter the salami, mortadella, and chopped tomato on top.

5 Dot with the ricotta cheese and then evenly sprinkle over the scallions and oregano. Season to taste with salt and pepper.

6 Fold over the other half of the dough to form a half moon shape. Press the edges together well to prevent the filling from coming out.

7 Place the calzone on a cookie sheet and brush with beaten egg to glaze. Make a small hole in the top with a knife in order to allow any steam to escape during cooking.

8 Bake in a preheated oven, 400°F/200°C, for 20 minutes, or until golden. Serve immediately.

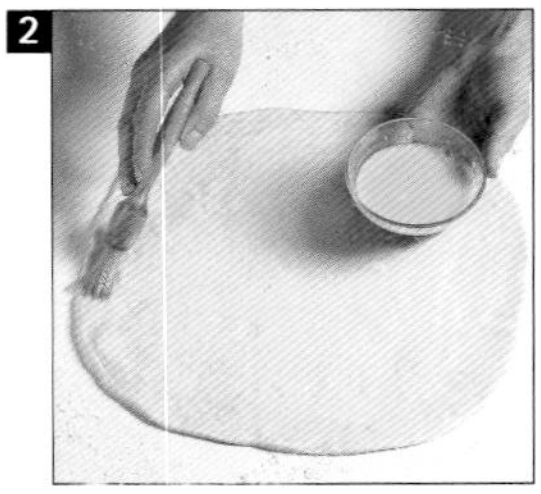

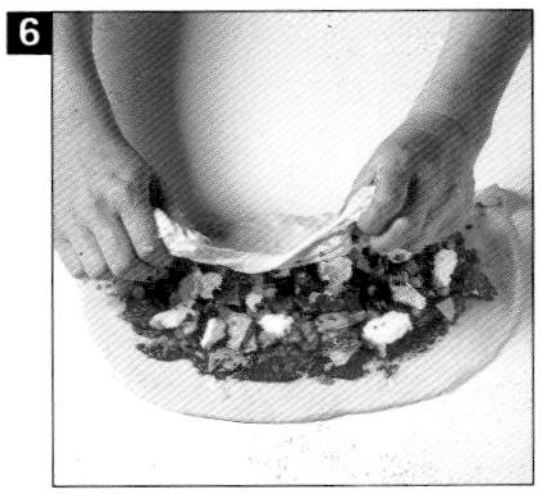

Stuffed Cannelloni

Cannelloni, the thick, round pasta tubes, make perfect containers for close-textured sauces of all kinds.

NUTRITIONAL INFORMATION

Calories	520	Sugars	5g
Protein	21g	Fat	39g
Carbohydrate	23g	Saturates	18g

30 mins · 1¼ hrs

SERVES 4

INGREDIENTS

- 8 dried cannelloni tubes
- 1 tbsp olive oil
- ⅓ cup freshly grated Parmesan cheese
- fresh herb sprigs, to garnish

FILLING

- 2 tbsp butter
- 10½ oz/300 g frozen spinach, thawed and chopped
- ½ cup ricotta cheese
- ⅓ cup freshly grated Parmesan cheese
- ¼ cup chopped ham
- pinch of freshly grated nutmeg
- 2 tbsp heavy cream
- 2 eggs, lightly beaten
- salt and pepper

SAUCE

- 2 tbsp butter
- scant ¼ cup all-purpose flour
- 1¼ cups milk
- 2 bay leaves
- pinch of freshly grated nutmeg

1

3

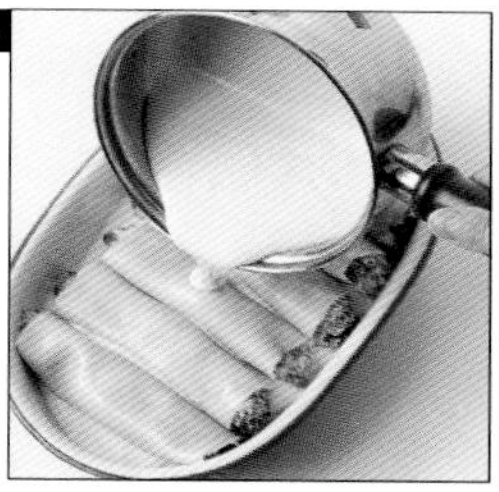

5

1 To make the filling, melt the butter in a pan over low heat and cook the spinach for 2–3 minutes. Remove from the heat and stir in the ricotta and Parmesan cheeses and the ham. Season to taste with nutmeg and salt and pepper. Beat in the cream and eggs to make a thick paste.

2 Bring a pan of lightly salted water to a boil. Add the pasta and the oil, return to a boil, and cook for 10–12 minutes or until tender, but still firm to the bite. Drain and let cool.

3 To make the sauce, melt the butter in a pan. Stir in the flour and cook, stirring, for 1 minute. Gradually stir in the milk. Add the bay leaves and simmer, stirring, for 5 minutes. Add the nutmeg and salt and pepper to taste. Remove from the heat and discard the bay leaves.

4 Spoon the filling into a pastry bag and fill the cannelloni.

5 Spoon a little sauce into the base of an ovenproof dish. Arrange the cannelloni in the dish in a single layer and pour over the remaining sauce. Sprinkle over the Parmesan cheese and bake in a preheated oven, 375°F/190°C, for 40–45 minutes. Garnish and serve.

Tom's Toad-in-the-Hole

This unusual recipe uses chicken and Cumberland sausage which is then made into individual bite-size cakes.

NUTRITIONAL INFORMATION

Calories	470	Sugars	4g
Protein	28g	Fat	27g
Carbohydrate	30g	Saturates	12g

1¼ hrs — 30 mins

SERVES 4-6

INGREDIENTS

- 1 cup all-purpose flour
- 1 egg, beaten
- scant 1 cup milk
- 5 tbsp water
- 2 tbsp beef drippings
- 9 oz/250 g chicken breasts
- 9 oz/250 g Cumberland sausage
- salt
- chicken or onion gravy, to serve (optional)

1 Mix the flour and salt in a bowl, make a well in the centre and add the beaten eggs. Add half the milk, and using a wooden spoon, work in the flour slowly.

2 Beat the mixture until smooth, then add the remaining milk and water. Beat again until the mixture is smooth. Let the mixture stand for at least 1 hour.

3 Add the drippings to individual baking pans or to 1 large baking pan. Cut up the chicken and sausage so that you get a generous piece in each individual pan or several scattered around the large pan.

4 Heat the pans in a preheated oven, 425°F/220°C, for 5 minutes until very hot. Remove the pans from the oven and pour in the batter, leaving space for the mixture to expand.

5 Return the pans to the oven to cook for 35 minutes until risen and golden brown. Do not open the oven door for at least 30 minutes.

6 Serve while hot with chicken or onion gravy, if desired, or on its own.

VARIATION

Use skinless, boneless chicken legs instead of chicken breast in the recipe. Cut up as directed. Instead of Cumberland sausage, use your favorite variety of sausage.

1

2

3

Braised Fennel & Linguine

This aniseed-flavored vegetable gives that certain extra punch to this delicious creamy pasta dish.

NUTRITIONAL INFORMATION

Calories 650	Sugars 6g
Protein 14g	Fat 39g
Carbohydrate ... 62g	Saturates 22g

20 mins 50 mins

SERVES 4

INGREDIENTS

- 6 fennel bulbs
- ⅔ cup vegetable bouillon
- 2 tbsp butter
- 6 slices rindless smoked bacon, diced
- 6 shallots, quartered
- ¼ cup all-purpose flour
- scant ½ cup heavy cream
- 1 tbsp Madeira
- 1 lb/450 g dried linguine
- 1 tbsp olive oil
- salt and pepper

1 Trim the fennel bulbs, then peel off and reserve the outer layer of each. Cut the bulbs into quarters and put them in a large pan with the bouillon and the reserved outer layers. Bring to a boil, lower the heat, and simmer for 5 minutes.

2 Using a perforated spoon, transfer the fennel to a large dish. Discard the outer layers of the fennel bulb. Bring the vegetable bouillon to a boil and allow to reduce by half. Set aside.

3 Melt the butter in a skillet. Add the bacon and shallots and cook over a low heat, stirring occasionally, for 4 minutes. Add the flour, reduced bouillon, cream, and Madeira and cook, stirring constantly, for 3 minutes or until the sauce is smooth. Season to taste with salt and pepper and pour over the fennel.

4 Bring a pan of lightly salted water to a boil. Add the pasta and oil, bring back to a boil, and cook for 8–10 minutes or until tender, but still firm to the bite. Drain and transfer to an ovenproof dish.

5 Add the fennel and the sauce and braise in a preheated oven, 350°F/180°C, for 20 minutes until the fennel is tender and piping hot. Serve immediately.

COOK'S TIP

Fennel will keep in the salad drawer of the refrigerator for 2–3 days, but it is best eaten as fresh as possible. Cut surfaces turn brown quickly, so do not prepare it too much in advance of cooking.

Eggplant Pasta Cake

This recipe would make a stunning dinner party dish, yet it contains simple ingredients and is easy to make.

NUTRITIONAL INFORMATION

Calories	201	Sugars	4g
Protein	14g	Fat	7g
Carbohydrate	22g	Saturates	4g

55 mins

35 mins

SERVES 4

INGREDIENTS

- butter, for greasing
- 1 medium eggplant
- 10½ oz/300 g dried tricolor pasta shapes
- ½ cup low-fat soft cheese with garlic and herbs
- 1½ cups passata (strained tomatoes)
- scant ¾ cup freshly grated Parmesan cheese
- 1½ tsp dried oregano
- 2 tbsp dry white bread crumbs
- salt and pepper

1 Grease and line an 8-inch/20-cm round spring-form cake pan.

2 Trim the eggplant and cut lengthwise into slices about ¼ inch/5 mm thick. Place in a bowl, sprinkle with salt, and let stand for 30 minutes to remove any bitter juices. Rinse well under cold running water and drain.

3 Bring a pan of water to a boil and blanch the eggplant slices for 1 minute. Drain and pat dry with paper towels. Set aside.

4 Bring a large pan of lightly salted water to a boil. Add the pasta shapes, bring back to a boil, and cook for 8–10 minutes, until tender, but still firm to the bite. Drain well and return to the pan. Add the soft cheese and allow it to melt over the pasta.

5 Stir in the passata, Parmesan cheese, and oregano, and season to taste with salt and pepper. Set aside.

6 Arrange the eggplant slices over the base and sides of the pan, overlapping them and leaving no gaps. Pile the pasta mixture into the pan, packing it down, and sprinkle with the bread crumbs. Bake in a preheated oven, 375°F/190°C, for 20 minutes. Remove from the oven and let stand for 15 minutes.

7 Loosen the cake round the edge with a spatula and release from the pan. Turn out the pasta cake, eggplant side uppermost, and serve hot.

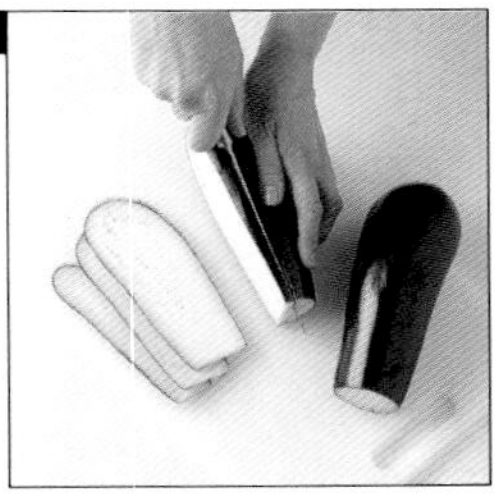

2

6

6

Fruity Lamb Casserole

The sweet spicy blend of cinnamon, coriander, and cumin is the perfect complement to the tender lamb and apricots in this warming casserole.

NUTRITIONAL INFORMATION

Calories	384	Sugars	16g
Protein	32g	Fat	22g
Carbohydrate	17g	Saturates	9g

5 mins

1¼ hrs

SERVES 4

INGREDIENTS

- 1 lb/450 g lean lamb, trimmed and cut into 1-inch/2.5-cm cubes
- 1 tsp ground cinnamon
- 1 tsp ground coriander
- 1 tsp ground cumin
- 2 tsp olive oil
- 1 red onion, finely chopped
- 1 garlic clove, crushed
- 14 oz/400 g canned chopped tomatoes
- 2 tbsp tomato paste
- 4½ oz/125 g no-soak dried apricots
- 1 tsp superfine sugar
- 1¼ cups vegetable bouillon
- salt and pepper
- 1 small bunch fresh cilantro, to garnish
- brown rice, steamed couscous or bulgar wheat, to serve

1 Place the meat in a mixing bowl and add the cinnamon, coriander, cumin, and oil. Mix thoroughly so that the lamb is well coated in the spices.

2 Heat a non-stick skillet for a few seconds, then add the lamb. Reduce the heat and cook for 4–5 minutes, stirring, until browned all over. Transfer the lamb to a large casserole.

3 In the same skillet, cook the onion, garlic, tomatoes, and tomato paste for 5 minutes. Season to taste with salt and pepper. Stir in the apricots and sugar, add the bouillon, and bring to a boil.

4 Spoon the sauce over the lamb and mix well. Cover and cook in a preheated oven, 350°F/180°C, for 1 hour, removing the lid for the last 10 minutes.

5 Coarsely chop the cilantro and sprinkle it over the casserole to garnish. Serve the lamb straight from the casserole with brown rice, steamed couscous, or bulgar wheat.

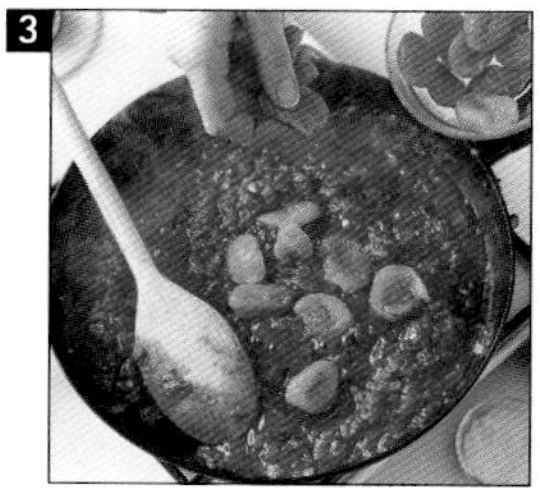

Hot Pot Chops

A hot pot is a lamb casserole, made with carrots and onions and with a potato topping. The leg steaks used here are an interesting alternative.

NUTRITIONAL INFORMATION

Calories	250	Sugars	2g
Protein	27g	Fat	12g
Carbohydrate	8g	Saturates	5g

10 mins · 30 mins

SERVES 4

INGREDIENTS

- 4 lean, boneless lamb leg steaks, 4½ oz/125 g each
- 1 small onion, thinly sliced
- 1 carrot, thinly sliced
- 1 potato, thinly sliced
- 1 tsp olive oil
- 1 tsp dried rosemary
- salt and pepper
- fresh rosemary, to garnish
- freshly steamed green vegetables, to serve

1 Using a sharp knife, trim any excess fat from the lamb steaks. Season both sides of the steaks with salt and pepper to taste and arrange them in a single layer on a cookie sheet.

2 Alternate layers of sliced onion, carrot, and potato on top of each lamb steak.

3 Brush the tops of the potato lightly with oil, season well with salt and pepper to taste, and then sprinkle with a little dried rosemary.

4 Bake the hot pot chops in a preheated oven, 350°F.180°C, for 25–30 minutes until the lamb is tender and cooked through.

5 Drain the lamb on paper towels and transfer to a warm serving plate.

6 Garnish with fresh rosemary and serve accompanied with a selection of steamed green vegetables.

1
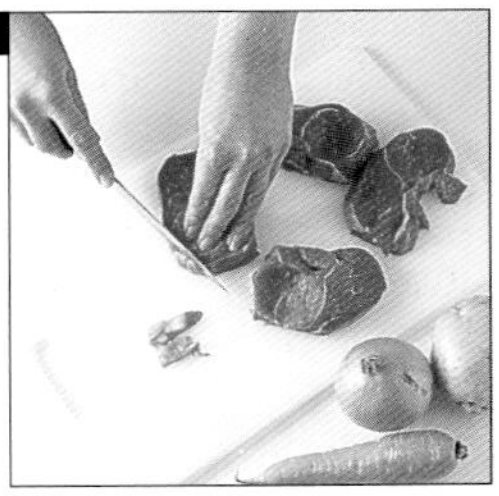

2
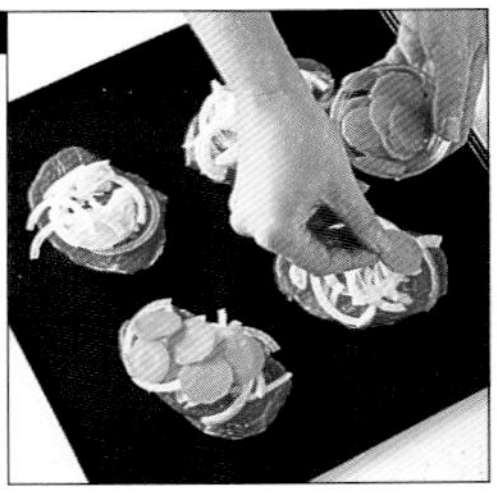

3
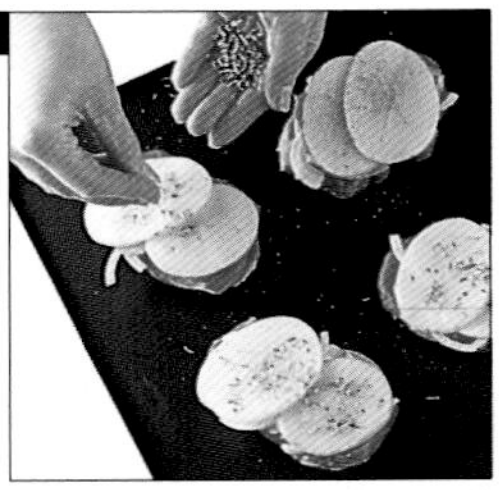

VARIATION

This recipe would work equally well with boneless chicken breasts. Pound the chicken slightly with a meat mallet so that the pieces are the same thickness throughout.

Beef & Tomato Gratin

A satisfying bake of lean ground beef, zucchini, and tomatoes, cooked in a low-fat "custard" with a cheese crust.

NUTRITIONAL INFORMATION

Calories	278	Sugars	10g
Protein	29g	Fat	10g
Carbohydrate	20g	Saturates	5g

10 mins — 1¼ hrs

SERVES 4

I N G R E D I E N T S

- 12 oz/350 g lean ground beef
- 1 large onion, finely chopped
- 1 tsp dried mixed herbs
- 1 tbsp all-purpose flour
- 1¼ cups beef bouillon
- 1 tbsp tomato paste
- 2 large tomatoes, thinly sliced
- 4 zucchini, thinly sliced
- 2 tbsp cornstarch
- 1¼ cups skim milk
- ¾ cup ricotta cheese
- 1 egg yolk
- scant ¾ cup freshly grated Parmesan cheese
- salt and pepper

TO SERVE

- crusty bread
- steamed vegetables

1 In a large skillet, dry-cook the beef and onion over low heat, stirring occasionally, for 4–5 minutes until the meat is browned.

2 Stir in the dried mixed herbs, flour, beef bouillon, and tomato paste, and season to taste with salt and pepper. Bring to a boil and simmer gently for 30 minutes until the mixture has thickened.

3 Transfer the beef mixture to an ovenproof gratin dish. Cover with a layer of sliced tomatoes and then add a layer of sliced zucchini. Blend the cornstarch with a little milk to a smooth paste. Pour the remaining milk into a pan and bring to a boil. Add the cornstarch mixture and cook, stirring constantly, for 1–2 minutes until thickened. Remove the pan from the heat and beat in the ricotta cheese and egg yolk. Season well with salt and pepper.

4 Spread the white sauce over the layer of zucchini. Place the dish on a cookie sheet and sprinkle the grated Parmesan cheese evenly over the top. Bake in a preheated oven, 375°F/190°C, for 25–30 minutes until golden brown. Serve with crusty bread and vegetables.

1

3

4

Rich Beef Stew

This wonderful slow-cooked beef stew is flavored with oranges, red wine, and porcini mushrooms.

NUTRITIONAL INFORMATION

Calories	388	Sugars	15g
Protein	30g	Fat	21g
Carbohydrate	16g	Saturates	9g

45 mins | 1¾ hrs

SERVES 4

INGREDIENTS

- 1 tbsp oil
- 1 tbsp butter
- 8 oz/225 g pearl onions, peeled and halved
- 1 lb 5 oz/600 g stewing steak, diced into 1½-inch/4-cm chunks
- 1¼ cups beef bouillon
- ⅔ cup red wine
- 4 tbsp chopped fresh oregano
- 1 tbsp sugar
- 1 orange
- 1 oz/25 g porcini or other dried mushrooms
- 8 oz/225 g fresh plum tomatoes
- cooked rice or potatoes, to serve

1 Heat the oil and butter in a large skillet. Add the onions and fry over low heat, stirring occasionally, for 5 minutes or until golden. Remove the onions with a perforated spoon, set aside, and keep warm.

2 Add the beef to the skillet and cook, stirring, for 5 minutes or until browned all over.

3 Return the onions to the skillet and add the bouillon, wine, oregano, and sugar, stirring to mix well. Transfer the mixture to a casserole dish.

2

3

4

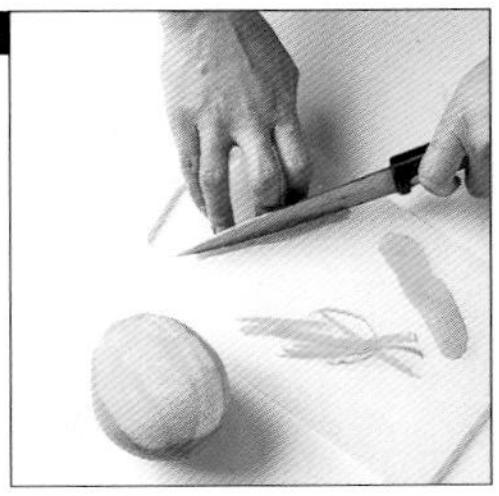

4 Pare the zest from the orange and cut it into strips. Slice the orange flesh into rings. Add the orange rings and the zest to the casserole. Cook in a preheated oven, 350°F/180°C, for 1¼ hours.

5 Meanwhile, soak the porcini or other dried mushrooms in a small bowl containing 4 tablespoons of warm water for 30 minutes.

6 Peel and halve the tomatoes. Add the tomatoes, mushrooms, and mushroom soaking liquid to the casserole. Cook for a further 20 minutes until the beef is tender and the juices thickened. Serve with cooked rice or potatoes.

Creamed Strips of Sirloin

This quick, easy, and elegant dish tastes superb and would make a delicious treat for a special occasion.

NUTRITIONAL INFORMATION

Calories	796	Sugars	2g
Protein	29g	Fat	63g
Carbohydrate	26g	Saturates	39g

15 mins | 30 mins

SERVES 4

INGREDIENTS

- 6 tbsp butter
- 1 lb/450 g sirloin steak, trimmed and cut into thin strips
- 2⅓ cups sliced white mushrooms
- 1 tsp mustard
- pinch of freshly grated ginger root
- 2 tbsp dry sherry
- ⅔ cup heavy cream
- salt and pepper
- 4 slices hot toast, cut into triangles, to serve

PASTA

- 1 lb/450 g dried rigatoni pasta
- 2 tbsp olive oil
- 2 sprigs fresh basil
- 4 oz/115 g butter

1 Melt the butter in a large skillet and gently cook the steak over low heat, stirring frequently, for 6 minutes. Using a perforated spoon, transfer the steak to an ovenproof dish and keep warm.

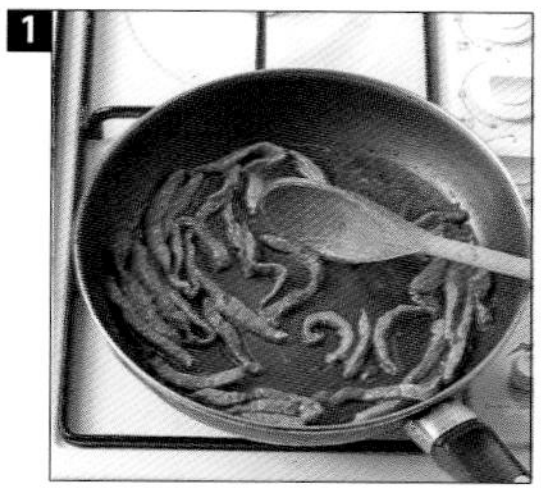

2 Add the sliced mushrooms to the skillet and cook for 2–3 minutes in the juices remaining in the pan. Add the mustard and ginger and season with salt and pepper to taste. Cook for 2 minutes, then add the sherry and cream. Cook for a further 3 minutes, then pour the cream sauce over the steak.

3 Bake the steak and cream mixture in a preheated oven, 375°F/190°C, for 10 minutes.

4 Meanwhile, cook the pasta. Bring a large pan of lightly salted water to a boil. Add the rigatoni, olive oil, and 1 of the basil sprigs, return to a boil, and cook for 8–10 minutes until tender, but still firm to the bite. Drain the pasta and transfer to a warm serving plate. Toss the pasta with the butter and garnish with a sprig of basil.

5 Serve the creamed steak strips with the pasta and triangles of warm toast.

COOK'S TIP

Dried pasta will keep for up to 6 months. Keep it in the packet and reseal it once you have opened it, or transfer the pasta to an airtight jar.

Fresh Spaghetti & Meatballs

This well-loved Italian dish is famous across the world. Make the most of it by using high-quality steak for the meatballs.

NUTRITIONAL INFORMATION

Calories	665	Sugars	9g
Protein	39g	Fat	24g
Carbohydrate	77g	Saturates	8g

45 mins

1¼ hrs

SERVES 4

INGREDIENTS

- 2½ cups fresh brown bread crumbs
- ⅔ cup milk
- 2 tbsp butter
- ¼ cup whole-wheat flour
- generous ¾ cup beef bouillon
- 14 oz/400 g canned chopped tomatoes
- 2 tbsp tomato paste
- 1 tsp sugar
- 1 tbsp finely chopped fresh tarragon
- 1 large onion, chopped
- 4 cups ground steak
- 1 tsp paprika
- 4 tbsp olive oil
- 1 lb/450 g fresh spaghetti
- salt and pepper
- fresh tarragon sprigs, to garnish

2

2

4

1 Place the bread crumbs in a bowl, add the milk, and set aside to soak for about 30 minutes.

2 Melt half of the butter in a pan. Add the flour and cook, stirring constantly, for 2 minutes. Gradually stir in the beef bouillon and cook, stirring constantly, for a further 5 minutes. Add the tomatoes, tomato paste, sugar, and tarragon. Season well and simmer for 25 minutes.

3 Mix the onion, steak, and paprika into the bread crumbs and season to taste. Shape the mixture into 14 meatballs.

4 Heat the oil and remaining butter in a skillet and cook the meatballs, turning, until brown all over. Place in a deep casserole, pour over the tomato sauce, cover, and bake in a preheated oven, 350°F/180°C, for 25 minutes.

5 Bring a large pan of lightly salted water to a boil. Add the fresh spaghetti, bring back to a boil, and cook for about 2–3 minutes or until tender, but still firm to the bite.

6 Meanwhile, remove the meatballs from the oven and let them cool for 3 minutes. Serve the meatballs and their sauce with the spaghetti, garnished with tarragon sprigs.

Layered Meat Loaf

The rich, cheese-flavored pasta layer comes as a pleasant surprise inside this lightly spiced meat loaf.

NUTRITIONAL INFORMATION

Calories	412	Sugars	3g
Protein	21g	Fat	30g
Carbohydrate	15g	Saturates	13g

35 mins

1½ hrs

SERVES 6

INGREDIENTS

2 tbsp butter, plus extra for greasing
1 small onion, finely chopped
1 small red bell pepper, seeded and chopped
1 garlic clove, chopped
4 cups ground beef
scant ½ cup fresh white bread crumbs
½ tsp cayenne pepper
1 tbsp lemon juice
½ tsp grated lemon zest
2 tbsp chopped fresh parsley
3¼ oz/90 g dried short pasta, such as fusilli
1 tbsp olive oil
1 cup Italian Cheese Sauce (see page 15)
4 bay leaves
6 oz/175 g fatty bacon
salt and pepper
salad greens, to serve

2

2

4

1 Melt the butter in a pan over medium heat and cook the onion and bell pepper for about 3 minutes. Stir in the garlic and cook for 1 minute.

2 Put the meat into a bowl and mash with a wooden spoon until sticky. Add the onion mixture, bread crumbs, cayenne pepper, lemon juice, lemon zest, and parsley. Season to taste and set aside.

3 Bring a pan of salted water to a boil. Add the pasta and oil, bring back to a boil, and cook for 8–10 minutes until almost tender, but still firm to the bite. Drain thoroughly and stir into the Italian Cheese Sauce.

4 Grease a 2-lb 4-oz/1-kg loaf pan and arrange the bay leaves in the base. Stretch the bacon slices with the back of a knife and line the bottom and sides of the pan with them. Spoon in half the meat mixture and smooth the surface. Cover with the pasta mixed with Italian Cheese Sauce, then spoon in the remaining meat mixture. Level the top and cover with foil.

5 Bake the meat loaf in a preheated oven, 350°F/180°C, for 1 hour or until the juices run clear when the point of a sharp knife is inserted into the center and the loaf has shrunk away from the sides of the pan. Pour off any fat and turn out the loaf onto a serving dish. Serve with salad greens.

Meatballs in Red Wine Sauce

A different twist is given to this popular, traditional pasta dish with a rich, but wonderfully subtle sauce.

NUTRITIONAL INFORMATION

Calories	811	Sugars	7g
Protein	30g	Fat	43g
Carbohydrate	76g	Saturates	12g

45 mins

1½ hrs

SERVES 4

INGREDIENTS

- ⅔ cup milk
- generous 2½ cups fresh white bread crumbs
- 2 tbsp butter
- 9 tbsp olive oil
- 3 cups sliced oyster mushrooms
- ¼ cup whole-wheat flour
- generous ¾ cup beef bouillon
- ⅔ cup red wine
- 4 tomatoes, peeled and chopped
- 1 tbsp tomato paste
- 1 tsp brown sugar
- 1 tbsp finely chopped fresh basil
- 12 shallots, chopped
- 4 cups ground steak
- 1 tsp paprika
- 1 lb/450 g dried egg tagliatelle
- salt and pepper
- fresh basil sprigs, to garnish

1 Pour the milk into a bowl, add the bread crumbs, and set aside to soak for 30 minutes.

2 Heat half of the butter and 4 tablespoons of the oil in a pan. Cook the mushrooms for 4 minutes,. Stir in the flour and cook, stirring, for 2 minutes. Add the bouillon and wine and simmer for 15 minutes. Add the tomatoes, tomato paste, sugar, and basil. Season and simmer for 30 minutes.

3 Mix the shallots, steak, and paprika with the bread crumbs and season to taste with salt and pepper. Shape the mixture into 14 meatballs.

4 Heat 4 tablespoons of the rest of the oil and the remaining butter in a large skillet. Cook the meatballs, turning frequently, until brown all over. Transfer to a deep casserole, pour over the red wine and the mushroom sauce, cover, and bake in a preheated oven, 350°F/180°C, for 30 minutes.

5 Bring a pan of salted water to a boil. Add the pasta and the remaining oil, bring back to a boil, and cook for 8–10 minutes or until tender, but still firm to the bite. Drain and transfer to a serving dish. Remove the casserole from the oven and cool for 3 minutes. Pour the meatballs and sauce onto the pasta, garnish, and serve.

3

3

4

Sicilian Spaghetti Cake

Any variety of long pasta, such as fettuccine or tagliatelle, could be used for this very tasty dish from Sicily.

NUTRITIONAL INFORMATION

Calories	876	Sugars	10g
Protein	37g	Fat	65g
Carbohydrate	39g	Saturates	18g

30 mins 50 mins

SERVES 4

INGREDIENTS

- ⅔ cup olive oil, plus extra for brushing
- 2 eggplants
- generous 3 cups finely ground lean beef
- 1 onion, chopped
- 2 garlic cloves, crushed
- 2 tbsp tomato paste
- 14 oz/400 g canned chopped tomatoes
- 1 tsp Worcestershire sauce
- 1 tsp chopped fresh oregano or marjoram or ½ tsp dried oregano or marjoram
- ½ cup pitted black olives, sliced
- 1 green, red, or yellow bell pepper, seeded and chopped
- 6 oz/175 g dried spaghetti
- generous 1 cup freshly grated Parmesan cheese
- salt and pepper

1 Brush an 8-inch/20-cm loose-bottomed circular cake pan with olive oil, place a disc of baking parchment in the bottom, and brush with oil. Trim the eggplants and cut into slanting slices, ¼ inch/5 mm thick. Heat some of the oil in a skillet. Fry a few slices of eggplant at a time until lightly browned, turning once, and adding more oil as necessary. Drain on paper towels.

2 Put the ground beef, onion, and garlic into a pan and cook over low heat, stirring frequently, until browned all over. Add the tomato paste, tomatoes, Worcestershire sauce, and herbs. Season to taste with salt and pepper. Simmer gently for 10 minutes, stirring occasionally, then add the olives and bell pepper and cook for a further 10 minutes.

3 Bring a large pan of salted water to a boil. Add the spaghetti, bring back to a boil, and cook for 8–10 minutes or until tender, but still firm to the bite. Drain the spaghetti thoroughly. Turn the spaghetti into a bowl and mix in the meat mixture and grated Parmesan cheese, tossing together with 2 forks.

4 Lay overlapping slices of eggplant over the base of the cake pan and up the sides. Add the meat mixture, pressing it down, and cover with the remaining eggplant slices.

5 Stand the cake pan in a baking pan and cook in a preheated oven, 400°F/200°C, for 40 minutes. Let stand for 5 minutes, then loosen around the edges and invert onto a warmed serving dish, releasing the pan clip. Remove the baking parchment. Serve immediately.

1

3

4

Beef & Pasta Bake

The combination of Italian and Indian ingredients makes a surprisingly delicious recipe. Marinate the steak in advance to save time.

NUTRITIONAL INFORMATION

Calories	1050	Sugars	4g
Protein	47g	Fat	81g
Carbohydrate	37g	Saturates	34g

6¼ hrs

1¼ hrs

SERVES 4

INGREDIENTS

- 2 lb/900 g steak, cubed
- ⅔ cup beef bouillon
- 1 lb/450 g dried macaroni
- 1¼ cups heavy cream
- ½ tsp garam masala
- salt
- fresh cilantro and slivered almonds, to garnish

KORMA PASTE

- ½ cup blanched almonds
- 6 garlic cloves
- 3 tsp coarsely chopped fresh ginger root
- 6 tbsp beef bouillon
- 1 tsp ground cardamom
- 4 cloves, crushed
- 1 tsp cinnamon
- 2 large onions, chopped
- 1 tsp coriander seeds
- 2 tsp ground cumin seeds
- pinch of cayenne pepper
- 6 tbsp sunflower oil

1 To make the korma paste, grind the almonds finely using a pestle and mortar. Put the ground almonds and the rest of the korma paste ingredients into a food processor or blender and process to make a very smooth paste.

2 Put the steak in a shallow dish and spoon over the korma paste, turning to coat the steak well. Set aside in the refrigerator to marinate for 6 hours.

3 Transfer the steak and korma paste to a large pan and simmer over low heat, adding a little beef bouillon if required, for 35 minutes.

4 Meanwhile, bring a large pan of lightly salted water to a boil. Add the macaroni, bring back to a boil, and cook for 10 minutes until tender, but still firm to the bite. Drain the pasta thoroughly and transfer to a deep casserole. Add the steak, heavy cream, and garam masala.

5 Bake in a preheated oven, 400°F/200°C, for 30 minutes. Remove the casserole from the oven and let stand for about 10 minutes.

6 Garnish the bake with fresh cilantro leaves and slivered almonds and serve immediately.

1

2

3

Lasagna Verde

The sauce in this delicious baked pasta dish can be used as an alternative sauce for spaghetti bolognese.

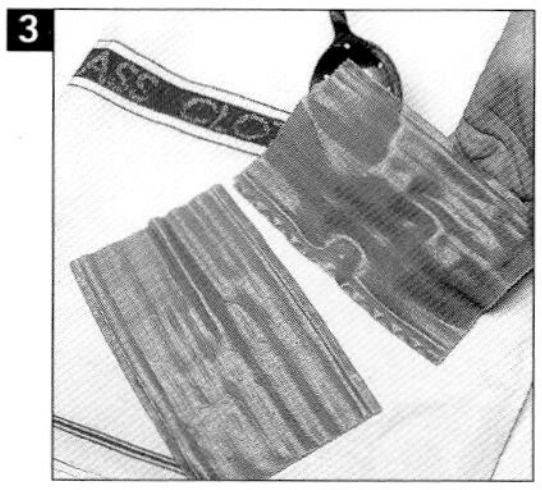

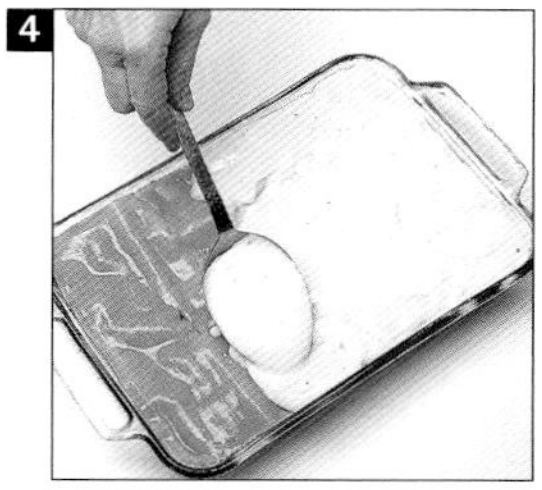

NUTRITIONAL INFORMATION

Calories 619	Sugars 7g
Protein 29g	Fat 45g
Carbohydrate . . .21g	Saturates 19g

1¾ hrs

55 mins

SERVES 6

INGREDIENTS

- Ragù Sauce (see page 15)
- 1 tbsp olive oil
- 8 oz/225 g lasagna verde
- butter, for greasing
- Béchamel Sauce (see page 92)
- ⅔ cup freshly grated Parmesan cheese
- salt
- salad greens, tomato salad, or black olives, to serve

1 Begin by making the Ragù Sauce as described on page 15, but cook for 10–12 minutes longer than the time given, in an uncovered pan, to allow the excess liquid to evaporate. It needs to be reduced to a thick paste.

2 Have ready a large pan of boiling, salted water and add the olive oil. Drop the pasta sheets into the boiling water, a few at a time, and return the water to a boil before adding further pasta sheets. If you are using fresh lasagna, cook the sheets for a total of 8 minutes. If you are using dried or partly pre-cooked pasta, cook it according to the directions given on the packet.

3 Remove the pasta sheets from the pan with a perforated spoon or tongs. Spread them in a single layer on damp dish cloths until required.

4 Grease a rectangular ovenproof dish, about 10–11 inches/25–28 cm long. To assemble the dish, spoon a little of the meat sauce into the prepared dish, cover with a layer of lasagna, then spoon over a little Béchamel Sauce, and sprinkle with some of the grated Parmesan cheese. Continue making layers in this way, covering the final layer of lasagna with the remaining Béchamel Sauce.

5 Sprinkle the remaining cheese on top and bake in a preheated oven, 375°F/190°C, for 40 minutes or until the sauce is golden brown and bubbling. Serve with salad greens, a tomato salad, or a bowl of black olives.

Pasticcio

A recipe that has both Italian and Greek origins, this dish may be served hot or cold, cut into thick, satisfying squares.

NUTRITIONAL INFORMATION

Calories	590	Sugars	8g
Protein	34g	Fat	39g
Carbohydrate	23g	Saturates	16g

35 mins

1¼ hrs

SERVES 6

INGREDIENTS

8 oz/225 g dried fusilli, or other short pasta shapes
1 tbsp olive oil
4 tbsp heavy cream
salt
fresh rosemary sprigs, to garnish

SAUCE

2 tbsp olive oil, plus extra for brushing
1 onion, thinly sliced
1 red bell pepper, seeded and chopped
2 cloves garlic, chopped
1 lb 6 oz/625 g lean ground beef
14 oz/400 g canned chopped tomatoes
½ cup dry white wine
2 tbsp chopped fresh parsley
1¾ oz/50 g canned anchovies, drained and chopped
salt and pepper

TOPPING

1¼ cups plain yogurt
3 eggs
pinch of freshly grated nutmeg
½ cup freshly grated Parmesan cheese

1

4

5

1 To make the sauce, heat the oil in a large skillet and cook the onion and red bell pepper for 3 minutes. Stir in the garlic and cook for 1 minute more. Stir in the beef and cook, stirring frequently, until it is no longer pink.

2 Add the tomatoes and wine, stir and bring to a boil. Simmer, uncovered, for 20 minutes or until the sauce is fairly thick. Stir in the parsley and anchovies and season to taste.

3 Bring a large pan of lightly salted water to a boil. Add the pasta and olive oil, return to a boil, and cook for 8–10 minutes until tender, but still firm to the bite. Drain the pasta, then transfer to a bowl. Stir in the cream and set aside.

4 To make the topping, beat together the yogurt and eggs and season with nutmeg, and salt and pepper, to taste.

5 Brush a shallow ovenproof dish with oil. Spoon in half the pasta and cover with half the meat sauce. Repeat the layers, then spread the topping over the final layer. Sprinkle the cheese on top.

6 Bake in a preheated oven, 375°F/190°C, for 25 minutes or until the topping is golden brown and bubbling. Garnish with sprigs of rosemary and serve.

Neapolitan Veal Cutlets

The delicious combination of apple, onion, and mushrooms perfectly complements the delicate flavor of veal.

NUTRITIONAL INFORMATION

Calories	1071	Sugars	13g
Protein	74g	Fat	59g
Carbohydrate	66g	Saturates	16g

20 mins — 45 mins

SERVES 4

INGREDIENTS

- ¾ cup butter
- 4 veal cutlets, 250 g/9 oz each, trimmed
- 1 large onion, sliced
- 2 apples, peeled, cored, and sliced
- 6 oz/175 g white mushrooms
- 1 tbsp chopped fresh tarragon
- 8 black peppercorns
- 1 tbsp sesame seeds
- 14 oz/400 g dried marille
- scant ½ cup extra virgin olive oil
- 2 large beefsteak tomatoes, cut in half
- leaves of 1 sprig fresh basil
- ¾ cup mascarpone cheese
- salt and pepper
- fresh basil leaves, to garnish

1 Melt cup of the butter in a skillet. Cook the veal over low heat for 5 minutes on each side. Transfer to a dish and keep warm.

2 Cook the onion and apples in the skillet, stirring frequently, until lightly browned. Transfer to a dish, place the veal on top, and keep warm.

3 Melt the remaining butter in the skillet. Add the mushrooms, tarragon, and peppercorns and cook over low heat, stirring occasionally, for 3 minutes. Sprinkle over the sesame seeds.

4 Bring a pan of lightly salted water to a boil. Add the pasta and 1 tablespoon of the olive oil, bring back to a boil, and cook for 8–10 minutes or until tender, but still firm to the bite. Drain well and transfer to an ovenproof dish.

5 Broil or fry the tomatoes and basil for 2–3 minutes.

6 Top the pasta with the mascarpone cheese and sprinkle over the remaining olive oil. Place the onions, apples, and veal cutlets on top of the pasta. Spoon the mushrooms, peppercorns, and pan juices onto the cutlets, place the tomatoes and basil leaves around the edge, and place in a preheated oven, 300°F/150°C, for 5 minutes.

7 Season to taste with salt and pepper, garnish with fresh basil leaves, and serve immediately.

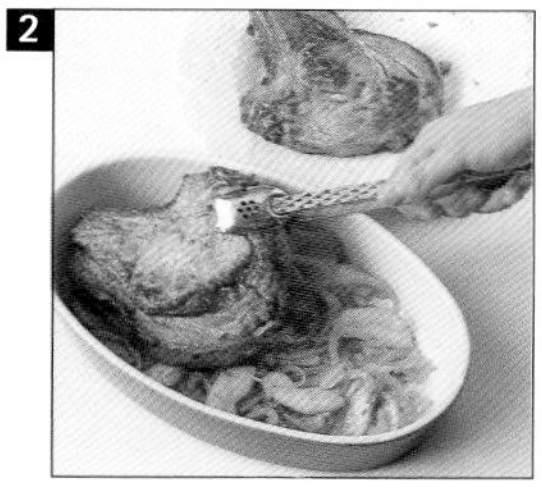

Vegetarian & Vegan

Anyone who ever thought that vegetarian meals were dull will be proved wrong by the rich variety of dishes in this chapter. You'll recognize influences from Middle Eastern

and Italian cooking, such as the Stuffed Vegetables, Roman Focaccia, and Sun-dried Tomato Loaf, but there are also traditional recipes such as Upside-down Cake and Fruit Crumble. They all make exciting treats at any time of year and for virtually any occasion. Don't be afraid to substitute some of your own personal favorite ingredients where ever appropriate.

Mushroom Cannelloni

Thick pasta tubes are filled with a mixture of seasoned, chopped mushrooms, and baked in a rich fragrant tomato sauce.

NUTRITIONAL INFORMATION

Calories	156	Sugar	8g
Protein	6g	Fats	1g
Carbohydrates	21g	Saturates	0.2g

35 mins — 1½ hrs

SERVES 4

INGREDIENTS

- 12 oz/350 g crimini mushrooms
- 1 onion, finely chopped
- 1 clove garlic, crushed
- 1 tbsp chopped fresh thyme
- ½ tsp ground nutmeg
- 4 tbsp dry white wine
- scant 1 cup fresh white bread crumbs
- 12 dried quick-cook cannelloni
- salt and pepper
- Parmesan shavings, to garnish (optional)

TOMATO SAUCE

- 1 large red bell pepper
- ¾ cup dry white wine
- scant 2 cups passata (strained tomatoes)
- 2 tbsp tomato paste
- 2 bay leaves
- 1 tsp superfine sugar

1 Finely chop the mushrooms and place in a pan with the onion and garlic. Stir in the thyme, nutmeg, and 4 tablespoons of wine. Bring to a boil, cover, and simmer for 10 minutes. Stir in the bread crumbs to bind the mixture together and season to taste with salt and pepper. Remove the pan from the heat and let cool for 10 minutes.

2 To make the sauce, halve and seed the bell pepper, place on the broiler rack, and cook under a preheated broiler for 8–10 minutes until charred. Let cool for 10 minutes.

3 Once the bell pepper has cooled, peel off the charred skin. Chop the flesh and place in a food processor with the wine. Blend until smooth, then pour into a pan.

4 Mix the remaining sauce ingredients with the bell pepper and wine. Bring to a boil and simmer for 10 minutes. Discard the bay leaves.

5 Cover the base of an ovenproof dish with a thin layer of sauce. Fill the cannelloni with the mushroom mixture and place in the dish. Spoon over the remaining sauce, cover with foil, and bake in a preheated oven, 400°F/200°C for 35–40 minutes. Garnish with Parmesan shavings, if desired, and serve immediately.

1

4

5

COOK'S TIP

Crimini mushrooms, also known as champignons de Paris, are common cultivated mushrooms that may have brown or white caps.

Pasta & Bean Casserole

A satisfying winter dish, this is a slow-cooked, one-pot meal. The navy beans need to be soaked overnight, so prepare well in advance.

NUTRITIONAL INFORMATION

Calories	323	Sugars	5g
Protein	13g	Fat	12g
Carbohydrate	41g	Saturates	2g

25 mins — 3½ hrs

SERVES 6

INGREDIENTS

- generous 1 cup dried navy beans, soaked overnight and drained
- 8 oz/225 g dried penne, or other short pasta shapes
- 6 tbsp olive oil
- 3½ cups vegetable bouillon
- 2 large onions, sliced
- 2 cloves garlic, chopped
- 2 bay leaves
- 1 tsp dried oregano
- 1 tsp dried thyme
- 5 tbsp red wine
- 2 tbsp tomato paste
- 2 celery stalks, sliced
- 1 fennel bulb, sliced
- scant 2 cups sliced mushrooms
- 8 oz/225 g tomatoes, sliced
- 1 tsp dark muscovado sugar
- scant 1 cup dry white bread crumbs
- salt and pepper

TO SERVE

- salad greens
- crusty bread

1 Put the beans in a large pan, cover them with water, and bring to a boil. Boil the beans rapidly for 20 minutes, then drain them.

2 Cook the pasta for only 3 minutes in a large pan of boiling salted water, adding 1 tablespoon of the oil. Drain in a strainer and set aside.

3 Put the beans in a large flameproof casserole, pour on the vegetable bouillon, and stir in the remaining olive oil, the onions, garlic, bay leaves, herbs, wine, and tomato paste.

4 Bring to a boil, cover the casserole, and cook in a preheated oven, 350°F/180°C, for 2 hours.

5 Remove the casserole from the oven and add the reserved pasta, the celery, fennel, mushrooms, and tomatoes, and season to taste with salt and pepper.

6 Stir in the sugar and sprinkle on the bread crumbs. Cover the casserole, return it to the oven, and continue cooking for 1 further hour. Serve hot straight from the casserole with salad greens and crusty bread.

3

5

6

Brazil Nut & Mushroom Pie

The button mushrooms give this wholesome vegan pie a wonderful aromatic flavor. The pie can be frozen uncooked and baked from frozen.

NUTRITIONAL INFORMATION

Calories	784	Sugars	5g
Protein	17g	Fat	58g
Carbohydrate	52g	Saturates	19g

45 mins

50 mins

SERVES 4

INGREDIENTS

PIE DOUGH

- 1¾ cups plain whole-wheat flour
- ⅓ cup vegan margarine, cut into small pieces
- 4 tbsp water
- soy milk, to glaze

FILLING

- 2 tbsp vegan margarine
- 1 onion, chopped
- 1 clove garlic, finely chopped
- scant 2 cups sliced white mushrooms
- 1 tbsp all-purpose flour
- ⅔ cup vegetable bouillon
- 1 tbsp tomato paste
- generous 1 cup chopped Brazil nuts
- 1⅔ cup fresh whole-wheat bread crumbs
- 2 tbsp chopped fresh parsley
- ½ tsp pepper

1 To make the pie dough, strain the flour into a mixing bowl and add any bran remaining in the strainer. Rub in the vegan margarine with your fingertips until the mixture resembles fine bread crumbs. Stir in the water and bring together to form a dough. Wrap and chill in the refrigerator for 30 minutes.

2 To make the filling, melt half of the margarine in a skillet. Add the onion, garlic, and mushrooms and cook over low heat, stirring occasionally, for 5 minutes until softened. Add the flour and cook for 1 minute, stirring constantly. Gradually add the bouillon, stirring until the sauce is smooth and beginning to thicken. Stir in the tomato paste, Brazil nuts, bread crumbs, parsley, and pepper. Let cool slightly.

3 On a lightly floured surface, roll out two-thirds of the pie dough and use it to line an 8-inch/20-cm loose-bottomed quiche/tart pan or pie dish. Spread the filling in the pie shell. Brush the edges of the pie dough with soy milk. Roll out the remaining pie dough to fit the top of the pie. Seal the edges, make a slit in the top of the pie dough, and brush with soy milk.

4 Bake in a preheated oven, 400°F/200°C, for 30–40 minutes until golden brown. Serve immediately.

1

2

2

Lentil & Red Bell Pepper Tart

This savory tart combines lentils and red bell peppers in a tasty whole-wheat shell. The tart is suitable for vegans.

NUTRITIONAL INFORMATION

Calories	374	Sugars	5g
Protein	13g	Fat	17g
Carbohydrate	44g	Saturates	7g

15–20 mins 50 mins

SERVES 6

I N G R E D I E N T S

P I E D O U G H

1¾ cups plain whole-wheat flour

⅓ cup vegan margarine, cut into small pieces

4 tbsp water

F I L L I N G

¾ cup red lentils, rinsed

1¼ cups vegetable bouillon

1 tbsp vegan margarine

1 onion, chopped

2 red bell peppers, seeded, and diced

1 tsp yeast extract

1 tbsp tomato paste

3 tbsp chopped fresh parsley

pepper

1 To make the pie dough, strain the flour in a mixing bowl and add any bran remaining in the strainer. Rub in the vegan margarine with your fingertips until the mixture resembles fine bread crumbs. Stir in the water and bring together to form a dough. Wrap and chill in the refrigerator for 30 minutes.

1
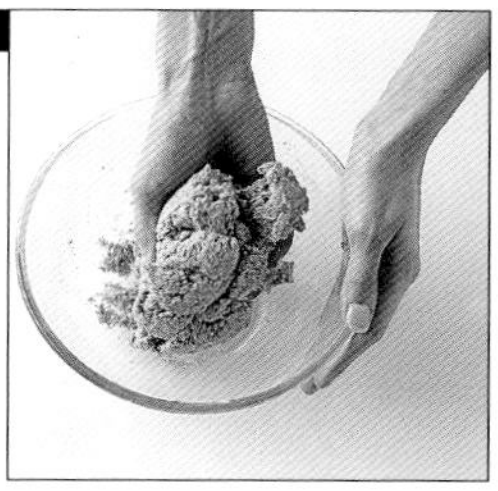

2 Meanwhile, make the filling. Put the lentils in a pan with the bouillon, bring to a boil, and then simmer for 10 minutes until the lentils are tender and can be mashed to a paste.

2

3 Melt the margarine in a small pan, add the chopped onion and diced red bell peppers, and cook over low heat, stirring occasionally, until just soft.

4 Add the lentil paste, yeast extract, tomato paste, and parsley. Season with pepper. Mix until well combined.

4

5 On a lightly floured surface, roll out the dough and line a 9½-inch/24-cm loose-bottomed quiche pan. Prick the base of the pie dough with a fork and spoon the lentil mixture into the pie shell.

6 Bake in a preheated oven, 400°F/200°C, for 30 minutes, until the filling is firm. Serve immediately.

VARIATION

Add corn kernels to the flan in step 4 for a colorful and tasty change, if you prefer.

Stuffed Vegetables

You can fill your favorite vegetables with this nutty-tasting combination of cracked wheat, tomatoes, and cucumber.

NUTRITIONAL INFORMATION

Calories	194	Sugars	7g
Protein	5g	Fat	4g
Carbohydrate	36g	Saturates	0.5g

40 mins — 25 mins

SERVES 4

INGREDIENTS

- 4 large beefsteak tomatoes
- 4 zucchini
- 2 orange bell peppers
- salt and pepper

FILLING

- 1¼ cups cracked wheat
- ¼ cucumber
- 1 red onion
- 2 tbsp lemon juice
- 2 tbsp chopped fresh cilantro
- 2 tbsp chopped fresh mint
- 1 tbsp olive oil
- 2 tsp cumin seeds

TO SERVE

- warm pita bread
- hummus

1 Cut off the tops of the tomatoes and reserve. Using a teaspoon, scoop out the tomato pulp, chop, and place in a bowl. Season the tomato shells, then turn them upside down on absorbent paper towels.

1

2 Trim the zucchini and cut a V-shaped groove lengthwise down each one. Finely chop the cut-out zucchini flesh and add to the tomato pulp. Season the zucchini shells and set aside. Halve the bell peppers. Leaving the stalks intact, cut out the seeds and discard. Season the bell pepper shells and set aside.

2

3 To make the filling, soak the cracked wheat according to the instructions on the packet. Finely chop the cucumber and add to the reserved tomato pulp and zucchini mixture. Finely chop the red onion, and add to the vegetable mixture with the lemon juice, herbs, olive oil, cumin, and seasoning, and mix together well.

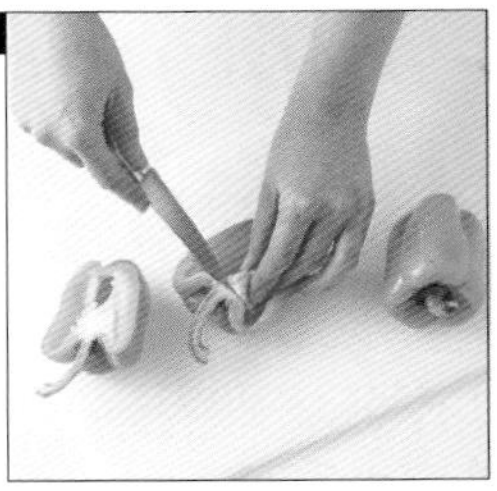
2

4 When the wheat has soaked, mix with the vegetables, and stuff into the tomato, zucchini, and bell pepper shells. Place the tops on the tomatoes, transfer to a roasting pan, and bake in a preheated oven, 400°F/200°C, for 20–25 minutes until cooked through. Drain and serve with pita bread and hummus.

COOK'S TIP

It is a good idea to blanch vegetables (except for tomatoes) before stuffing. Blanch bell peppers, zucchini, and eggplants for 5 minutes.

Spicy Black-eye Peas

A hearty casserole of black-eyed peas in a rich, sweet tomato sauce flavored with molasses and mustard.

NUTRITIONAL INFORMATION

Calories	233	Sugars	21g
Protein	11g	Fat	4g
Carbohydrate	42g	Saturates	1g

15 mins

2½ hrs

SERVES 4

INGREDIENTS

- 2 cups black-eyed peas, soaked overnight in cold water
- 1 tbsp vegetable oil
- 2 onions, chopped
- 1 tbsp clear honey
- 2 tbsp molasses
- 4 tbsp dark soy sauce
- 1 tsp dry mustard powder
- 4 tbsp tomato paste
- scant 2 cups vegetable bouillon
- 1 bay leaf
- 1 sprig each of fresh rosemary, thyme, and sage
- 1 small orange
- 1 tbsp cornstarch
- 2 red bell peppers, seeded and diced
- pepper
- 2 tbsp chopped fresh flat-leaf parsley, to garnish
- crusty bread, to serve

1 Rinse the peas and place in a pan. Cover with water, bring to a boil, and boil rapidly for 10 minutes. Drain and place in a casserole dish.

2 Meanwhile, heat the oil in a skillet and cook the onions over low heat, stirring occasionally, for 5 minutes. Stir in the honey, molasses, soy sauce, mustard, and tomato paste. Pour in the bouillon, bring to a boil, and pour over the peas.

3 Tie the bay leaf and herbs together with a clean piece of string and add to the casserole. Using a vegetable peeler, pare off 3 pieces of orange zest and mix into the peas, along with plenty of pepper. Cover and cook in a preheated oven, 300°F/150°C, for 1 hour.

4 Extract the juice from the orange and blend with the cornstarch to form a paste. Remove the casserole from the oven and stir the cornstarch paste into the peas along with the red bell peppers. Cover, return to the oven, and cook for 1 further hour, until the sauce is rich and thick and the peas are tender. Discard the herbs and orange zest.

5 Garnish the casserole with chopped fresh parsley and serve immediately with crusty bread.

1

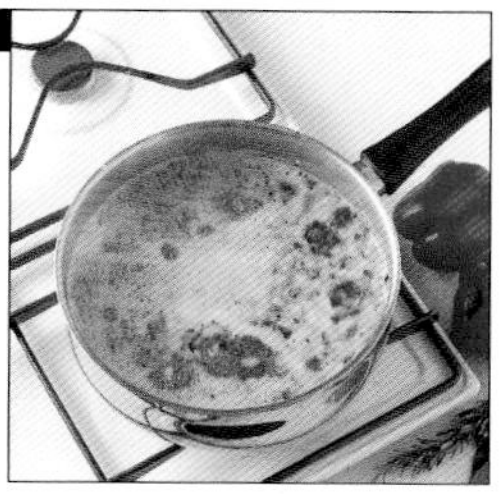

2

3

Garlic & Sage Bread

This freshly made bread is an ideal accompaniment to salads and soups and is suitable for vegans.

NUTRITIONAL INFORMATION

Calories	207	Sugars	3g
Protein	9g	Fat	2g
Carbohydrate	42g	Saturates	0g

1¼ hrs   30 mins

SERVES 6

INGREDIENTS

- vegan margarine, for greasing
- 2¼ cups brown bread flour
- 1 sachet active dry yeast
- 3 tbsp chopped fresh sage
- 2 tsp sea salt
- 3 cloves garlic, finely chopped
- 1 tsp clear honey
- ⅔ cup lukewarm water

1 Grease a cookie sheet with vegan margarine. Strain the flour into a large mixing bowl and stir in the bran remaining in the strainer.

2 Stir in the dry yeast, sage, and half of the sea salt. Reserve 1 teaspoon of the chopped garlic for sprinkling and stir the rest into the bowl. Add the honey with the lukewarm water and mix together to form a dough.

3 Turn the dough out onto a lightly floured counter and knead it for about 5 minutes. Alternatively, use an electric mixer with a dough hook.

4 Place the dough in a greased bowl, cover, and let rise in a warm place until doubled in size.

5 Knead the dough again for a few minutes, shape it into a circle (see Cook's Tip), and place on the cookie sheet.

6 Cover and let rise for a further 30 minutes or until springy to the touch. Sprinkle with the rest of the sea salt and garlic.

7 Bake the loaf in a preheated oven, 400°F/200°C, for 25–30 minutes. Transfer to a wire rack to cool completely before slicing and serving.

3

5

6

COOK'S TIP

Roll the dough into a long sausage and then curve it into a circular shape.

Roman Focaccia

Roman focaccia makes a delicious snack on its own or served with a selection of vegetarian cheeses and salad for a quick supper.

NUTRITIONAL INFORMATION

Calories	119	Sugars	2g
Protein	3g	Fat	2g
Carbohydrate	24g	Saturates	0.3g

1 hr

45 mins

Makes 16 squares

INGREDIENTS

- ¼ oz/7 g dried yeast
- 1 tsp granulated sugar
- 1¼ cups lukewarm water
- 1 lb/450 g white bread flour
- 2 tsp salt
- 3 tbsp fresh rosemary, chopped
- 2 tbsp olive oil
- 1 lb/450 g mixed red and white onions, sliced into rings
- 4 garlic cloves, sliced

1 Place the yeast and the sugar in a bowl and mix with cup of the water. Let the mixture ferment in a warm place for 15 minutes.

2 Strain the flour with the salt into a large bowl. Add the yeast mixture, half of the rosemary, and the remaining water, and mix to form a smooth dough. Knead the dough for 4 minutes.

3 Cover the dough with oiled plastic wrap and let rise for 30 minutes or until doubled in size.

4 Meanwhile, heat the oil in a large pan. Add the onions and garlic and cook over low heat for 5 minutes or until softened. Cover the pan and continue to cook for a further 7–8 minutes or until the onions are lightly caramelized.

5 Knead the dough again for 1–2 minutes, then roll out to a square. It should be no more than ¼ inch/5 mm thick because it will rise during cooking. Place the dough on a large cookie sheet, pushing out the edges until even.

6 Spread the onions evenly over the dough, and sprinkle the surface with the remaining rosemary.

7 Bake in a preheated oven, 400°F/200°C, for 25–30 minutes or until a golden brown color. Cut the focaccia into 16 squares and serve immediately while it is still warm.

2

4

5

Sun-dried Tomato Loaf

This delicious tomato bread is great with cheese or soup or for making an unusual sandwich. This recipe makes one loaf.

2

5

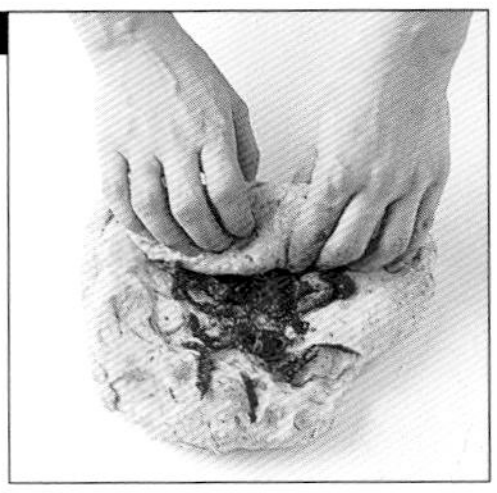

6

NUTRITIONAL INFORMATION

Calories	403	Sugars	5g
Protein	12g	Fat	2g
Carbohydrate	91g	Saturates	0.3g

$1\frac{3}{4}$ hrs

35 mins

SERVES 4

INGREDIENTS

- ¼ oz/7 g dried yeast
- 1 tsp granulated sugar
- 1¼ cups lukewarm water
- 1 lb/450 g white bread flour
- 1 tsp salt
- 2 tsp dried basil
- 2 tbsp sun-dried tomato paste or tomato paste
- vegan margarine, for greasing
- 12 sun-dried tomatoes in oil, drained and cut into strips

1 Place the yeast and sugar in a bowl and mix with cup of the water. Let the mixture ferment in a warm place for 15 minutes.

2 Strain the flour and salt into a bowl. Make a well in the center and add the basil, yeast mixture, tomato paste, and half of the remaining water. Using a wooden spoon, draw the flour into the liquid and mix to form a dough, adding the rest of the water gradually.

3 Turn out onto a floured counter and knead for 5 minutes. Cover with oiled plastic wrap and let stand in a warm place for 30 minutes or until doubled in size.

4 Lightly grease a 2-lb/900-g loaf pan with vegan margarine.

5 Remove the dough from the bowl and knead in the sun-dried tomatoes. Knead again for 2–3 minutes.

6 Place the dough in the pan and let rise for 30–40 minutes or until it has doubled in size again. Bake in a preheated oven, 375°F/190°C, for 30–35 minutes or until golden and the base sounds hollow when tapped. Cool on a wire rack.

COOK'S TIP

You could make mini sun-dried tomato loaves for children. Divide the dough into 8 equal portions, leave to rise, and bake in mini-loaf pans for 20 minutes. Alternatively, make 12 small rounds, leave to rise, and bake for 12–15 minutes.

Roasted Bell Pepper Bread

Bell peppers become wonderfully sweet and mild when they are roasted, and make this bread delicious.

NUTRITIONAL INFORMATION

Calories	426	Sugars	4g
Protein	12g	Fat	4g
Carbohydrate	90g	Saturates	1g

1¾ hrs

1 hr 5 mins

SERVES 4

INGREDIENTS

- vegan margarine, for greasing
- 1 red bell pepper, halved and seeded
- 1 yellow bell pepper, halved and seeded
- 2 sprigs rosemary
- 1 tbsp olive oil
- ¼ oz/7 g dried yeast
- 1 tsp granulated sugar
- 1¼ cups lukewarm water
- 1 lb/450 g white bread flour
- 1 tsp salt

1 Grease a 9-inch/23-cm deep circular cake pan with vegan margarine.

2 Place the bell peppers and rosemary in a shallow roasting pan. Pour over the oil and roast in a preheated oven, 400°F/200°C, for 20 minutes or until slightly charred. Remove the skin from the bell peppers and cut the flesh into slices.

3 Place the yeast and sugar in a small bowl and mix with cup of lukewarm water. Let the mixture ferment in a warm place for 15 minutes.

4 Strain the flour and salt together into a large bowl. Stir in the yeast mixture and the remaining water and mix to form a smooth dough.

5 Knead the dough for about 5 minutes until smooth. Cover with oiled plastic wrap and let rise for about 30 minutes or until doubled in size.

6 Cut the dough into 3 equal portions. Roll the portions into circles slightly larger than the cake pan.

7 Place 1 circle in the bottom of the pan so that it reaches up the sides of the pan by about ¾ inch/2 cm. Top with half of the bell pepper mixture.

8 Place the second circle of dough on top, followed by the remaining bell pepper mixture. Place the last circle of dough on top, pushing the edges of the dough down the sides of the pan.

9 Cover the dough with oiled plastic wrap and let rise for 30–40 minutes. Return to the oven and bake for 45 minutes until golden or the bottom sounds hollow when lightly tapped. Transfer to a wire rack to cool slightly, then cut into slices and serve warm.

2

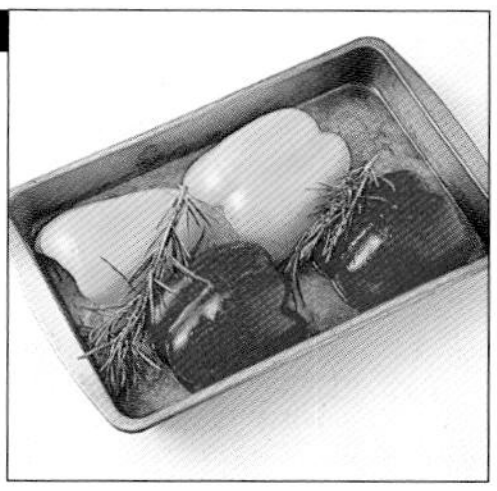

6

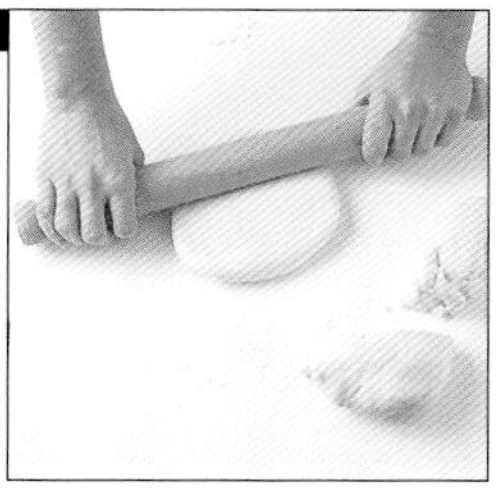

7

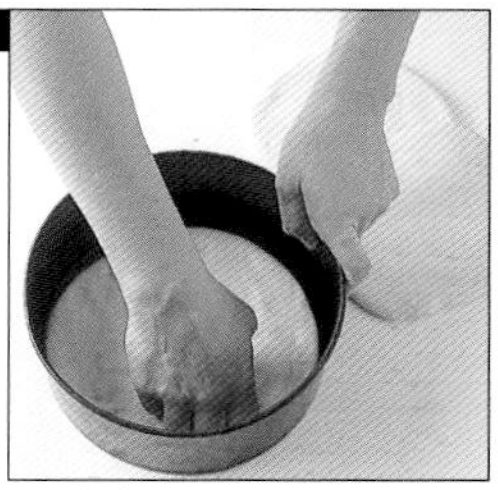

Apricot Slices

These vegan slices are ideal for children's lunches. They are full of flavor and made with healthy ingredients.

NUTRITIONAL INFORMATION

Calories	198	Sugars	13g
Protein	4g	Fat	9g
Carbohydrate	25g	Saturates	2g

50 mins

1 hr

MAKES 12

INGREDIENTS

PIE DOUGH

- ⅓ cup vegan margarine, cut into small pieces, plus extra for greasing
- 1¾ cups whole-wheat flour
- ½ cup finely ground mixed nuts
- 4 tbsp water
- soy milk, to glaze

FILLING

- 1 cup dried apricots
- grated zest of 1 orange
- 1¼ cups apple juice
- 1 tsp ground cinnamon
- ⅓ cup raisins

1 Lightly grease a 9-inch/23-cm square cake pan. To make the pie dough, place the flour and nuts in a mixing bowl and rub in the margarine with your fingertips until the mixture resembles bread crumbs. Stir in the water and bring together to form a dough. Wrap and chill in the refrigerator for 30 minutes.

1

2 To make the filling, place the apricots, orange zest, and apple juice in a pan and bring to a boil. Simmer gently for 30 minutes until the apricots are mushy. Cool slightly, then process in a food processor or blender to a paste. Alternatively, press the mixture through a fine strainer. Stir in the cinnamon and raisins.

2

3 Divide the pie dough in half, roll out one half, and use to line the bottom of the prepared pan. Spread the apricot paste over the top and brush the edges of the pastry with water. Roll out the rest of the dough to fit over the top of the apricot paste. Press down and seal the edges.

3

4 Prick the top of the pie dough with a fork and brush with soy milk. Bake in a preheated oven, 400°F/200°C, for 20–25 minutes until the pastry is golden. Let cool slightly before cutting into 12 bars. Serve the slices either warm or cold.

COOK'S TIP

These slices will keep in an airtight container for 3–4 days.

Baked Cheesecake

This cheesecake has a rich creamy texture, but contains no dairy produce at all, as it is made with bean curd.

NUTRITIONAL INFORMATION

Calories	282	Sugars	17g
Protein	9g	Fat	15g
Carbohydrate	29g	Saturates	4g

2¼ hrs — 45 mins

SERVES 6

INGREDIENTS

- 4 tbsp vegan margarine, melted, plus extra for greasing
- 2¼ cups graham cracker crumbs
- ⅓ cup chopped pitted dates
- 4 tbsp lemon juice
- zest of 1 lemon
- 3 tbsp water
- 12 oz/350 g firm bean curd
- ⅔ cup apple juice
- 1 banana, mashed
- 1 tsp vanilla extract
- 1 mango, peeled, pitted, and chopped

1 Lightly grease a 7-inch/18-cm circular loose-bottomed cake pan with a little vegan margarine.

2 Mix together the graham cracker crumbs and melted margarine in a bowl. Press the mixture into the base of the prepared pan.

3 Put the chopped dates, lemon juice, lemon zest, and water into a pan and bring to a boil. Simmer gently for 5 minutes until the dates are soft, then mash them roughly with a fork.

4 Place the mixture in a blender or food processor with the bean curd, apple juice, mashed banana, and vanilla extract and process until the mixture forms a thick, smooth paste.

5 Pour the bean curd paste onto the prepared cracker crumb base.

6 Bake in a preheated oven, 350°F/180°C, for 30–40 minutes, until lightly golden. Let cool in the pan, then chill thoroughly before serving.

7 Place the chopped mango in a blender and process until smooth. Serve it as a sauce with the cheesecake.

2

3

4

VARIATION

Silken bean curd may be substituted for the firm bean curd to give a softer texture; it will take 40–50 minutes to set.

Upside-down Cake

This recipe shows how a classic favorite can be adapted for vegans by using vegetarian margarine and oil instead of butter and eggs.

NUTRITIONAL INFORMATION

Calories	354	Sugars	31g
Protein	3g	Fat	15g
Carbohydrate	56g	Saturates	2g

15 mins

50 mins

SERVES 6

INGREDIENTS

¼ cup vegan margarine, cut into small pieces, plus extra for greasing

15 oz/425 g canned unsweetened pineapple pieces, drained, juice reserved

4 tsp cornstarch

¼ cup brown sugar

½ cup water

zest of 1 lemon

SPONGE CAKE

4 tbsp sunflower oil

⅓ cup brown sugar

⅔ cup water

1¼ cups all-purpose flour

2 tsp baking powder

1 tsp ground cinnamon

3

4

4

1 Grease a deep 7-inch/18-cm cake pan with a little vegan margarine.

2 Mix the reserved pineapple juice with the cornstarch to a smooth paste. Put the paste in a pan with the sugar, margarine, and water and stir over low heat until the sugar has dissolved. Bring to a boil and simmer for 2–3 minutes until thickened. Let cool slightly.

3 To make the sponge cake, heat the oil, sugar, and water in a pan until the sugar has dissolved, but do not allow to boil. Remove from the heat and let cool. Sift the flour, baking powder, and ground cinnamon into a bowl. Pour in the cooled sugar syrup and beat well to form a batter.

4 Place the pineapple pieces and lemon zest on the bottom of the prepared pan and pour over 4 tablespoons of the pineapple syrup. Spoon the sponge batter on top, leveling the surface.

5 Bake in a preheated oven, 350°F/180°C, for 35–40 minutes until set and a toothpick inserted into the center comes out clean. Invert onto a plate, let stand for 5 minutes, then remove the pan. Serve with the remaining syrup.

Date & Apricot Tart

There is no need to add any extra sugar to this filling because the dried fruit is naturally sweet. This tart is suitable for vegans.

NUTRITIONAL INFORMATION

Calories	359	Sugars	34g
Protein	7g	Fat	15g
Carbohydrate	53g	Saturates	2g

45 mins

50 mins

SERVES 8

INGREDIENTS

- 1¾ cups all-purpose whole-wheat flour
- ½ cup ground mixed nuts
- ⅓ cup vegan margarine, cut into small pieces
- 4 tbsp water
- 1 cup chopped dried apricots
- 1⅓ cups chopped pitted dates
- scant 2 cups apple juice
- 1 tsp ground cinnamon
- grated zest of 1 lemon
- soy custard, to serve (optional)

1 Place the flour and ground nuts in a mixing bowl and rub in the margarine with your fingertips until the mixture resembles bread crumbs. Stir in the water and bring together to form a dough. Wrap the dough and chill in the refrigerator for 30 minutes.

2 Meanwhile, place the apricots and dates in a pan, together with the apple juice, cinnamon, and lemon zest. Bring to a boil, cover, and simmer over low heat for about 15 minutes until the fruit has softened. Remove the pan from the heat and mash the fruit to a paste.

3 Reserve a small ball of dough for making lattice strips. On a lightly floured counter, roll out the rest of the dough to form a circle and use it to line a 9-inch/23-cm loose-bottomed quiche pan.

4 Spread the fruit filling over the base of the dough. Roll out the reserved dough and cut into strips ½-inch/1-cm wide. Cut the strips to fit the tart and twist them across the top of the fruit to form a decorative lattice pattern. Moisten the edges of the strips with water and seal them firmly around the rim.

5 Bake in a preheated oven, 400°F/200°C, for 25–30 minutes, until golden brown.

6 Cut into the tart into slices and serve immediately with soy custard, if using.

Fruit Crumble

Any fruits in season can be used in this wholesome pudding. It is suitable for vegans as it contains no dairy produce.

NUTRITIONAL INFORMATION

Calories	426	Sugars	37g
Protein	8g	Fat	16g
Carbohydrate	67g	Saturates	4g

10 mins

30 mins

SERVES 6

INGREDIENTS

- vegan margarine, for greasing
- 6 dessert pears, peeled, cored, quartered, and sliced
- 1 tbsp chopped preserved ginger
- 1 tbsp molasses
- 2 tbsp orange juice

TOPPING

- 1½ cups all-purpose flour
- 6 tbsp vegan margarine, cut into small pieces
- ¼ cup slivered almonds
- ⅓ cup porridge oats
- 1¾ oz/50 g molasses
- soy custard, to serve

2

3

4

1 Lightly grease a 4-cup/1-litre ovenproof dish with vegan margarine.

2 Prepare the pears. In a bowl, mix together the pears, ginger, molasses, and orange juice. Spoon the mixture into the prepared dish.

3 To make the crumble topping, strain the flour into a mixing bowl. Add the margarine and rub it in with your fingertips until the mixture resembles fine bread crumbs. Stir in the slivered almonds, porridge oats, and molasses. Mix well until thoroughly combined.

4 Sprinkle the crumble topping evenly over the pear and ginger mixture in the dish, pressing it down gently with the back of a spoon.

5 Bake in a preheated oven, 375°F/190°C, for 30 minutes, until the topping is golden and the fruit tender. Serve the crumble immediately with soy custard, if using.

VARIATION

Stir 1 teaspoon ground allspice into the crumble mixture in step 3 for added flavor, if you prefer.

Eggless Sponge

This is a healthy, but still absolutely delicious variation of the classic sponge layer cake and is suitable for vegans.

NUTRITIONAL INFORMATION

Calories	273	Sugars	27g
Protein	3g	Fat	9g
Carbohydrate	49g	Saturates	1g

1¼ hrs — 30 mins

SERVES 6

INGREDIENTS

- vegan margarine, for greasing
- 1¾ cups whole-wheat self-rising flour
- 2 tsp baking powder
- ¾ cup superfine sugar
- 6 tbsp sunflower oil
- 1 cup water
- 1 tsp vanilla extract
- 4 tbsp strawberry or raspberry reduced-sugar spread
- superfine sugar, for dusting

1 Grease two 8-inch/20-cm layer pans and line them with baking parchment.

2 Strain the self-rising flour and baking powder into a large mixing bowl, stirring in any bran remaining in the strainer. Stir in the superfine sugar.

3 Pour in the sunflower oil, water, and vanilla extract. Mix well with a wooden spoon for about 1 minute until the mixture is smooth, then divide among the prepared pans.

4 Bake in a preheated oven, 350°F/180°C, for about 25–30 minutes until the center of the cakes springs back when lightly touched.

3

3

3

5 Let the sponge cakes cool slightly in the pans before turning them out and transferring to a wire rack to cool completely.

6 Remove the baking parchment and place one sponge cake on a serving plate. Cover with the low-sugar spread and place the other sponge on top. Dust the eggless sponge cake with a little superfine sugar before serving.

VARIATION

To make a chocolate-flavored sponge, replace 2 tablespoons of the flour with unsweetened cocoa. To make a citrus-flavored sponge, add the grated rind of ½ lemon or orange to the flour in step 2. To make a coffee-flavored sponge, replace 2 teaspoons of the flour with instant coffee powder.

Desserts

Confirmed pudding lovers feel a meal is lacking if there isn't a tempting dessert to finish off the menu. Yet it is often possible to combine indulgence with healthy

ingredients. A lot of the recipes in this chapter contain fruit, which is the perfect ingredient for healthy desserts that are still deliciously tempting, such as Blackberry Pudding, Raspberry Shortcake, One Roll Fruit Pie, Apple Tart Tatin, and Baked Bananas. Some desserts are also packed full of protein-rich nuts, such as Pine Nut Tart and Almond Cheesecakes.

Eve's Pudding

This is a popular family favorite pudding with soft apples on the bottom and a light buttery sponge on top.

NUTRITIONAL INFORMATION

Calories	365	Sugars	40g
Protein	5g	Fat	14g
Carbohydrate	58g	Saturates	7g

15 mins | 45 mins

SERVES 6

INGREDIENTS

- butter, for greasing
- 1 lb/450 g cooking apples, peeled, cored, and sliced
- ⅓ cup granulated sugar
- 1 tbsp lemon juice
- ⅓ cup golden raisins
- 6 tbsp butter
- ⅓ cup superfine sugar
- 1 egg, beaten
- 1¼ cups self-rising flour
- 3 tbsp milk
- ¼ cup slivered almonds
- custard or heavy cream, to serve

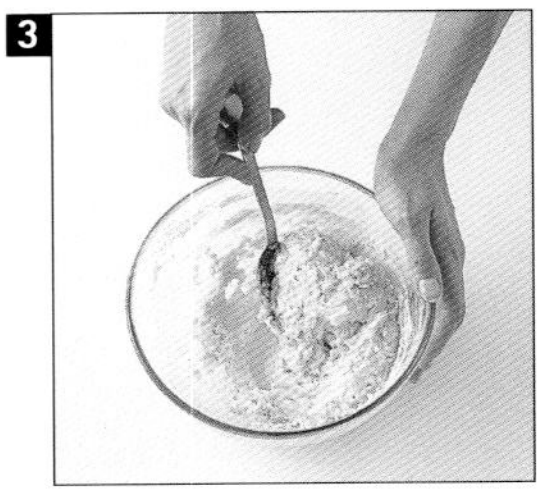

1 Grease a 3½-cup/900-ml ovenproof dish with a little butter.

2 Mix the apples with the sugar, lemon juice, and golden raisins. Spoon the mixture into the prepared dish.

3 In a bowl, cream the butter and superfine sugar together until pale. Add the egg, a little at a time.

4 Carefully fold in the self-rising flour and stir in the milk to give a soft, dropping consistency.

5 Spread the mixture evenly over the apples and sprinkle the top with the slivered almonds.

6 Bake in a preheated oven, 350°F/180°C, for 40–45 minutes until the sponge topping is golden brown. Serve the pudding piping hot, accompanied by custard or heavy cream.

COOK'S TIP

To increase the almond flavor of this pudding, add ¼ cup ground almonds with the flour in step 4.

Queen of Puddings

This is a slightly different version of an old favorite made with the addition of orange zest and marmalade to give a delicious orange flavor.

NUTRITIONAL INFORMATION

Calories	289	Sugars	40g
Protein	5g	Fat	14g
Carbohydrate	58g	Saturates	7g

25 mins 45 mins

SERVES 8

INGREDIENTS

- 2 tbsp butter, plus extra for greasing
- 2½ cups milk
- 1¼ cups superfine sugar
- finely grated zest of 1 orange
- 4 eggs, separated
- 1⅔ cups fresh bread crumbs
- 6 tbsp orange marmalade
- salt

1 Grease a 6-cup/1.5-litre ovenproof dish with a little butter.

2 To make the custard, heat the milk in a pan with the butter, ¼ cup of the superfine sugar, and the grated orange zest, until just warm.

3

6

7
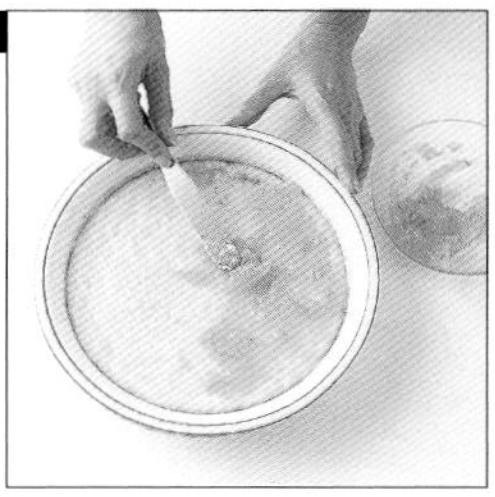

3 Whisk the egg yolks in a bowl. Gradually pour the warm milk over the eggs, stirring constantly.

4 Stir the bread crumbs into the pan, then transfer the mixture to the prepared dish and let stand for about 15 minutes.

5 Bake in a preheated oven, 350°F/180°C, for 20–25 minutes until the custard has just set. Remove the dish from the oven but do not turn the oven off.

6 To make the meringue, whisk the egg whites with a pinch of salt until they stand in soft peaks. Whisk in the remaining sugar, a little at a time.

7 Spread the orange marmalade over the cooked custard. Top with the meringue, spreading it right to the edges of the dish.

8 Return the pudding to the oven and bake for a further 20 minutes until the meringue is crisp and golden.

COOK'S TIP

If you prefer a crisper meringue, bake the pudding in the oven for an extra 5 minutes.

Bread & Butter Pudding

Everyone has their own favorite recipe for this dish. This one has added marmalade and grated apples for a really rich and unique taste.

NUTRITIONAL INFORMATION

Calories	427	Sugars	63g
Protein	9g	Fat	13g
Carbohydrate	74g	Saturates	7g

45 mins   1 hr

SERVES 6

INGREDIENTS

- 4 tbsp butter, softened
- 4–5 slices white or brown bread
- 4 tbsp chunky orange marmalade
- grated zest of 1 lemon
- ½–¾ cup golden raisins
- ¼ cup chopped candied peel
- 1 tsp ground cinnamon or allspice
- 1 cooking apple, peeled, cored, and coarsely grated
- scant ½ cup brown sugar
- 3 eggs
- generous 2 cups milk
- 2 tbsp raw brown sugar

1 Use the softened butter to grease an ovenproof dish and to spread on the slices of bread, then spread the bread with the marmalade.

2 Place a layer of bread in the bottom of the dish and sprinkle with the lemon zest, half the golden raisins, half the candied peel, half the spice, all of the apple, and half the brown sugar. Add another layer of bread, cutting it so that it fits the dish.

3 Sprinkle over most of the remaining golden raisins and all the remaining candied peel, spice, and brown sugar, scattering it evenly over the bread. Top with a final layer of bread, again cutting to fit the dish.

4 Lightly beat together the eggs and milk and then carefully strain the mixture over the bread in the dish. If time allows, set the pudding aside to stand for 20–30 minutes.

5 Sprinkle the top of the pudding with the raw brown sugar and scatter over the remaining golden raisins. Cook in a preheated oven, 400°F/200°C, for 50–60 minutes, until risen and golden brown. Serve immediately or let cool and serve cold.

Plum Cobbler

This is a favorite dessert which can easily be adapted to suit all types of fruit if plums are not available.

NUTRITIONAL INFORMATION

Calories	430	Sugars	46g
Protein	7g	Fat	12g
Carbohydrate	79g	Saturates	7g

10 mins — 40 mins

SERVES 6

INGREDIENTS

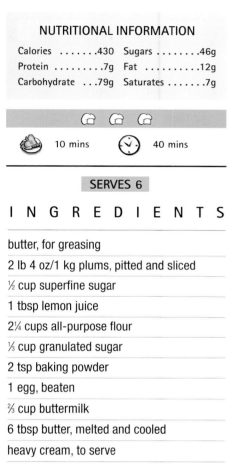

- butter, for greasing
- 2 lb 4 oz/1 kg plums, pitted and sliced
- ½ cup superfine sugar
- 1 tbsp lemon juice
- 2¼ cups all-purpose flour
- ⅓ cup granulated sugar
- 2 tsp baking powder
- 1 egg, beaten
- ⅔ cup buttermilk
- 6 tbsp butter, melted and cooled
- heavy cream, to serve

1 Lightly grease an 8-cup/2-litre ovenproof dish with a little butter.

2 In a large bowl, combine the plums, superfine sugar, lemon juice, and ¼ cup of the all-purpose flour.

3 Spoon the coated plums into the bottom of the prepared ovenproof dish, spreading them out evenly.

4 Combine the remaining flour, granulated sugar, and baking powder in a bowl.

5 Add the beaten egg, buttermilk, and cooled melted butter. Mix everything gently together to form a soft dough.

6 Place spoonfuls of the dough on top of the fruit mixture until it is almost completely covered.

7 Bake in a preheated oven, 375°F/190°C, for about 35–40 minutes until golden brown and bubbling.

8 Serve the pudding piping hot, with heavy cream.

3

5

6

COOK'S TIP

If you cannot find buttermilk, try using sour cream.

Blackberry Pudding

A delicious dessert to make when blackberries are in abundance! If blackberries are unavailable, try using currants or gooseberries.

NUTRITIONAL INFORMATION

Calories	455	Sugars	47g
Protein	7g	Fat	18g
Carbohydrate	70g	Saturates	11g

15–20 mins | 30 mins

SERVES 4

INGREDIENTS

- butter, for greasing
- 1 lb/450 g blackberries
- ⅓ cup superfine sugar, plus extra for sprinkling
- 1 egg
- ⅓ cup brown sugar
- 6 tbsp butter, melted
- ½ cup milk
- scant 1 cup self-rising flour

1 Lightly grease a large 3 ½-cup/900-ml ovenproof dish with a little butter.

2 In a large mixing bowl, gently mix together the blackberries and superfine sugar until well combined.

3

5

6

3 Transfer the blackberry and sugar mixture to the prepared ovenproof dish, spreading it out evenly.

4 Beat the egg and brown sugar in a separate mixing bowl. Stir in the melted butter and milk.

5 Strain the flour into the egg and butter mixture and fold together lightly to form a smooth batter.

6 Carefully spread the batter over the blackberry and sugar mixture in the ovenproof dish.

7 Bake the pudding in a preheated oven, 350°F/180°C, for about 25–30 minutes until the topping is firm and golden.

8 Sprinkle the pudding with a little sugar and serve hot.

VARIATION

You can add 2 tablespoons of unsweetened cocoa to the batter in step 5, if you prefer a chocolate flavor.

Raspberry Shortcake

For this lovely summery dessert, two crisp rounds of shortbread are sandwiched together with fresh raspberries and lightly whipped cream.

NUTRITIONAL INFORMATION

Calories	496	Sugars	14g
Protein	4g	Fat	41g
Carbohydrate	30g	Saturates	26g

40 mins — 15 mins

SERVES 8

INGREDIENTS

- ⅓ cup butter, diced, plus extra for greasing
- 1 ½ cups self-rising flour
- ⅓ cup superfine sugar
- 1 egg yolk
- 1 tbsp rose water
- 2 ½ cups whipping cream, whipped lightly
- 1⅓ cups raspberries, plus extra for decoration

TO DECORATE

- confectioners' sugar
- fresh mint leaves

COOK'S TIP

The shortcake can be made a few days in advance and stored in an airtight container until required.

1 Lightly grease 2 cookie sheets with a little butter.

2 To make the shortcake, strain the flour into a bowl.

3 Rub the butter into the flour with your fingertips until the mixture resembles bread crumbs.

4 Stir the sugar, egg yolk, and rose water into the mixture and bring together with your fingers to form a soft dough. Divide the dough in half.

5 Roll each piece of dough into an 8-inch/20-cm circle on a lightly floured surface. Carefully lift each one onto a prepared cookie sheet. Crimp the edges of the dough.

6 Bake in a preheated oven, 375°F/190°C, for 15 minutes until lightly golden. Transfer the shortcakes to a wire rack and let cool.

7 Mix the cream with the raspberries and spoon on top of one of the shortcakes. Top with the other shortcake circle, dust with a little confectioners' sugar, and decorate with the extra raspberries and mint leaves.

3

4

5

Pavlova

This delicious dessert originated in Australia. Serve it with sharp fruits, such as summer berries, to balance the sweetness of the meringue.

NUTRITIONAL INFORMATION

Calories	354	Sugars	34g
Protein	3g	Fat	24g
Carbohydrate	34g	Saturates	15g

1 hr 10 mins   1¼ hrs

MAKES 6

INGREDIENTS

- 3 egg whites
- ¾ cup superfine sugar
- 1 ¼ cups heavy cream, lightly whipped
- fresh fruit of your choice (raspberries, strawberries, peaches, passion fruit, ground cherries)
- salt

1 Line a cookie sheet with a sheet of baking parchment.

2 Whisk the egg whites with a pinch of salt in a large bowl until they form soft peaks.

3 Whisk in the sugar, a little at a time, whisking well after each addition until all of the sugar has been incorporated and the meringue is smooth and glossy.

4 Spoon three-quarters of the meringue onto the cookie sheet, forming a circle 8 inches/20-cm in diameter.

5 Place spoonfuls of the remaining meringue all around the edge of the circle to join up to make a nest shape.

6 Bake in a preheated oven, 275°F/140°C, for 1¼ hours.

7 Turn the heat off, but leave the pavlova in the oven until it is completely cold.

8 To serve, place the pavlova on a serving dish. Spread with the lightly whipped cream, then arrange the fresh fruit on top.

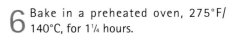

2

3
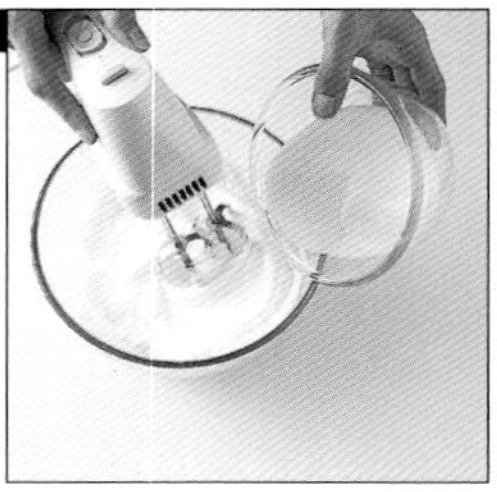

5

COOK'S TIP

If you are worried about creating the right shape, draw a circle on the baking parchment, turn the paper over, then spoon the meringue inside the outline.

One Roll Fruit Pie

This is an easy way to make a pie—once you have rolled out the pie dough and filled it with fruit, you just turn the edges in.

NUTRITIONAL INFORMATION

Calories	282	Sugars	17g
Protein	9g	Fat	15g
Carbohydrate	29g	Saturates	4g

2¼ hrs — 45 mins

SERVES 8

INGREDIENTS

PIE DOUGH

- ⅓ cup butter, cut into small pieces, plus extra for greasing
- 1½ cups all-purpose flour
- 1 tbsp water
- 1 egg, separated
- sugar lumps, crushed, for sprinkling

FILLING

- 1½ lb/600 g prepared fruit (rhubarb, gooseberries, plums, damsons)
- ⅓ cup brown sugar
- 1 tbsp ground ginger

1 Grease a large cookie sheet with a little butter and set aside until required.

2 To make the pie dough, place the flour and butter in a mixing bowl and rub in the butter with your fingertips until the mixture resembles bread crumbs. Add the water and work the mixture together until a soft dough has formed. Wrap and chill in the refrigerator for 30 minutes.

3 Roll out the chilled dough to a circle about 14 inches/ 35 cm in diameter.

4 Transfer the dough circle to the center of the prepared cookie sheet. Brush the dough with the egg yolk.

5 To make the filling, mix the prepared fruit with the brown sugar and ground ginger and pile it into the center of the dough.

6 Turn in the edges of the dough circle all the way around. Brush the surface of the dough with the egg white and sprinkle with the crushed sugar lumps.

7 Bake in a preheated oven, 400°F/200°C, for 35 minutes or until golden brown. Serve warm.

2

4

6

COOK'S TIP

If the pie dough breaks when you are shaping it into a circle, don't panic—just patch and seal, as the overall effect of this tart is quite rough.

Fruit Crumble Tart

This tart has a double helping of flavors, with a succulent fruit filling covered in a crumbly topping.

NUTRITIONAL INFORMATION

Calories	499	Sugars	26g
Protein	7g	Fat	30g
Carbohydrate	53g	Saturates	16g

1 hr 20 mins — 25 mins

SERVES 8

INGREDIENTS

SWEET PIE DOUGH

- 1¼ cups all-purpose flour
- 2 tbsp superfine sugar
- ½ cup butter, cut into small pieces
- 1 tbsp water

FILLING

- 1½ cups raspberries
- 1 lb/450 g plums, halved, pitted, and roughly chopped
- 3 tbsp raw brown sugar

TO SERVE

- light cream

TOPPING

- scant 1 cup all-purpose flour
- ⅓ cup raw brown sugar
- ⅓ cup butter, cut into small pieces
- ⅔ cup chopped mixed nuts
- 1 tsp ground cinnamon

1 To make the dough, place the flour, sugar, and butter in a bowl and rub in the butter with your fingertips. Add the water and work the mixture together until a soft dough has formed. Wrap and chill in the refrigerator for 30 minutes.

2 Roll out the dough on a lightly floured surface and line the bottom of a 9½-inch/24-cm loose-bottomed tart pan. Prick the base of the dough with a fork and chill for about 30 minutes.

3 To make the filling, toss the raspberries and plums together with the sugar and spoon into the tart shell.

4 To make the crumble topping, combine the flour, sugar, and butter in a bowl. Work the butter into the flour with your fingertips until the mixture resembles coarse bread crumbs. Stir in the nuts and ground cinnamon.

5 Sprinkle the topping over the fruit and press down gently with the back of a spoon. Bake in a preheated oven, 400°F/200°C, for 20–25 minutes until the topping is golden. Serve the tart immediately with light cream.

1

3

5

Cheese & Apple Tart

The chopped apples, dates and the brown sugar combined with cheese make this a sweet tart with a savory twist to it.

NUTRITIONAL INFORMATION

Calories	360	Sugars	26g
Protein	11g	Fat	18g
Carbohydrate	43g	Saturates	6g

15 mins — 50 mins

SERVES 8

I N G R E D I E N T S

- butter, for greasing
- 1½ cups self-rising flour
- 1 tsp baking powder
- pinch of salt
- ⅓ cup brown sugar
- generous 1 cup pitted dates, chopped
- 1lb 2 oz/500 g dessert apples, cored and chopped
- ¼ cup chopped walnuts
- ¼ cup sunflower oil
- 2 eggs
- 1¾ cups grated Red Leicester or Cheddar cheese

2

3

5

1 Grease a 9½-inch/23-cm loose-bottomed tart pan with a little butter and line with baking parchment.

2 Strain the flour, baking powder, and salt into a large bowl. Stir in the brown sugar and the chopped dates, apples, and walnuts. Mix together until thoroughly combined.

3 Beat the oil and eggs together and add the mixture to the dry ingredients. Stir with a wooden spoon until well combined.

4 Spoon half of the mixture into the prepared pan and level the surface with the back of a spoon.

5 Sprinkle with the grated cheese, then spoon over the remaining cake mix, spreading it to the edges of the pan.

6 Bake in a preheated oven, 350°F/180°C, for 45–50 minutes or until golden and firm to the touch.

7 Let the tart cool slightly in the pan. Remove the tart from the pan and serve warm.

COOK'S TIP

This is a deliciously moist tart. Any leftovers should be stored in the refrigerator and heated to serve.

Apple Tart Tatin

This attractive, French up-side-down apple tart is always a popular choice for a comforting dessert.

NUTRITIONAL INFORMATION

Calories	340	Sugars	23g
Protein	2g	Fat	22g
Carbohydrate	37g	Saturates	12g

15 mins — 30 mins

SERVES 8

INGREDIENTS

- generous ½ cup butter
- scant ⅔ cup superfine sugar
- 4 eating apples, cored and quartered
- 9 oz/250 g ready-made shortcrust pie dough, thawed if frozen
- crème fraîche, to serve

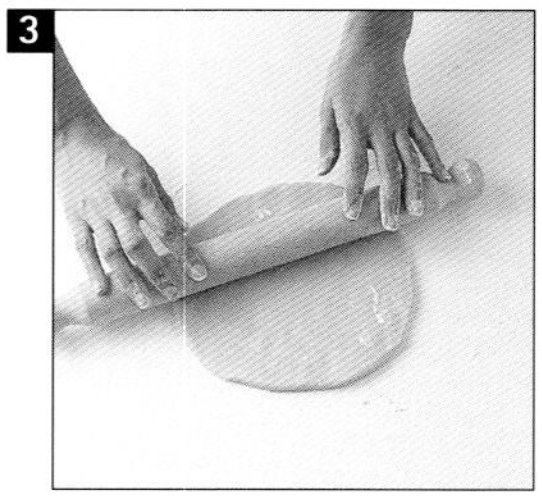

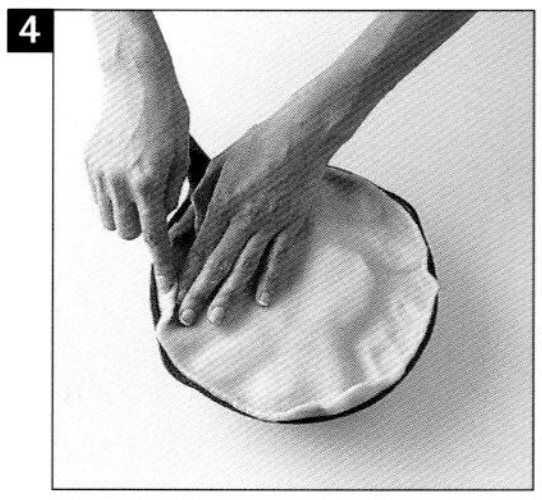

1 Heat the butter and sugar in a 9-inch/23-cm ovenproof skillet over medium heat for about 5 minutes until the mixture begins to caramelize. Remove the pan from the heat.

2 Arrange the apple quarters, skin side down, in the pan, taking care as the butter and sugar will be very hot. Place the skillet back on the heat and simmer for 2 minutes.

3 Roll out the pie dough on a lightly floured surface to form a circle just a little larger than the skillet.

4 Place the pie dough over the apples, press down, and carefully tuck in the edges to seal the apples under the layer of pie dough.

5 Bake in a preheated oven, 400°F/200°C, for 20–25 minutes until the pie dough is golden. Remove from the oven and let cool for about 10 minutes.

6 Place a serving plate over the skillet and, holding them firmly together, invert so that the dough forms the base of the turned-out tart. Serve warm with crème fraîche.

VARIATION

Replace the apples with pears, if you prefer. Leave the skin on the pears, cut them into quarters, and then remove the core.

Treacle Tart

This is an old-fashioned dessert which still delights people time after time. It is very quick to make if you use ready-made pastry.

NUTRITIONAL INFORMATION

Calories	378	Sugars	36g
Protein	4g	Fat	17g
Carbohydrate	57g	Saturates	8g

20 mins   40 mins

SERVES 8

INGREDIENTS

- 9 oz/250 g ready-made shortcrust pie dough, thawed if frozen
- 1 cup light corn syrup
- scant 2 cups fresh white bread crumbs
- ½ cup heavy cream
- finely grated zest of ½ lemon or orange
- 2 tbsp lemon or orange juice
- custard or light cream, to serve

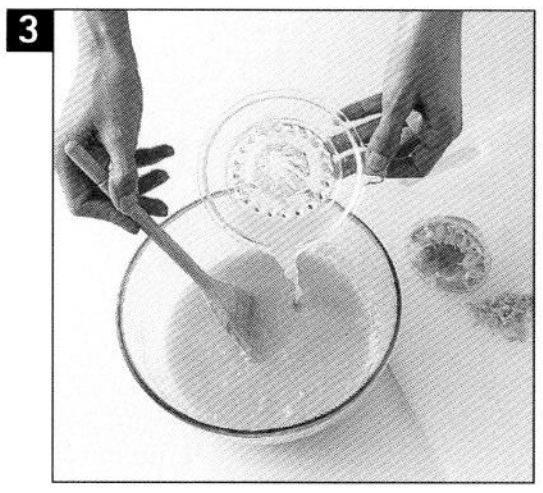

1 Roll out the pie dough to line an 8-inch/20-cm loose-bottomed tart pan, reserving the dough trimmings. Prick the base of the pie dough with a fork and let chill in the refrigerator.

2 Cut out small shapes from the reserved dough trimmings, such as leaves, stars, or hearts, to decorate the top of the tart.

3 In a bowl, combine the light corn syrup, bread crumbs, heavy cream, grated lemon or orange zest, and lemon or orange juice.

4 Pour the mixture into the tart shell and decorate the edges of the tart with the dough cut-outs.

5 Bake in a preheated oven, 375°F/190°C, for 35–40 minutes or until the filling is just set.

6 Let the tart cool slightly in the tin. Turn out and serve hot or cold with custard or light cream.

VARIATION

Use the pie dough trimmings to create a lattice pattern on top of the tart, if preferred.

Apple & Mincemeat Tart

The fresh apple brings out the flavor of the sweet rich mincemeat and makes it a beautifully moist filling for pies and tarts.

NUTRITIONAL INFORMATION

Calories	402	Sugars	44g
Protein	2g	Fat	19g
Carbohydrate	58g	Saturates	12g

1¼ hrs   50 mins

SERVES 8

INGREDIENTS

SWEET PIE DOUGH

- 1¼ cups all-purpose flour
- 2 tbsp superfine sugar
- ½ cup butter, cut into small pieces
- 1 tbsp water

FILLING

- 14½ oz/410 g jar mincemeat
- 3 eating apples, cored and grated
- 1 tbsp lemon juice
- 2 tbsp light corn syrup
- 3 tbsp butter

1 To make the dough, place the flour and superfine sugar in a large mixing bowl and rub in the butter with your fingertips until the mixture resembles bread crumbs.

2 Add the water and work the mixture together until a soft dough has formed. Wrap and chill in the refrigerator for 30 minutes.

3 On a lightly floured surface, roll out the dough and line a 9½ inch/24-cm loose-bottomed tart pan. Prick the dough with a fork and chill in the refrigerator for 30 minutes.

4 Line the tart shell with foil and baking beans. Bake the shell in a preheated oven, 375°F/190°C, for 15 minutes. Remove the foil and beans and cook for 15 minutes.

5 Combine the mincemeat with the apples and lemon juice and spoon into the baked tart shell.

6 Melt the syrup and butter together in a small pan over low heat. Pour the syrup mixture over the mincemeat filling in the tart.

7 Return the tart to the oven and bake for about 20 minutes or until firm. Serve warm.

4

5

6

VARIATION

Add 2 tablespoons of sherry to spice up the mincemeat, if you wish.

Custard Tart

This is a classic egg custard tart which should be served as fresh as possible for the best flavor and texture.

NUTRITIONAL INFORMATION

Calories	268	Sugars	5g
Protein	5g	Fat	19g
Carbohydrate	20g	Saturates	12g

1¼ hrs

1 hr

SERVES 8

INGREDIENTS

SWEET PIE DOUGH

1¼ cups all-purpose flour

2 tbsp superfine sugar

½ cup butter, cut into small pieces

1 tbsp water

FILLING

3 eggs

⅔ cup light cream

⅔ cup milk

freshly grated nutmeg

TO SERVE

whipped cream (optional)

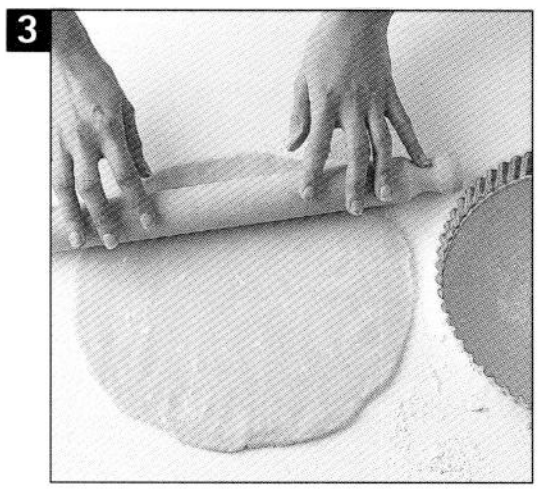
3

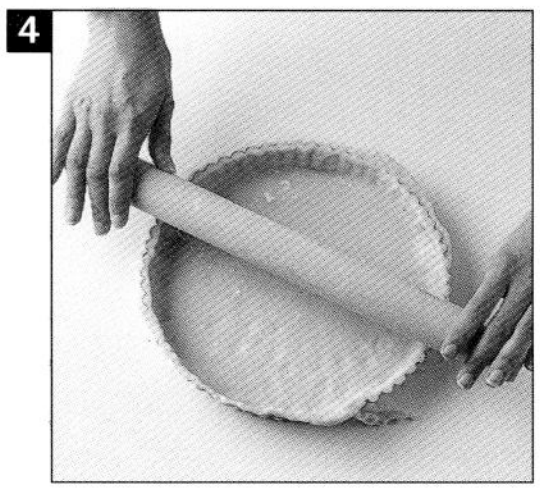
4

7

1 To make the dough, place the flour and sugar in a mixing bowl and rub in the butter with your fingertips.

2 Add the water and mix together until a soft dough has formed. Wrap and chill in the refrigerator for about 30 minutes.

3 Roll out the dough to form a circle slightly larger than a 9½-inch/ 24-cm/ loose-bottomed tart pan.

4 Line the pan with the dough, trimming off the edges. Prick the dough with a fork and chill in the refrigerator for 30 minutes.

5 Line the tart shell with foil and baking beans. Bake in a preheated oven, 375°F/190°C, for 15 minutes. Remove the foil and baking beans and bake the tart shell for a further 15 minutes.

6 To make the filling, whisk together the eggs, cream, milk, and nutmeg. Pour the filling into the prepared tart shell.

6 Return the tart to the oven and cook for for a further 25–30 minutes or until the filling is just set. Serve with whipped cream, if wished.

COOK'S TIP

Baking the pie shell blind ensures that the finished tart has a crisp base.

Lemon Tart

No-one will be able to resist this tart with its buttery pastry and a sharp, melt-in-the-mouth lemon filling.

NUTRITIONAL INFORMATION

Calories	363	Sugars	18g
Protein	5g	Fat	25g
Carbohydrate	32g	Saturates	15g

1 hr 50 mins — 50 mins

SERVES 8

INGREDIENTS

SWEET PIE DOUGH

- 1¼ cups all-purpose flour
- 2 tbsp superfine sugar
- ½ cup butter, cut into small pieces
- 1 tbsp water

FILLING

- ⅔ cup heavy cream
- ½ cup superfine sugar
- 4 eggs
- grated zest of 3 lemons
- ¾ cup lemon juice
- confectioners' sugar, for dusting

1 To make the dough, place the flour and sugar in a bowl and rub in the butter with your fingertips until the mixture resembles bread crumbs. Add the water and mix until a soft dough has formed. Wrap and chill in the refrigerator for 30 minutes.

2 On a lightly floured surface, roll out the dough and line a 9½-inch/24-cm loose-bottomed tart pan. Prick the dough with a fork and chill in the refrigerator for 30 minutes.

3 Line the tart shell with foil and baking beans and bake in a preheated oven, 375°F/190°C, for 15 minutes. Remove the foil and baking beans and cook for a further 15 minutes.

4 To make the filling, whisk the cream, sugar, eggs, lemon zest, and juice together. Place the tart shell, still in its pan, on a cookie sheet, and pour in the filling (see Cook's Tip).

5 Return the tart to the oven for about 20 minutes or until the filling is just set. Let cool, then lightly dust with confectioners' sugar before serving.

1

2

4

COOK'S TIP

To avoid any spillage, pour half of the filling into the pie shell, place in the oven, and pour in the remaining filling.

Orange Tart

This is a variation of the classic lemon tart—in this recipe fresh bread crumbs are used to create a thicker texture.

NUTRITIONAL INFORMATION

Calories	450	Sugars	17g
Protein	6g	Fat	31g
Carbohydrate	40g	Saturates	19g

1 hr 20 mins — 1¼ hrs

SERVES 6-8

INGREDIENTS

SWEET PIE DOUGH

1¼ cups all-purpose flour

2 tbsp superfine sugar

½ cup butter, cut into small pieces

1 tbsp water

FILLING

grated zest of 2 oranges

scant ⅔ cup orange juice

scant 1 cup fresh white bread crumbs

2 tbsp lemon juice

⅔ cup light cream

4 tbsp butter

¼ cup superfine sugar

2 eggs, separated

salt

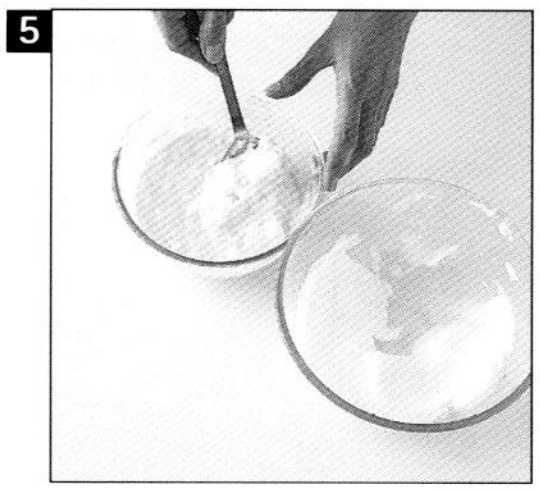

1 To make the dough, place the flour and sugar in a bowl and rub in the butter with your fingertips until the mixture resembles bread crumbs. Add the water and work the mixture together until a soft dough has formed. Wrap and chill in the refrigerator for 30 minutes.

2 Roll out the dough on a lightly floured surface to a circle and line a 9½-inch/24-cm loose-bottomed tart pan. Prick the dough with a fork and chill in the refrigerator for 30 minutes.

3 Line the tart shell with foil and baking beans and bake in a preheated oven, 375°F/190°C, for 15 minutes. Remove the foil and beans and cook for a further 15 minutes.

4 To make the filling, combine the orange zest and juice with the bread crumbs in a bowl. Stir in the lemon juice and light cream. Melt the butter and sugar in a small pan over low heat. Remove the pan from the heat, add the 2 egg yolks, a pinch of salt, and the bread crumb mixture, and stir.

5 In a mixing bowl, whisk the egg whites with a pinch of salt until they form soft peaks. Fold them into the egg yolk mixture.

6 Pour the filling mixture into the tart shell. Bake in a preheated oven, 325°F/170°C, for about 45 minutes or until just set. Let cool slightly and serve warm.

Coconut Cream Tart

Decorate this tart with some fresh tropical fruit, such as mango or pineapple, and extra shredded coconut, toasted.

NUTRITIONAL INFORMATION

Calories	740	Sugars	37g
Protein	9g	Fat	52g
Carbohydrate	62g	Saturates	35g

2¼ hrs   40 mins

SERVES 6-8

INGREDIENTS

SWEET PIE DOUGH

1¼ cups all-purpose flour

2 tbsp superfine sugar

½ cup butter, cut into small pieces

1 tbsp water

FILLING

scant 2 cups milk

4½ oz/125 g creamed coconut

3 egg yolks

½ cup superfine sugar

generous ⅓ cup all-purpose flour, sifted

¼ cup shredded coconut

generous ¼ cup chopped candied pineapple

2 tbsp rum or pineapple juice

1⅓ cups whipping cream, whipped

1 To make the dough, place the flour and sugar in a bowl and rub in the butter with your fingertips until the mixture resembles bread crumbs. Add the water and work the mixture together until a soft dough has formed. Wrap and chill in the refrigerator for 30 minutes.

2 On a lightly floured surface, roll out the dough to a circle and line a 9½-inch/24-cm loose-bottomed tart pan. Prick the dough with a fork and chill in the refrigerator for 30 minutes.

3 Line the tart shell with foil and baking beans and bake in a preheated oven, 375°F/190°C, for 15 minutes. Remove the foil and baking beans and cook for a further 15 minutes. Let cool.

4 To make the filling, bring the milk and creamed coconut to just below boiling point in a small pan over a low heat, stirring to melt the coconut.

5 In a bowl, whisk the egg yolks with the sugar until pale and fluffy. Whisk in the flour. Pour the hot milk over the egg mixture, stirring constantly. Return the mixture to the pan and heat gently, stirring constantly, for about 8 minutes until thick. Let cool.

6 Stir the coconut, pineapple, and rum or juice into the coconut cream filling. Spread the filling in the tart shell. Cover with the whipped cream and chill in the refrigerator until required.

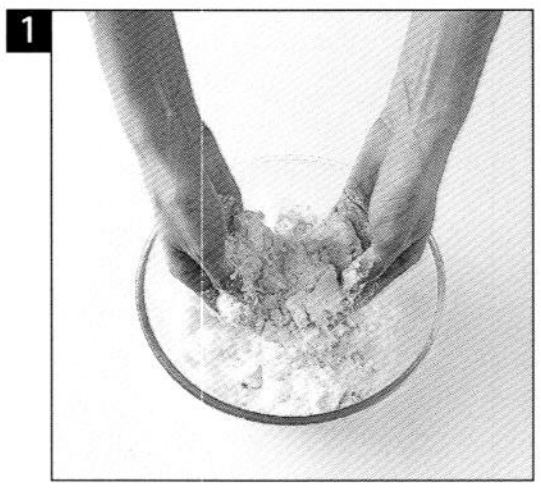

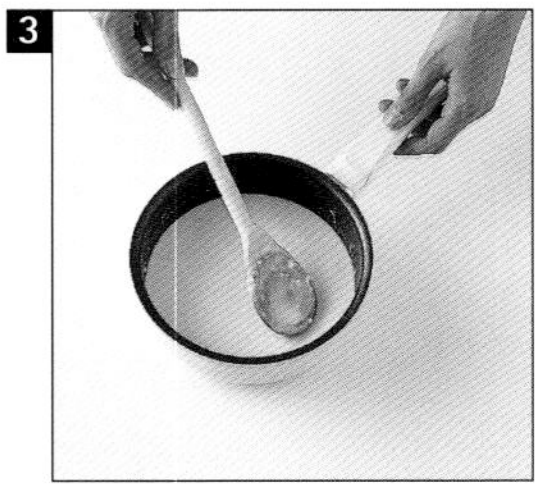

Pine Nut Tart

This tart has a sweet filling made with creamy cheese and it is topped with pine nuts for a decorative finish and contrasting texture.

NUTRITIONAL INFORMATION

Calories	512	Sugars	22g
Protein	10g	Fat	37g
Carbohydrate	37g	Saturates	18g

2¼ hrs

1 hr 5 mins

SERVES 8

INGREDIENTS

SWEET PIE DOUGH

- 1¼ cups all-purpose flour
- 2 tbsp superfine sugar
- ½ cup butter, cut into small pieces
- 1 tbsp water

FILLING

- 1½ cups curd cheese
- 4 tbsp heavy cream
- 3 eggs
- ½ cup superfine sugar
- grated zest of 1 orange
- 1 cup pine nuts

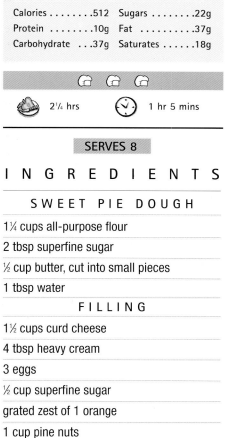

1 To make the dough, place the flour and sugar in a bowl and rub in the butter with your fingertips until the mixture resembles bread crumbs. Add the water and work the mixture together until a soft dough has formed. Wrap and chill in the refrigerator for 30 minutes.

2 On a lightly floured surface, roll out the dough and line a 9½-inch/24-cm loose-bottomed tart pan. Prick the dough with a fork and chill for 30 minutes.

3 Line the tart shell with foil and baking beans and bake in a preheated oven, 375°F/190°C, for 15 minutes. Remove the foil and beans and cook the shell for a further 15 minutes.

4 To make the filling, beat together the curd cheese, cream, eggs, sugar, orange zest, and half of the pine nuts. Pour the filling into the tart shell and sprinkle over the remaining pine nuts.

5 Bake in the oven, 325°F/170°C, for about 35 minutes or until the filling is just set. Let cool before serving.

1

2

4

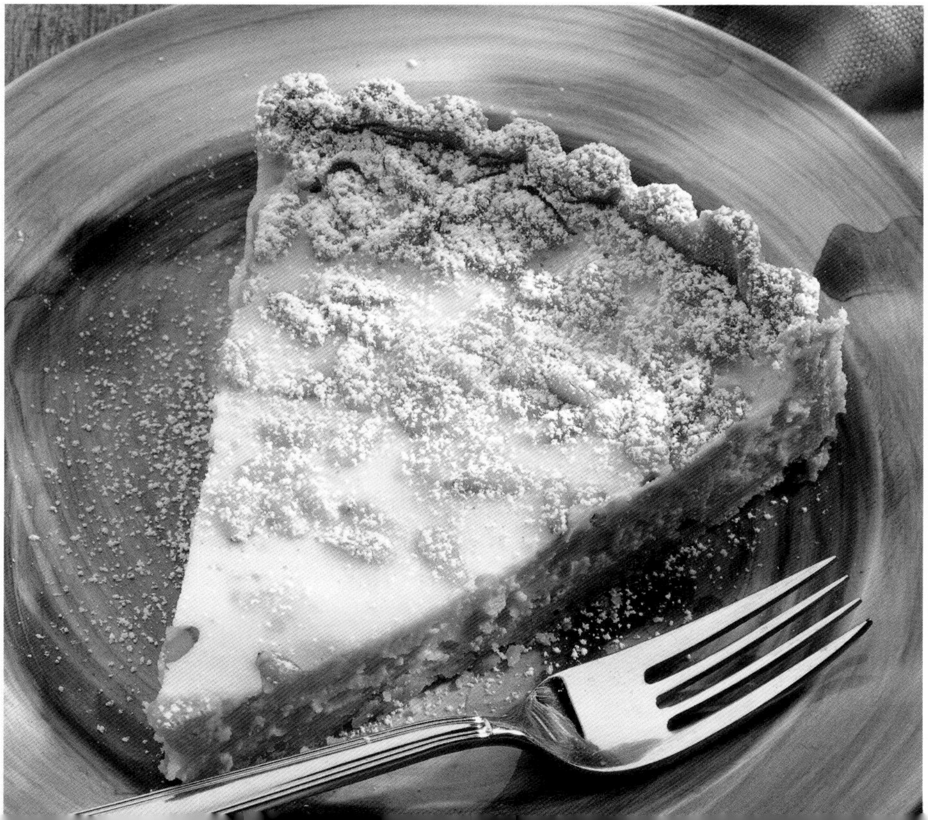

VARIATION

Replace the pine nuts with slivered almonds, if you prefer.

Candied Peel & Nut Tart

This very rich tart is not for the faint-hearted. Serve it in thin slices – even to dessert enthusiasts and those with a sweet tooth.

NUTRITIONAL INFORMATION

Calories	643	Sugars	34g
Protein	9g	Fat	47g
Carbohydrate	49g	Saturates	23g

2¼ hrs — 20 mins

SERVES 8

INGREDIENTS

SWEET PIE DOUGH

- 1¼ cups all-purpose flour
- 2 tbsp superfine sugar
- ½ cup butter, cut into small pieces
- 1 tbsp water

FILLING

- 6 tbsp butter
- ¼ cup superfine sugar
- 2¾ oz/75 g set honey
- generous ¾ cup heavy cream
- 1 egg, beaten
- scant 1 cup mixed nuts
- generous 1 cup candied peel

VARIATION

Substitute walnuts or pecan nuts for the mixed nuts, if you prefer.

1 To make the dough, place the flour and sugar in a bowl and rub in the butter with your fingertips until the mixture resembles bread crumbs. Add the water and work the mixture together until a soft dough has formed. Wrap and chill in the refrigerator for 30 minutes.

2 On a lightly floured surface, roll out the dough and line a 9½-inch/24-cm loose-bottomed tart pan. Prick the dough with a fork and chill in the refrigerator for 30 minutes.

3 Line the tart shell with foil and baking beans and bake in a preheated oven, 375°F/190°C, for 15 minutes. Remove the foil and baking beans and cook for a further 15 minutes.

4 To make the filling, melt the butter, sugar, and honey in a small pan over low heat. Stir in the cream and beaten egg, then add the nuts and candied peel. Cook over a low heat, stirring constantly, for 2 minutes until the mixture is a pale golden color.

5 Pour the filling into the tart shell and return the tart to the oven for 15–20 minutes or until the filling is just set. Let cool, then serve in slices.

1

2

4

Apricot & Cranberry Tart

This frangipane tart, made with fresh cranberries, is ideal for Thanksgiving. If you wish, brush the warm tart with melted apricot jelly.

NUTRITIONAL INFORMATION

Calories	752	Sugars	40g
Protein	9g	Fat	55g
Carbohydrate	59g	Saturates	28g

1 hr 20 mins

1½ hrs

SERVES 8

INGREDIENTS

SWEET PIE DOUGH

- 1¼ cups all-purpose flour
- 2 tbsp superfine sugar
- ½ cup butter, cut into small pieces
- 1 tbsp water

FILLING

- scant 1 cup sweet butter
- 1 cup superfine sugar
- 1 egg
- 2 egg yolks
- ⅓ cup all-purpose flour, strained
- 1⅔ cups ground almonds
- 4 tbsp heavy cream
- 14½ oz/410 g canned apricot halves, drained
- generous 1 cup fresh cranberries

1 To make the dough, place the flour and sugar in a bowl and rub in the butter with your fingertips until the mixture resembles bread crumbs. Add the water and work the mixture together until a soft dough has formed. Wrap and chill in the refrigerator for 30 minutes.

2 Roll out the dough and line a 9½-inch/24-cm loose-bottomed tart pan. Prick the dough with a fork and chill in the refrigerator for 30 minutes.

3 Line the tart shell with foil and baking beans and bake in a preheated oven, 375°F/190°C, for 15 minutes. Remove the foil and baking beans and cook for a further 10 minutes.

4 To make the filling, cream together the butter and sugar until light and fluffy. Beat in the egg and egg yolks, then stir in the flour, almonds, and cream.

5 Place the apricot halves and cranberries on the bottom of the tart shell and spoon the filling over the top.

6 Return the tart to the oven and bake for about 1 hour or until the topping is just set. Let cool slightly, then serve warm or cold.

Mincemeat & Grape Jalousie

This jalousie makes a good Thanksgiving dessert. Its festive filling and flavor is a great alternative to small mince pies.

NUTRITIONAL INFORMATION

Calories	796	Sugars	73g
Protein	9g	Fat	35g
Carbohydrate	118g	Saturates	3g

1 hr 5 mins — 45 mins

SERVES 4

INGREDIENTS

- butter, for greasing
- 1lb 2 oz/500 g ready-made puff pie dough, thawed if frozen
- 14½ oz/410 g jar mincemeat
- 1 cup grapes, seeded and halved
- 1 egg, lightly beaten
- raw brown sugar, for sprinkling

1 Lightly grease a cookie sheet with a little butter.

2 On a lightly floured surface, roll out the puff pie dough and cut it into 2 rectangles.

3 Place dough rectangle on the prepared cookie sheet and brush the edges with water.

4 Combine the mincemeat and grapes in a mixing bowl. Spread the mixture evenly over the dough rectangle on the cookie sheet, leaving a 1-inch/2.5-cm border all around the edges.

5 Fold the second pie dough rectangle in half lengthwise, and carefully cut a series of parallel lines across the folded edge, leaving a 1-inch/2.5-cm border.

6 Open out the second rectangle and lay it over the mincemeat filling. Seal down the edges of the pie dough and press together well.

7 Flute and crimp the edges of the dough. Lightly brush with the beaten egg to glaze and sprinkle with raw brown sugar.

8 Bake in a preheated oven, 425°F/220°C, for 15 minutes. Lower the heat to 350°F/180°C and cook for a further 30 minutes until the jalousie is well risen and golden brown.

9 Carefully transfer the jalousie to a wire rack with a fish slice or spatula. Let cool completely before serving.

COOK'S TIP

For an enhanced festive flavour, stir 2 tablespoons of sherry into the mincemeat.

Pear Tarts

These tarts are made with ready-made puff pie dough which is available from most stores. The finished result is rich and buttery.

NUTRITIONAL INFORMATION

Calories 250	Sugars 15g
Protein 3g	Fat 14g
Carbohydrate ...30g	Saturates 3g

35 mins   20 mins

SERVES 6

INGREDIENTS

9 oz/250 g ready-made puff pie dough, thawed if frozen

2 tbsp brown sugar

2 tbsp butter, plus extra for brushing

1 tbsp finely chopped preserved ginger

3 pears, peeled, halved, and cored

cream, to serve

2

5

6

1 Roll out the puff pie dough on a lightly floured surface. Cut or stamp out 6 circles, each about 4 inches/10 cm in diameter.

2 Place the circles on a large cookie sheet and chill in the refrigerator for 30 minutes.

3 Cream together the brown sugar and butter in a small bowl, then stir in the chopped preserved ginger.

4 Prick the pastry circles with a fork and spread a little of the ginger mixture onto each one.

5 Slice the pears halves lengthwise, keeping them intact at the tip. Fan out the slices slightly.

6 Place a fanned-out pear half on top of each pie dough circle. Make small flutes around the edge of the circles with the back of a knife blade and brush each pear half with melted butter.

7 Bake in a preheated oven, 400°F/200°C, for 15–20 minutes, until the pastry is well risen and golden. Let cool slightly before serving the tarts warm with a little cream.

COOK'S TIP

If you prefer, serve these tarts with vanilla ice cream for a delicious dessert.

Crème Brûlée Tarts

Serve these melt-in-your-mouth tarts with fresh fruit, such as mixed summer berries if wished.

NUTRITIONAL INFORMATION

Calories	635	Sugars	17g
Protein	6g	Fat	53g
Carbohydrate	36g	Saturates	32g

2 hrs 20 mins — 25 mins

SERVES 6

INGREDIENTS

SWEET PIE DOUGH

- 1¼ cups all-purpose flour
- 2 tbsp superfine sugar
- ½ cup butter, cut into small pieces.
- 1 tbsp water

FILLING

- 4 egg yolks
- ¼ cup superfine sugar
- 1¾ cups heavy cream
- 1 tsp vanilla extract
- raw brown sugar, for sprinkling

2

4

7

1 To make the dough, place the flour and sugar in a bowl and rub in the butter with your fingertips until the mixture resembles bread crumbs. Add the water and work the mixture together until a soft dough has formed. Wrap and chill in the refrigerator for 30 minutes.

2 On a lightly floured surface, roll out the dough to line 6 tart pans, each 4 inches/10 cm wide. Prick the bottom of the tart shells with a fork and chill in the refrigerator for 20 minutes.

3 Line the tart shells with foil and baking beans and bake in a preheated oven, 375°F/190°C, for 15 minutes. Remove the foil and beans and cook for a further 10 minutes until crisp and golden. Let cool.

4 Meanwhile, make the filling. In a bowl, beat the egg yolks and sugar until pale. Heat the cream and vanilla extract in a pan until just below boiling point, then pour it onto the egg mixture, whisking constantly.

5 Return the mixture to a clean pan and bring to just below a boil, stirring constantly until thick. Do not let the mixture boil or it will curdle.

6 Let the mixture cool slightly, then pour it into the tart pans. Let cool and then chill overnight in the refrigerator.

7 Sprinkle the tarts with the sugar. Place under a preheated hot broiler for a few minutes. Let cool, then chill for 2 hours before serving.

Mini Frangipane Tartlets

These little tartlets have an unusual lime-flavored pastry and are filled with a delicious almond frangipane mixture.

NUTRITIONAL INFORMATION

Calories	149	Sugars	9g
Protein	2g	Fat	9g
Carbohydrate	17g	Saturates	5g

45 mins   15 mins

SERVES 12

INGREDIENTS

- scant 1 cup all-purpose flour
- ⅓ cup butter, softened
- 1 tsp grated lime zest
- 1 tbsp lime juice
- ¼ cup superfine sugar
- 1 egg
- ¼ cup ground almonds
- ⅓ cup confectioners' sugar, strained
- ½ tbsp water

3

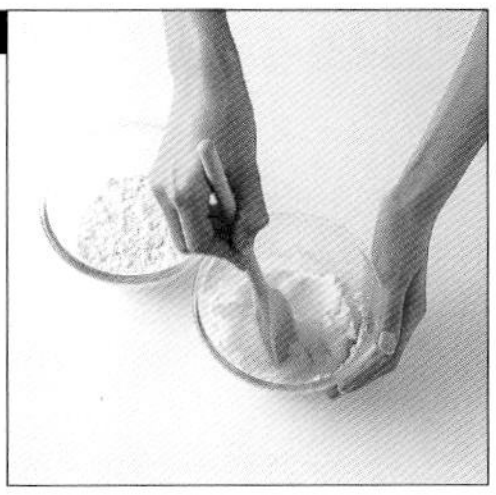
5

6

1 Reserve 5 teaspoons of the flour and 3 teaspoons of the butter and set aside until required.

2 Rub the remaining butter into the remaining flour with your fingertips until the mixture resembles fine bread crumbs. Stir in the lime zest, followed by the lime juice, and bring the mixture together to form a soft dough.

3 On a lightly floured surface, roll out the dough thinly. Stamp out 12 circles, 3-inch/7.5-cm in diameter and line a shallow muffin pan.

4 In a bowl, cream together the reserved butter with the superfine sugar until pale and fluffy.

5 Mix in the egg, then the ground almonds and the reserved flour.

6 Divide the mixture among the tartlet shells and smooth the tops.

7 Bake in a preheated oven, 400°F/200°C, for 15 minutes, until set and lightly golden. Remove the tartlets from the pan, place on wire racks, and let cool completely.

8 Mix the confectioners' sugar with the water. Drizzle a little of the frosting over each tartlet and serve.

COOK'S TIP

These tartlets can be made in advance. Store them in an airtight container and decorate them just before serving.

Paper-Thin Fruit Pies

A tasty treat for weight-watchers, serve these crisp pastry cases, filled with glazed fruit, hot with low-fat custard.

NUTRITIONAL INFORMATION

Calories	158	Sugars	12g
Protein	2g	Fat	10g
Carbohydrate	14g	Saturates	2g

20 mins   15 mins

SERVES 4

INGREDIENTS

- 1 medium eating apple
- 1 medium ripe pear
- 2 tbsp lemon juice
- 4 tbsp low-fat spread
- 4 sheets of phyllo pastry, thawed if frozen
- 2 tbsp low-sugar apricot jelly
- 1 tbsp unsweetened orange juice
- 1 tbsp finely chopped shelled pistachio nuts
- 2 tsp confectioners' sugar, for dusting
- low-fat custard, to serve

1 Core and thinly slice the apple and pear and toss them in the lemon juice.

2 Gently melt the low-fat spread in a small pan over low heat.

3 Cut the sheets of phyllo pastry into 4 and cover with a clean, damp dish cloth. Brush 4 non-stick large muffin pans, measuring 10 cm/4 inches across, with a little of the low-fat spread.

4 Working on each pie separately, brush 4 sheets of pastry with low-fat spread. Press a small sheet of pastry into the base of one pan. Arrange the other sheets on top at slightly different angles. Repeat with the other sheets to make another 3 pies.

5 Arrange the apple and pear slices alternately in the center of each phyllo pastry case and lightly crimp the edges of the pastry of each pie.

6 Mix the jelly and orange juice together until smooth and brush over the fruit. Bake in a preheated oven, 400°F/200°C, for 12–15 minutes. Sprinkle with the pistachio nuts, dust lightly with confectioners' sugar, and serve hot with low-fat custard.

3

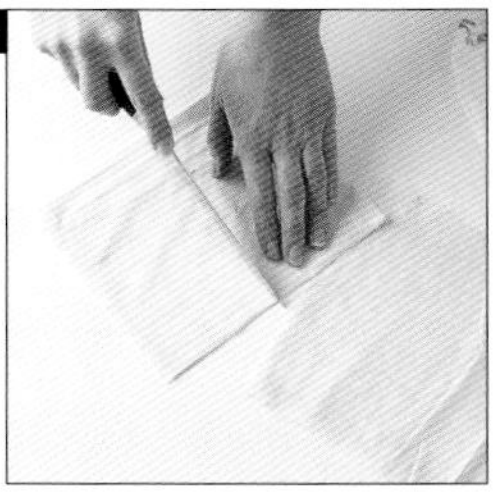

4

5

VARIATION

Other combinations of fruit are equally delicious. Try peach and apricot, raspberry and apple, or pineapple and mango.

Almond Cheesecakes

These creamy cheese desserts are so delicious that it's hard to believe that they are low in fat—a healthy and tasty option.

NUTRITIONAL INFORMATION

Calories	361	Sugars	29g
Protein	16g	Fat	15g
Carbohydrate	43g	Saturates	4g

1¼ hrs — 10 mins

SERVES 4

INGREDIENTS

- 12 amaretti cookies
- 1 egg white, lightly beaten
- 1 cup skim-milk soft cheese
- ½ tsp almond extract
- ½ tsp finely grated lime zest
- scant ¼ cup ground almonds
- 2 tbsp superfine sugar
- ⅓ cup golden raisins
- 2 tsp powdered gelatin
- 2 tbsp boiling water
- 2 tbsp lime juice

TO DECORATE

- 2 tbsp slivered toasted almonds
- strips of lime zest

1 Place the cookies in a clean plastic bag, seal the bag, and using a rolling pin, crush them into small pieces.

2 Place the amaretti crumbs in a bowl and stir in the egg white to bind them together.

3 Arrange 4 non-stick pastry rings or poached egg rings, 3½ inches/9 cm across, on a cookie sheet lined with baking parchment.

4 Divide the amaretti mixture into 4 equal portions and spoon it into the rings, pressing it down well. Bake in a preheated oven, 350°F/180°C, for about 10 minutes until crisp. Remove from the oven and let cool in the rings.

5 Put the soft cheese, almond extract, lime zest, ground almonds, sugar, and golden raisins in a bowl and beat thoroughly until well mixed.

6 Dissolve the gelatin in the boiling water and stir in the lime juice. Fold into the cheese mixture and spoon over the amaretti bases. Smooth over the tops and chill for 1 hour or until set.

7 Loosen the cheesecakes from the rings using a small spatula and transfer to serving plates. Decorate with slivered toasted almonds and strips of lime zest and serve.

1

4

6

Brown Sugar Pavlovas

This simple combination of fudgey meringue topped with mascarpone and raspberries is the perfect finale to any meal.

NUTRITIONAL INFORMATION

Calories	155	Sugars	34g
Protein	5g	Fat	0.2g
Carbohydrate	35g	Saturates	0g

1 hr 1 hr

SERVES 4

INGREDIENTS

- 2 large egg whites
- 1 tsp cornstarch
- 1 tsp raspberry vinegar
- ½ cup light brown sugar, crushed free of lumps
- 2 tbsp red currant jelly
- 2 tbsp unsweetened orange juice
- ¾ cup low-fat mascarpone cheese
- 1 cup raspberries, thawed if frozen
- rose-scented geranium leaves, to decorate (optional)

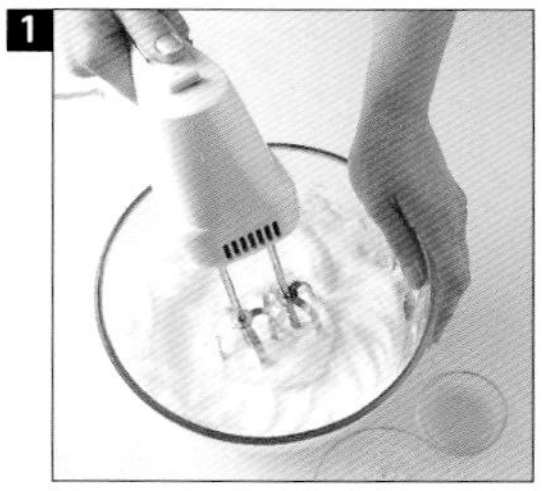

1 Line a large cookie sheet with baking parchment. Whisk the egg whites until very stiff and dry. Gently fold in the cornstarch and vinegar.

2 Gradually whisk in the sugar, a spoonful at a time, until the mixture is thick and glossy.

3 Divide the mixture into 4 and spoon onto the prepared cookie sheet, spaced well apart. Smooth each heap into a circle, about 4 inches/10 cm in diameter, and bake in a preheated oven, 300°F/150°C, for 40–45 minutes until crisp and a light golden brown color. Let cool on the cookie sheet.

4 Place the red currant jelly and orange juice in a small pan and heat, stirring, until melted. Let cool for 10 minutes.

5 Using a spatula, carefully remove each pavlova from the baking parchment and transfer to a serving plate. Top with the mascarpone and the raspberries. Glaze the fruit with the red currant jelly mixture, and decorate with the rose-scented geranium leaves if using.

COOK'S TIP

Make a large pavlova by forming the meringue into a circle, measuring 7 inches/18 cm across, on a lined cookie sheet, and baking for 1 hour.

Baked Pears with Cinnamon

This simple recipe is easy to prepare and cook but is deliciously warming. For a healthy treat, serve hot on a pool of low-fat custard.

NUTRITIONAL INFORMATION

Calories	207	Sugars	35g
Protein	3g	Fat	6g
Carbohydrate	37g	Saturates	2g

10 mins 25 mins

SERVES 4

INGREDIENTS

- 4 ripe pears
- 2 tbsp lemon juice
- ¼ cup light brown sugar
- 1 tsp ground cinnamon
- 5 tbsp low-fat spread
- low-fat custard, to serve
- lemon zest, finely grated, to decorate

1

2

2

1 Core and peel the pears, then slice them in half lengthwise, and brush all over with the lemon juice to prevent them from turning brown. Arrange the pears, cored side down, in a small non-stick roasting pan.

2 Place the sugar, cinnamon, and low-fat spread in a small pan and heat gently, stirring constantly, until the sugar has completely dissolved. Keep the heat as low as possible to stop too much water evaporating from the low-fat spread as it gets hot. Spoon the mixture over the pears.

3 Bake in a preheated oven, 400°F/200°C, for 20–25 minutes or until the pears are tender and golden, occasionally spooning the sugar mixture over the fruit during the cooking time.

4 To serve, heat the custard until it is piping hot and spoon a little over the bases of 4 warm dessert plates. Arrange 2 pear halves on each plate.

5 Decorate with grated lemon zest and serve immediately.

VARIATION

For alternative flavors, replace the cinnamon with ground ginger and serve the pears sprinkled with chopped preserved ginger in syrup. Alternatively, use ground allspice and spoon over some warmed dark rum to serve.

Baked Bananas

The orange-flavored cream can be prepared in advance but do not make up the banana parcels until just before you need to bake them.

NUTRITIONAL INFORMATION

Calories	784	Sugars	5g
Protein	17g	Fat	58g
Carbohydrate	52g	Saturates	19g

30 mins — 10 mins

SERVES 4

INGREDIENTS

- 4 bananas
- 2 passion fruit
- 4 tbsp orange juice
- 4 tbsp orange-flavored liqueur

ORANGE-FLAVORED CREAM

- ⅔ cup heavy cream
- 3 tbsp confectioners' sugar
- 2 tbsp orange-flavored liqueur

1

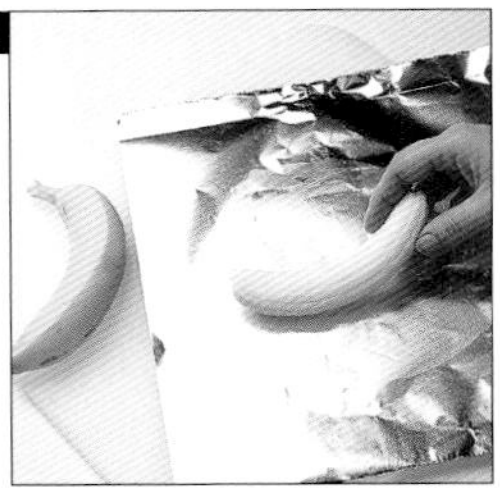
2

3

1 To make the orange-flavored cream, pour the heavy cream into a mixing bowl and sprinkle over the confectioners' sugar. Whisk the mixture until it is standing in soft peaks. Carefully fold in the orange-flavored liqueur and chill in the refrigerator until required.

2 Peel the bananas and place each one on a sheet of foil.

3 Cut the passion fruit in half and squeeze the juice of each half over each banana. Spoon over the orange juice and liqueur.

4 Fold the foil over the top of the bananas, tucking the ends in so that they are completely enclosed.

5 Bake the bananas in a preheated oven, 350°F/180°C, for about 10 minutes or until the bananas are just tender and piping hot. Check by piercing the foil parcel with a toothpick.

6 Transfer the foil parcels to warm, individual serving plates. Open out the foil parcels at the table and then serve immediately with the chilled orange-flavored cream.

VARIATION

Leave the bananas in their skins for a really quick dessert. Split the banana skins and pop in 1–2 cubes of chocolate. Wrap the bananas in foil and bake in a preheated oven, 350°F/180°C, for 10 minutes, or until the chocolate just melts.

Baked Apples with Berries

This winter dessert is a classic dish. Large, fluffy apples are hollowed out and filled with spices, almonds, and blackberries.

NUTRITIONAL INFORMATION

Calories	228	Sugars	31g
Protein	1g	Fat	2g
Carbohydrate	31g	Saturates	0.2g

10 mins — 45 mins

SERVES 4

INGREDIENTS

- 4 medium-size cooking apples
- 1 tbsp lemon juice
- 1 cup prepared blackberries, thawed if frozen
- 1 tbsp slivered almonds
- ½ tsp ground allspice
- ½ tsp finely grated lemon zest
- 2 tbsp raw brown sugar
- 1¼ cups ruby port
- 1 cinnamon stick, broken
- 2 tsp cornstarch blended with 2 tbsp cold water
- low-fat custard, to serve

1

2

3

1 Wash and dry the apples. Using a small sharp knife, make a shallow cut through the skin around the middle of each apple—this will help the apples to cook through.

2 Core the apples, brush the centers with the lemon juice to prevent them from browning, and stand them in an ovenproof dish.

3 In a bowl, combine the blackberries, almonds, allspice, lemon zest, and sugar. Using a teaspoon, spoon the mixture into the center of each apple.

4 Pour the port into the dish, add the cinnamon stick, and bake the apples in a preheated oven, 400°F/200°C, for 35–40 minutes or until tender and soft.

5 Drain the cooking juices into a small pan and set over low heat. Keep the apples warm.

6 Discard the cinnamon from the cooking juices and add the cornstarch mixture to the pan. Heat, stirring constantly, until thickened.

7 Heat the custard until piping hot. Pour the sauce over the apples and serve with the custard.

Italian Bread Pudding

This deliciously rich pudding is cooked with cream and apples and is delicately flavored with orange.

NUTRITIONAL INFORMATION

Calories	387	Sugars	31g
Protein	8g	Fat	20g
Carbohydrate	45g	Saturates	12g

45 mins | 25 mins

SERVES 4

INGREDIENTS

- 1 tbsp butter
- 2 small eating apples, peeled, cored, and sliced into rings
- generous ⅓ cup granulated sugar
- 2 tbsp white wine
- 3½ oz/100 g bread, sliced with crusts removed (slightly stale French baguette is ideal)
- 1¼ cups light cream
- 2 eggs, beaten
- pared zest of 1 orange, cut into thin sticks

1 Lightly grease a 5-cup/1.25-litre deep ovenproof dish with the butter.

2 Arrange the apple rings in the bottom of the dish. Sprinkle half of the sugar over the apples.

3 Pour the wine over the apples. Add the bread slices, pushing them down with your hands to flatten them slightly.

4 Mix the cream with the eggs, the remaining sugar, and the orange zest and pour the mixture over the bread. Set aside to soak for 30 minutes.

5 Bake the pudding in a preheated oven, 350°F/180°C, for 25 minutes until golden and set. Serve warm.

2

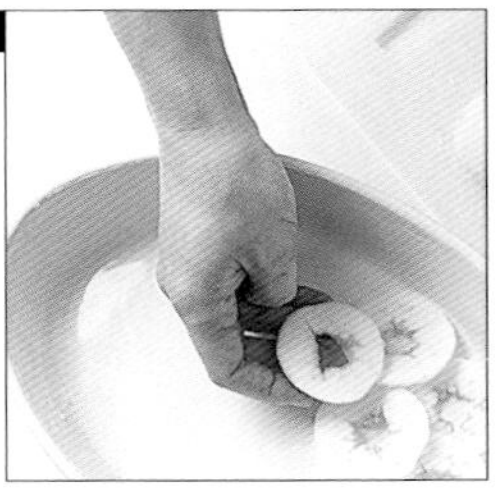

3

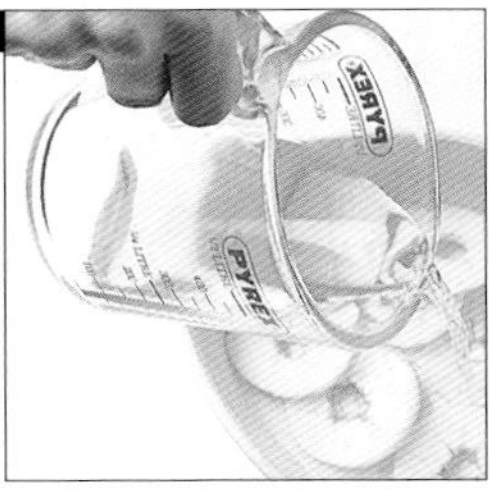

3

VARIATION

For a variation, try adding dried fruit, such as apricots, cherries, or dates to the pudding, if you prefer.

Tuscan Pudding

These baked mini-ricotta puddings are delicious served warm or chilled and will keep in the refrigerator for 3–4 days.

NUTRITIONAL INFORMATION

Calories 293	Sugars 28g
Protein 9g	Fat 17g
Carbohydrate ...28g	Saturates 9g

20 mins   15 mins

SERVES 4

INGREDIENTS

1 tbsp butter

⅔ cup mixed dried fruit

generous 1 cup ricotta cheese

3 egg yolks

¼ cup superfine sugar

1 tsp cinnamon

finely grated zest of 1 orange, plus extra to decorate

crème fraîche, to serve

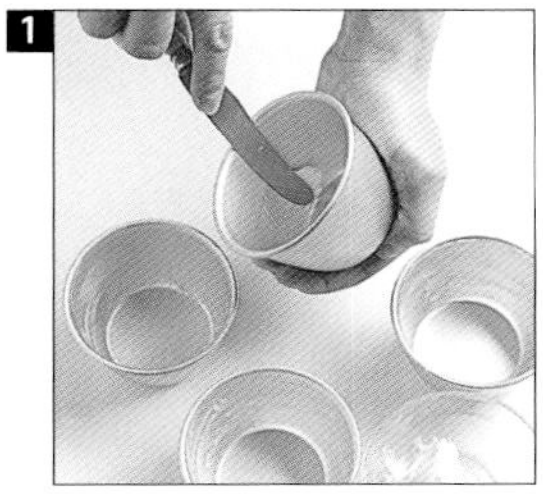

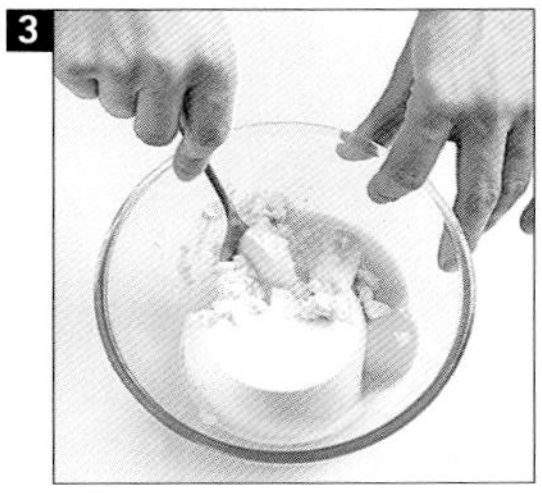

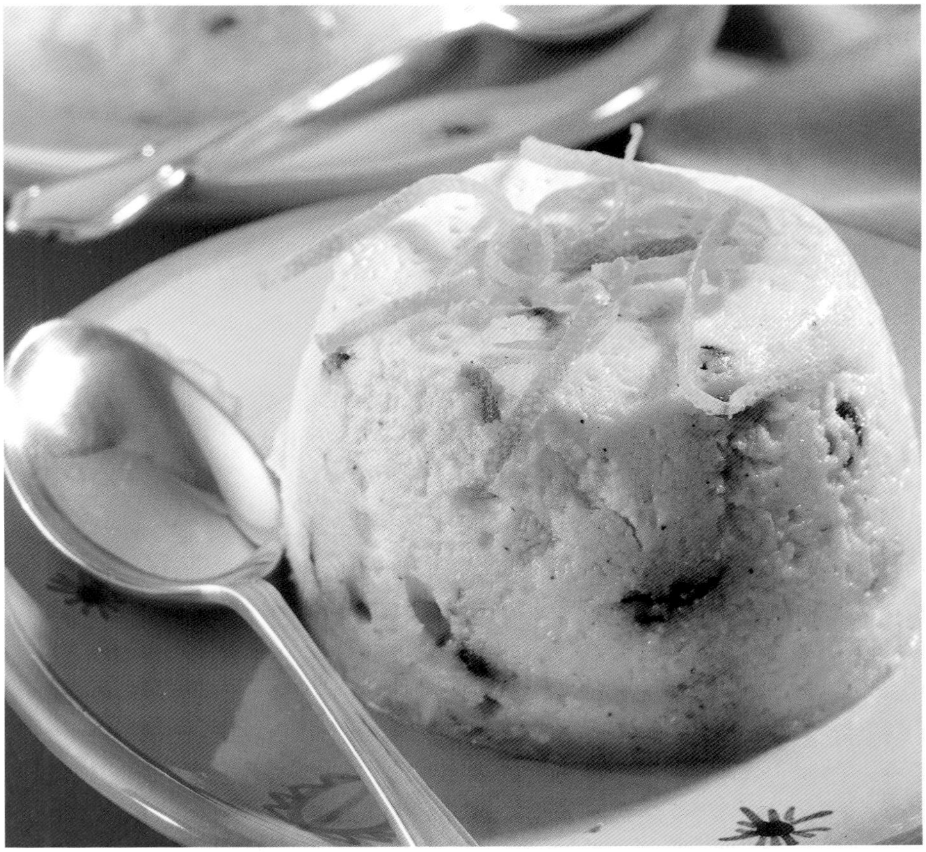

1 Lightly grease 4 mini ovenproof bowls or ramekin dishes with the butter.

2 Put the dried fruit in a bowl and cover with warm water. Set aside to soak for 10 minutes.

3 Beat the ricotta cheese with the egg yolks in a bowl. Stir in the superfine sugar, cinnamon, and orange zest and mix to combine.

4 Drain the dried fruit in a strainer set over a bowl. Mix the drained fruit with the ricotta cheese mixture.

5 Spoon the mixture into the bowls or ramekin dishes.

6 Bake in a preheated oven, 350°F/180°C, for 15 minutes. The tops should just be firm to the touch, but they should not brown.

7 Decorate the puddings with grated orange zest. Serve warm or chilled with a spoon of crème fraîche, if liked.

COOK'S TIP

Crème fraîche has a slightly sour, nutty taste and is very thick. It is suitable for cooking, but has the same fat content as heavy cream. It can be made by stirring cultured buttermilk into heavy cream and refrigerating overnight.

Mascarpone Cheesecake

The mascarpone gives this baked cheesecake a wonderfully tangy flavor. Ricotta cheese could be used as an alternative.

NUTRITIONAL INFORMATION

Calories	327	Sugars	25g
Protein	9g	Fat	18g
Carbohydrate	33g	Saturates	11g

15 mins | 50 mins

SERVES 8

INGREDIENTS

- 4 tbsp sweet butter, plus extra for greasing
- 3 cups ginger cookie crumbs
- 1 tablespoon chopped preserved ginger
- 2¼ cups mascarpone cheese
- finely grated zest and juice of 2 lemons
- ½ cup superfine sugar
- 2 large eggs, separated
- fruit coulis (see Cook's Tip), to serve

1 Grease and line the base of a 10-inch/25-cm spring-form cake pan or loose-bottomed pan.

2 Melt the butter in a pan and stir in the crushed cookies and chopped ginger. Use the mixture to line the pan, pressing the mixture about ¼ inch/5 mm up the sides.

1

2

2

3 Beat together the cheese, lemon zest and juice, sugar, and egg yolks until quite smooth.

4 Whisk the egg whites until they are stiff and fold into the cheese and lemon mixture.

5 Pour the mixture into the pan and bake in a preheated oven, 350°F/180°C, for 35–45 minutes until just set. Don't worry if it cracks or sinks—this is quite normal.

6 Leave the cheesecake in the pan to cool. Serve with fruit coulis (see Cook's Tip).

COOK'S TIP

Fruit coulis can be made by cooking 14 oz/400 g fruit, such as blueberries, for 5 minutes with 2 tablespoons of water. Strain the mixture, then stir in 1 tablespoon (or more to taste) of strained confectioners' sugar. Let cool before serving.

Baked Sweet Ravioli

These unusual and scrumptious little parcels are the perfect dessert for anyone with a really sweet tooth.

NUTRITIONAL INFORMATION

Calories	765	Sugars	56g
Protein	16g	Fat	30g
Carbohydrate	114g	Saturates	15g

1½ hrs — 20 mins

SERVES 4

INGREDIENTS

PASTA

- 3¾ cups all-purpose flour
- ⅔ cup butter, plus extra for greasing
- ¾ cup superfine sugar
- 4 eggs
- 1 oz/25 g yeast
- ½ cup lukewarm milk

FILLING

- ⅔ cup chestnut paste
- ½ cup unsweetened cocoa
- generous ¼ cup superfine sugar
- ½ cup chopped almonds
- 1 cup crushed amaretti cookies
- generous ½ cup orange marmalade

1 To make the sweet pasta dough, strain the flour into a mixing bowl, then add the butter, sugar, and 3 of the eggs and mix well to combine.

2 Mix together the yeast and warm milk in a small bowl and when thoroughly combined, mix into the dough.

3 Knead the dough for 20 minutes, cover with a clean cloth, and set aside in a warm place for 1 hour to rise.

4 In a separate bowl, mix together the chestnut paste, unsweetened cocoa, sugar, almonds, crushed amaretti cookies, and orange marmalade.

5 Grease 1 or 2 cookie sheets with a little butter.

6 Lightly flour the counter. Roll out the pasta dough into a thin sheet and cut into 2-inch/5-cm circles with a plain dough cutter.

7 Put a spoonful of filling onto each circle and then fold in half, pressing the edges to seal. Arrange on the prepared cookie sheet, spacing the ravioli out well.

8 Beat the remaining egg and brush all over the ravioli to glaze. Bake in a preheated oven, 350°F/180°C, for 20 minutes. Serve hot.

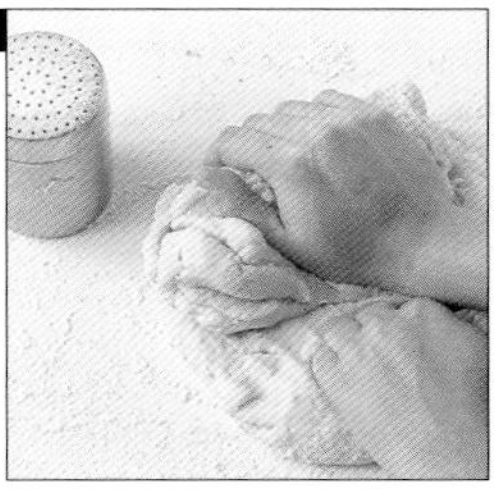
3

4

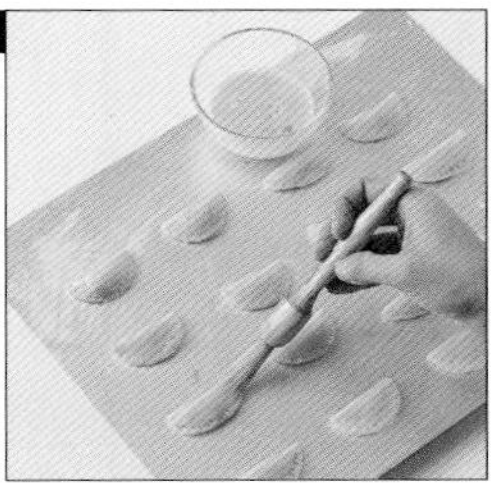
8

German Noodle Pudding

This rich and satisfying pudding is a traditional Jewish recipe that will quickly become popular with all the family.

NUTRITIONAL INFORMATION

Calories	719	Sugars	28g
Protein	20g	Fat	45g
Carbohydrate	62g	Saturates	25g

10 mins 45 mins

SERVES 4

INGREDIENTS

- 5 tbsp butter, plus extra for greasing
- 6 oz/175 g ribbon egg noodles
- ½ cup cream cheese
- 1 cup cottage cheese
- scant ½ cup superfine sugar
- 2 eggs, lightly beaten
- ½ cup sour cream
- 1 tsp vanilla extract
- a pinch of ground cinnamon
- 1 tsp grated lemon zest
- ¼ cup slivered almonds
- generous ¼ cup dry white bread crumbs
- confectioner's sugar, for dusting

1 Grease an ovenproof dish with butter.

2 Bring a large pan of water to a boil. Add the noodles and cook until almost tender. Drain and set aside.

3 Beat together the cream cheese, cottage cheese, and superfine sugar in a mixing bowl. Beat in the eggs, a little at a time. Stir in the sour cream, vanilla extract, cinnamon, and lemon zest, and fold in the noodles. Transfer the mixture to the prepared dish and smooth the surface.

4 Melt the butter in a skillet over low heat. Add the almonds and cook, stirring constantly, for about 1–1½ minutes, until lightly colored. Remove the skillet from the heat and stir the bread crumbs into the almonds.

5 Sprinkle the almond and bread crumb mixture over the pudding and bake in a preheated oven, 350°F/180°C, for 35–40 minutes, until just set.

6 Dust with a little confectioner's sugar and serve the pudding immediately.

3

3

5

VARIATION

Although not authentic, you could add 3 tablespoons of raisins with the lemon zest in step 3, if liked.

Honey & Nut Nests

Pistachio nuts and honey are combined with crisp cooked angel hair pasta in this unusual and charming dessert.

NUTRITIONAL INFORMATION

Calories 802	Sugars 53g
Protein 13g	Fat 48g
Carbohydrate ...85g	Saturates 16g

10 mins 1 hr

SERVES 4

INGREDIENTS

- 8 oz/225 g dried angel hair pasta
- ½ cup butter
- 1½ cups chopped pistachio nuts
- ½ cup sugar
- ⅓ cup clear honey
- ⅔ cup water
- 2 tsp lemon juice
- salt
- Greek-style yogurt, to serve

1 Bring a large pan of lightly salted water to a boil. Add the angel hair pasta, bring back to a boil, and cook for 8–10 minutes or until tender, but still firm to the bite. Drain the pasta and return to the pan. Add the butter and toss to coat the pasta thoroughly. Let cool.

2 Arrange 4 small tart or poaching rings on a cookie sheet. Divide the angel hair pasta into 8 equal quantities and spoon 4 of them into the rings. Press down lightly. Top the pasta with half of the nuts, then add the remaining pasta.

3 Bake in a preheated oven, 350°F/180°C, for 45 minutes, or until golden brown.

4 Meanwhile, put the sugar, honey, and water in a pan and bring to a boil over low heat, stirring constantly until the sugar has dissolved completely. Simmer for 10 minutes, add the lemon juice and simmer for a further 5 minutes.

5 Using a spatula, carefully transfer the angel hair nests to a serving dish. Pour over the honey syrup, sprinkle over the remaining nuts, and set aside to cool completely before serving. Serve at room temperature and hand the Greek-style yogurt separately.

2

2

2

COOK'S TIP

Angel hair pasta is also known as *capelli d'angelo*. Long and very fine, it is usually sold in small bunches that already resemble nests.

Banana Pies

These miniature pies require a little time to prepare, but are well worth the effort. A sweet banana filling is wrapped in dough and baked.

NUTRITIONAL INFORMATION

Calories	745	Sugars	24g
Protein	13g	Fat	30g
Carbohydrate	112g	Saturates	15g

45 mins | 25 mins

SERVES 4

INGREDIENTS

DOUGH

- 3½ cups all-purpose flour
- 5 tbsp shortening
- 5 tbsp sweet butter
- ½ cup water

FILLING

- 2 large bananas
- ⅓ cup finely chopped no-need-to-soak dried apricots
- pinch of nutmeg
- dash of orange juice
- 1 egg yolk, beaten
- confectioners' sugar, for dusting
- cream or ice cream, to serve

1 To make the dough, strain the flour into a large mixing bowl. Add the shortening and butter and rub into the flour with the fingertips until the mixture resembles bread crumbs. Gradually blend in the water to make a soft dough. Wrap in plastic wrap and chill in the refrigerator for 30 minutes.

2

2 Mash the bananas in a bowl with a fork and stir in the apricots, nutmeg, and orange juice, mixing well.

3 Roll the dough out on a lightly floured surface and cut out 16 circles, each 4 inches/10 cm across.

4
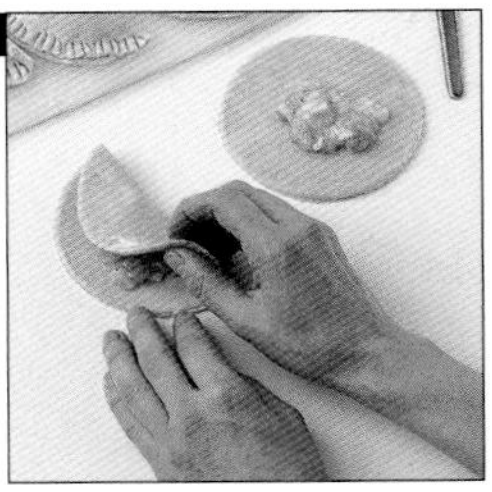

4 Spoon a little of the banana filling onto one half of each circle and fold the dough over the filling to make semicircles. Pinch the edges together and seal by pressing with the prongs of a fork.

5

5 Arrange the pies on a non-stick cookie sheet and brush them with the beaten egg yolk. Cut a small slit in each pie and cook in a preheated oven, 350°F/180°C, for about 25 minutes or until golden brown.

6 Dust the banana pies with confectioners' sugar and serve with cream or ice cream.

VARIATION

Use a fruit filling of your choice, such as apple or plum, as an alternative.

Chinese Custard Tarts

These small tarts are irresistible—custard is baked in a rich, sweet dough. The tarts may be served warm or cold.

NUTRITIONAL INFORMATION

Calories	474	Sugars	30g
Protein	9g	Fat	22g
Carbohydrate	64g	Saturates	12g

20 mins 30 mins

SERVES 4

INGREDIENTS

SWEET PIE DOUGH

1¼ cups all-purpose flour

scant ¼ cup superfine sugar

5 tbsp sweet butter

2 tbsp shortening

2 tbsp water

CUSTARD

2 small eggs

generous ¼ cup superfine sugar

¾ cup milk

½ tsp ground nutmeg, plus extra for sprinkling

cream, to serve

1 To make the dough, strain the flour into a bowl. Add the sugar and rub in the butter and shortening with your fingertips until the mixture resembles bread crumbs. Add the water and mix to form a firm dough.

2 Transfer the dough to a lightly floured counter and knead for 5 minutes until smooth. Cover with plastic wrap and chill in the refrigerator while you are preparing the filling.

3 To make the custard, beat the eggs and sugar together. Gradually add the milk and ground nutmeg and beat until well combined.

4 Separate the dough into 15 even-size pieces. Flatten the dough pieces into circles and press into shallow muffin pans.

5 Spoon the custard into the tart shells and cook in a preheated oven, 300°F/150°C, for 25–30 minutes.

6 Transfer the Chinese custard tarts to a wire rack, leave to cool slightly, then sprinkle with nutmeg. Serve warm or cold with cream.

3

4

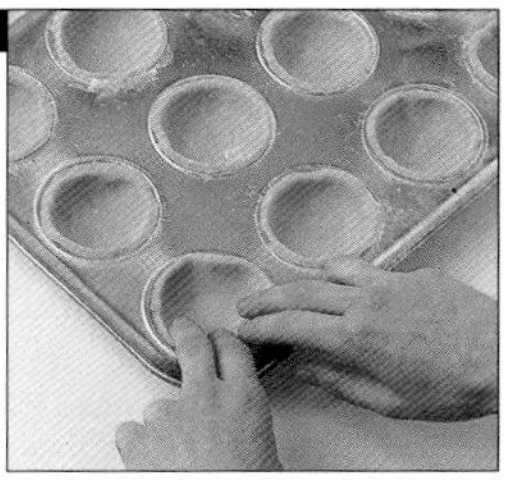

6

COOK'S TIP

For extra convenience, make the dough in advance, cover, and chill in the refrigerator until required.

Cakes & Bread

There is nothing more traditional than afternoon tea and cakes and this chapter gives a wickedly extravagant twist to some of those delicious tea-time classics—full of chocolate, spice, and all things nice, these recipes are a

treat to enjoy. The chapter includes a variety of different cakes depending on the time you have and the effort you want to spend. Small cakes include Fruity Muffins, Almond Slices, and Molasses Biscuits. These cakes are easier to prepare and cook than larger ones and are particular favorites.

Teacakes

These popular snacks are ideal split in half and toasted, then spread with butter. A luxury mix of dried fruit gives them a rich taste.

NUTRITIONAL INFORMATION

Calories	197	Sugars	11g
Protein	6g	Fat	3g
Carbohydrate	39g	Saturates	2g

3¼ hrs — 20 mins

MAKES 12

INGREDIENTS

- 2 tbsp butter, cut into small pieces, plus extra for greasing
- 3½ cups white bread flour
- 1 sachet active dry yeast
- ¼ cup superfine sugar
- 1 tsp salt
- 1¼ cups lukewarm milk
- ½ cup luxury dried fruit mix
- honey, for brushing

1 Grease several cookie sheets with a little butter.

2 Strain the flour into a large bowl. Stir in the dried yeast, sugar, and salt. Rub in the butter with your fingertips until the mixture resembles fine bread crumbs. Add the milk and mix all of the ingredients together to form a soft dough.

3 Place the dough on a lightly floured surface and knead for about 5 minutes. Alternatively, you can knead the dough with an electric mixer with a dough hook.

4 Form the dough into a ball and place in a greased bowl, cover, and let rise in a warm place for about 1–1½ hours until it has doubled in size.

5 Knead the dough again for a few minutes and knead in the fruit. Divide the dough into 12 circles and place on the prepared cookie sheets. Cover and let stand for a further 1 hour or until springy to the touch.

6 Bake in a preheated oven, 400°F/200°C, for 20 minutes.

7 Transfer the teacakes to a wire rack and brush with the honey while they are still warm. Let cool before serving them split in half, toasted if liked, and spread with butter.

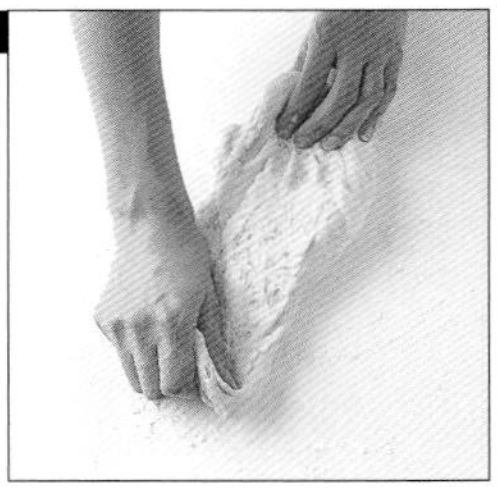
3

5

5

COOK'S TIP

It is important to have the milk at the right temperature: heat it until you can put your little finger into the milk and leave it there for 10 seconds without it feeling too hot.

Cinnamon Swirls

These cinnamon-flavored buns are delicious if they are served warm a few minutes after they come out of the oven.

NUTRITIONAL INFORMATION

Calories	160	Sugars	10g
Protein	4g	Fat	6g
Carbohydrate	24g	Saturates	4g

1 hr 25 mins 30 mins

MAKES 12

INGREDIENTS

- 2 tbsp butter, cut into small pieces, plus extra for greasing
- generous 1½ cups white bread flour
- ½ tsp salt
- 1 sachet active dry yeast
- 1 egg, lightly beaten
- ½ cup lukewarm milk
- 2 tbsp maple syrup

FILLING

- 4 tbsp butter, softened
- 2 tsp ground cinnamon
- ¼ cup brown sugar
- ⅓ cup currants

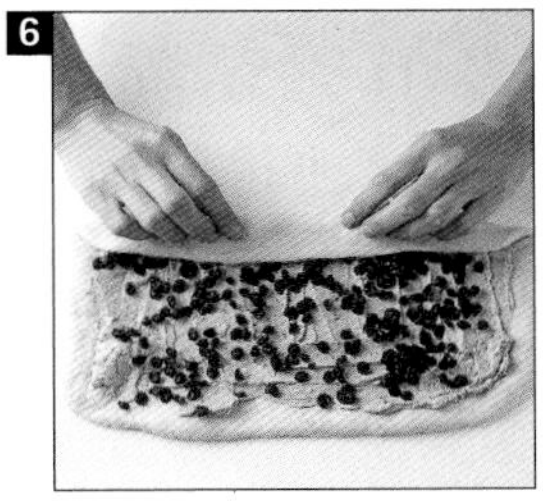

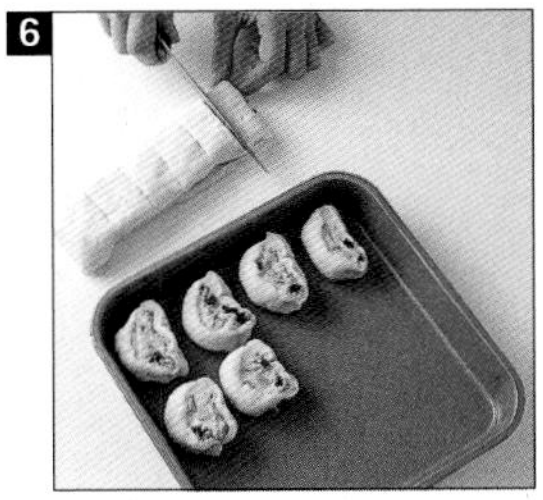

1 Grease a 9-inch/23-cm square baking pan with a little butter.

2 Strain the flour and salt into a mixing bowl. Stir in the dried yeast. Rub in the butter with your fingertips until the mixture resembles bread crumbs. Add the egg and milk and mix to form a dough.

3 Form the dough into a ball, place in a greased bowl, cover, and let stand in a warm place for about 40 minutes or until doubled in size.

4 Punch down the dough lightly for 1 minute, then roll out to a rectangle 12 x 9 inches/30 x 23 cm.

5 To make the filling, cream together the softened butter, cinnamon, and brown sugar until light and fluffy. Spread the filling evenly over the dough rectangle, leaving a 1-inch/2.5-cm border all around. Sprinkle the currants evenly over the top.

6 Roll up the dough from one of the long edges, and press down to seal. Cut the roll into 12 slices. Place them in the pan, cover, and let stand for 30 minutes.

7 Bake in a preheated oven, 375°F/190°C, for 20–30 minutes or until well risen. Brush with the syrup and let cool slightly before serving.

Cinnamon & Currant Loaf

This spicy, fruit tea bread is quick and easy to make. Serve it buttered and with a drizzle of honey for an afternoon snack.

NUTRITIONAL INFORMATION

Calories 439	Sugars 33g
Protein 7g	Fat 18g
Carbohydrate ...67g	Saturates 11g

1 hr 10 mins

1 hr 10 mins

SERVES 8

INGREDIENTS

- ⅔ cup butter, cut into small pieces, plus extra for greasing
- 2¾ cups all-purpose flour
- pinch of salt
- 1 tbsp baking powder
- 1 tbsp ground cinnamon
- ¾ cup brown sugar
- ¾ cup currants
- finely grated zest of 1 orange
- 5–6 tbsp orange juice
- 6 tbsp milk
- 2 eggs, lightly beaten

2

3

4

1 Grease a 2-lb/900-g loaf pan and line the bottom with baking parchment.

2 Strain the flour, salt, baking powder, and ground cinnamon into a bowl. Rub in the butter with your fingertips until the mixture resembles bread crumbs.

3 Stir in the sugar, currants, and orange zest. Beat the orange juice, milk, and eggs together and add to the dry ingredients. Mix well together.

4 Spoon the mixture into the prepared pan. Make a slight dip in the middle of the mixture to help it rise evenly.

5 Bake in a preheated oven, 350°F/180°C, for about 1–1 hour 10 minutes or until a fine metal skewer inserted into the center of the loaf comes out clean.

6 Let the loaf cool before turning it out of the pan. Transfer to a wire rack and let cool completely before slicing.

COOK'S TIP

Once you have added the liquid to the dry ingredients, work as quickly as possible, because the baking powder is activated by the liquid.

Banana & Cranberry Loaf

The addition of chopped nuts, mixed peel, fresh orange juice, and dried cranberries makes this a rich, moist tea bread.

NUTRITIONAL INFORMATION

Calories 388	Sugars 40g
Protein 5g	Fat 17g
Carbohydrate ...57g	Saturates 2g

45 mins   1 hr

SERVES 8

INGREDIENTS

- butter, for greasing
- 1¼ cups self-rising flour
- ½ tsp baking powder
- ¾ cup brown sugar
- 2 bananas, mashed
- ⅓ cup chopped mixed peel
- 2 tbsp chopped mixed nuts
- ¼ cup dried cranberries
- 5–6 tbsp orange juice
- 2 eggs, lightly beaten
- ⅔ cup sunflower oil
- ¾ cup confectioners' sugar, strained
- grated zest of 1 orange

2

3

3

1 Grease a 2-lb/900-g loaf pan with a little butter and line the bottom with baking parchment.

2 Strain the flour and baking powder together into a mixing bowl. Stir in the sugar, bananas, chopped mixed peel, nuts, and cranberries.

3 Stir the orange juice, eggs, and oil together, until thoroughly combined. Add the mixture to the dry ingredients and mix until well blended. Pour the mixture into the prepared pan.

4 Bake in a preheated oven, 350°F/180°C, for about 1 hour until firm to the touch or until a fine skewer inserted into the center of the loaf comes out clean.

5 Turn out the loaf onto a wire rack and let cool completely.

6 Mix the confectioners' sugar with a little water and drizzle the frosting over the loaf. Sprinkle the orange zest over the top. Let the icing set before serving the loaf in slices.

COOK'S TIP

This tea bread will keep for a couple of days. Wrap it carefully and store in a cool, dry place.

Banana & Date Loaf

This fruity bread is excellent for afternoon tea or morning coffee time with its moist texture and more-ish flavour.

NUTRITIONAL INFORMATION

Calories	432	Sugars	41g
Protein	7g	Fat	16g
Carbohydrate	70g	Saturates	10g

15 mins 1 hr

SERVES 6

INGREDIENTS

- ⅓ cup butter, cut into small pieces,plus extra for greasing
- generous 1½ cups self-rising flour
- ⅓ cup superfine sugar
- 2/3 cup chopped pitted dates
- 2 bananas, coarsely mashed
- 2 eggs, lightly beaten
- 2 tbsp clear honey

3

3

4

1 Grease a 2-lb/900-g loaf pan with a little butter and line the bottom with baking parchment.

2 Strain the flour into a mixing bowl. Rub the butter into the flour with your fingertips until the mixture resembles fine bread crumbs.

3 Add the sugar, chopped dates, bananas, beaten eggs, and honey to the dry ingredients. Mix together to form a soft dropping consistency.

4 Spoon the mixture into the prepared loaf pan, spreading it out evenly, and gently smooth the surface with the back of a knife.

5 Bake the loaf in a preheated oven, 325°F/160°C, for about 1 hour or until golden brown on top and a toothpick inserted into the center of the loaf comes out clean.

6 Let the loaf cool in the pan before turning out and transferring to a wire rack to cool completely.

7 Serve the loaf warm or cold, cut into thick slices.

COOK'S TIP

This tea bread will keep for several days if stored in an airtight container and kept in a cool, dry place.

Crown Loaf

This is a rich, sweet bread combining alcohol, nuts, and fruit in a decorative wreath shape. It is ideal for serving at Thanksgiving.

NUTRITIONAL INFORMATION

Calories	164	Sugars	14g
Protein	3g	Fat	6g
Carbohydrate	25g	Saturates	3g

1½ hrs — 30 mins

1 LOAF

INGREDIENTS

- 2 tbsp butter, cut into small pieces, plus extra for greasing
- generous 1½ cups white bread flour
- ½ tsp salt
- 1 sachet active dry yeast
- ½ cup lukewarm milk
- 1 egg, lightly beaten

FILLING

- 4 tbsp butter, softened
- ¼ cup brown sugar
- 2 tbsp chopped hazelnuts
- 1 tbsp chopped preserved ginger
- ⅓ cup mixed candied peel
- 1 tbsp rum or brandy
- 1 cup icing confectioners' sugar
- 2 tbsp lemon juice

2
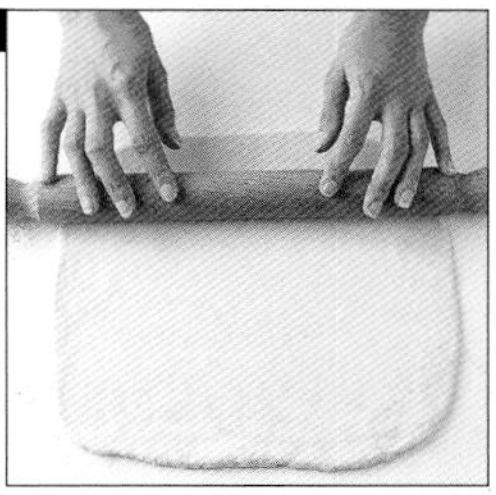

3

4
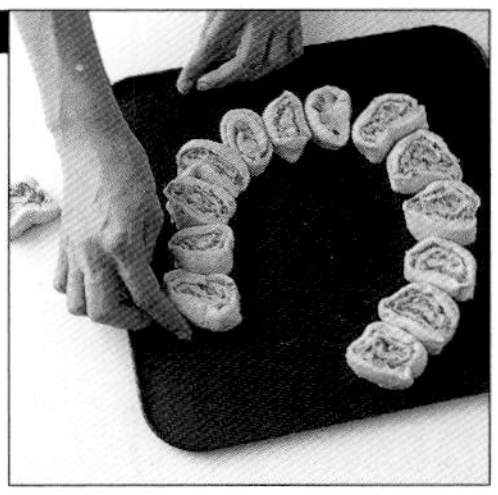

1 Grease a cookie sheet. Strain the flour and salt into a bowl. Stir in the yeast. Rub in the butter with your fingertips. Add the milk and egg and mix to form a dough.

2 Place the dough in a greased bowl, cover, and stand in a warm place for 40 minutes until doubled in size. Punch down the dough lightly for 1 minute. Roll out to a rectangle about 12 x 9 inches/ 30 x 23 cm.

3 To make the filling, cream together the butter and sugar until light and fluffy. Stir in the hazelnuts, ginger, candied peel, and rum or brandy. Spread the filling over the dough, leaving a 1-inch/2.5-cm border.

4 Roll up the dough, starting from one of the long edges, into a sausage shape. Cut into slices at 2-inch/5-cm intervals and place in a circle on the cookie sheet with the slices just touching. Cover and stand in a warm place to rise for 30 minutes.

5 Bake in a preheated oven, 325°F/ 190°C, for 20–30 minutes or until golden. Meanwhile, mix the confectioners' sugar with enough lemon juice to form a thin frosting.

6 Let the loaf cool slightly before drizzling with frosting. Let the frosting set slightly before serving.

Date & Honey Loaf

This bread is full of good things—chopped dates, sesame seeds, and honey. Toast thick slices and spread with soft cheese for a light snack.

NUTRITIONAL INFORMATION

Calories	240	Sugars	14g
Protein	6g	Fat	6g
Carbohydrate	44g	Saturates	1g

2 hrs 40 mins   30 mins

1 LOAF

INGREDIENTS

- butter, for greasing
- 1¾ cups white bread flour
- ½ cup brown bread flour
- ½ tsp salt
- 1 sachet active dry yeast
- generous ¾ cup lukewarm water
- 3 tbsp sunflower oil
- 3 tbsp honey
- ½ cup chopped pitted dates
- 2 tbsp sesame seeds

1 Grease a 2-lb/900-g loaf pan with a little butter.

2 Strain both types of flour into a large mixing bowl, and stir in the salt and dried yeast. Pour in the lukewarm water, sunflower oil, and honey. Mix together to form a dough.

3 Place the dough on a lightly floured counter and knead for about 5 minutes until smooth.

4 Place the dough in a greased bowl, cover, and let rise in a warm place for about 1 hour or until doubled in size.

5 Knead in the dates and sesame seeds. Shape the dough and place in the pan.

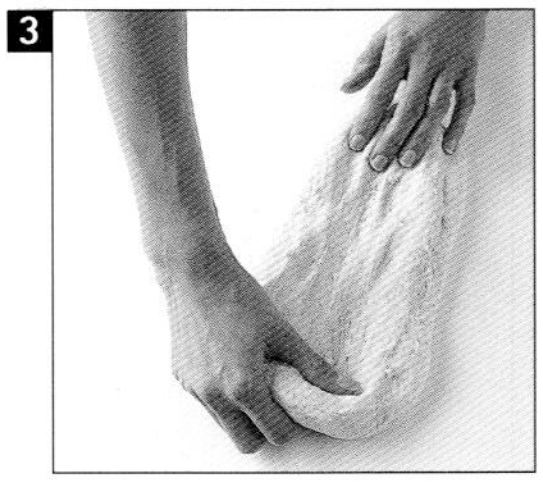

6 Cover and stand the loaf in a warm place for a further 30 minutes or until springy to the touch.

7 Bake in a preheated oven, 425°F/220°C, for 30 minutes or until a hollow sound is heard when the bottom of the loaf is tapped.

8 Transfer the loaf to a wire rack and let cool completely. Serve cut into thick slices with butter or soft cheese.

COOK'S TIP

If you cannot find a warm place, sit a bowl with the dough in it over a pan of warm water and cover.

Pumpkin Loaf

The pumpkin paste in this loaf makes it beautifully moist. It is delicious eaten at any time of the day.

NUTRITIONAL INFORMATION

Calories	456	Sugars	33g
Protein	7g	Fat	21g
Carbohydrate	62g	Saturates	12g

1½ hrs — 2 hrs 10 mins

SERVES 6

INGREDIENTS

- vegetable oil, for greasing
- 1 lb/450 g pumpkin flesh
- ½ cup butter, softened
- ¾ cup superfine sugar
- 2 eggs, lightly beaten
- generous 1½ cups all-purpose flour, strained
- 1½ tsp baking powder
- ½ tsp salt
- 1 tsp ground allspice
- 2 tbsp pumpkin seeds

1 Grease a 2-lb/900-g loaf pan with oil.

2 Chop the pumpkin into large pieces and wrap in buttered foil. Cook in a preheated oven, 400°F/200°C, for 30–40 minutes until they are tender.

3 Let the pumpkin cool completely before mashing well to make a thick paste.

4 In a bowl, cream the butter and sugar together until light and fluffy. Add the beaten eggs, a little at a time.

5 Stir in the pumpkin paste. Fold in the flour, baking powder, salt, and allspice.

6 Fold the pumpkin seeds gently through the mixture in a figure-eight movement. Spoon the mixture into the prepared loaf pan.

7 Bake in a preheated oven, 325°F/160°C, for about 1¼–1½ hours or until a skewer inserted into the center of the loaf comes out clean.

8 Transfer the loaf to a wire rack to cool and serve sliced and buttered, if wished.

2

4

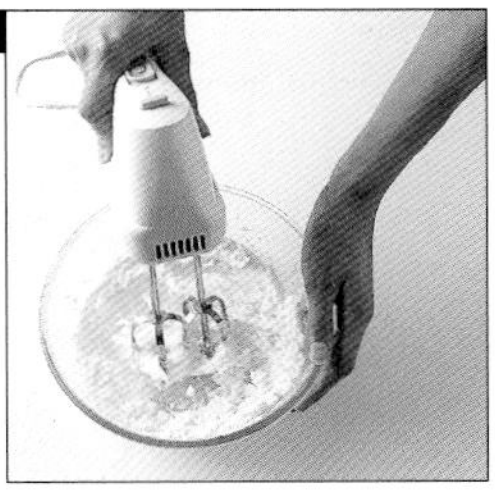

5

COOK'S TIP

To ensure that the pumpkin paste is dry, place it in a pan over medium heat for a few minutes, stirring frequently, until it is thick.

Tropical Fruit Bread

The flavors in this bread will bring a touch of sunshine to your breakfast table. The mango can be replaced with other dried fruits.

NUTRITIONAL INFORMATION

Calories	228	Sugars	10g
Protein	6g	Fat	7g
Carbohydrate	37g	Saturates	5g

1¼ hrs — 30 mins

1 LOAF

INGREDIENTS

- 2 tbsp butter, cut into small pieces, plus extra for greasing
- 2½ cups white bread flour
- 5 tbsp bran
- ½ tsp salt
- ½ tsp ground ginger
- 1 sachet active dry yeast
- 2 tbsp brown sugar
- 1 cup lukewarm water
- ½ cup candied pineapple, finely chopped
- 2 tbsp finely chopped dried mango
- ½ cup shredded coconut, toasted
- 1 egg, lightly beaten
- 2 tbsp shredded coconut

1

1

1

1 Grease a cookie sheet. Strain the flour into a large bowl. Stir in the bran, salt, ginger, dried yeast, and sugar. Rub in the butter with your fingertips, then add the water, and mix to form a dough.

2 On a lightly floured counter, knead the dough for 5–8 minutes or until smooth. Alternatively, use an electric mixer with a dough hook. Place the dough in a greased bowl, cover, and let rise in a warm place for 30 mins or until doubled in size.

3 Knead the pineapple, mango, and toasted coconut into the dough. Shape into a circle and place on the cookie sheet. Score the top with the back of a knife. Cover and let stand for a further 30 minutes in a warm place.

4 Brush the loaf with the beaten egg and sprinkle with the 2 tablespoons of shredded coconut. Bake in a preheated oven, 425°F/220°C, for 30 minutes or until golden brown on top.

5 Let the bread cool on a wire rack before serving.

COOK'S TIP

To test the bread after the second rising, gently poke the dough with your finger—it should spring back if it has risen enough.

Citrus Bread

This sweet loaf is flavored with citrus fruits. As with Tropical Fruit Bread (see opposite page), it is excellent served at breakfast.

NUTRITIONAL INFORMATION

Calories	195	Sugars	10g
Protein	5g	Fat	4g
Carbohydrate	37g	Saturates	2g

1¼ hrs — 30 mins

1 LOAF

INGREDIENTS

- 4 tbsp butter, cut into small pieces, plus extra for greasing
- 3½ cups white bread flour
- ½ tsp salt
- ¼ cup superfine sugar
- 1 sachet active dry yeast
- 5–6 tbsp orange juice
- 4 tbsp lemon juice
- 3–4 tbsp lime juice
- ⅔ cup lukewarm water
- 1 orange
- 1 lemon
- 1 lime
- 2 tbsp clear honey

1 Lightly grease a cookie sheet with a little butter.

2 Strain the flour and salt into a mixing bowl. Stir in the sugar and dried yeast.

3 Rub in the butter with your fingertips until the mixture resembles bread crumbs. Add all of the fruit juices and the water and mix to form a dough.

4 Place the dough on a lightly floured counter and knead for 5 minutes. Alternatively, use an electric mixer with a dough hook. Place the dough in a greased bowl, cover, and let rise in a warm place for 1 hour.

5 Meanwhile, grate the zest of the orange, lemon, and lime. Knead the fruit zests into the dough.

6 Divide the dough into 2 balls, making one slightly bigger than the other.

7 Place the larger ball on the cookie sheet and set the smaller one on top.

8 Push a floured finger through the center of the dough. Cover and let rise for about 40 minutes or until springy to the touch.

9 Bake in a preheated oven, 425°F/220°C, for 35 minutes. Remove from the oven and transfer to a wire rack. Glaze with the honey and let cool completely.

5

5

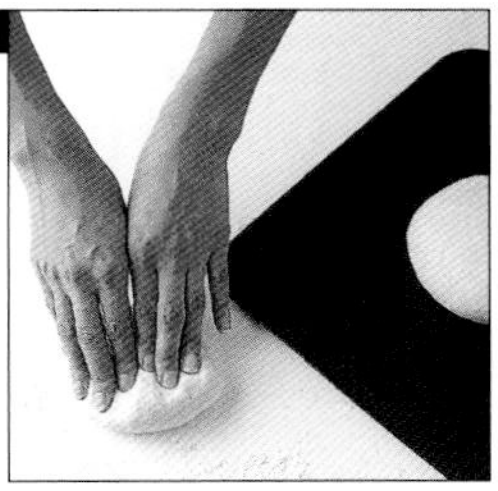

8

Chocolate Bread

For the chocoholics among us, this bread is not only great fun to make, it is also even better to eat.

NUTRITIONAL INFORMATION

Calories	228	Sugars	4g
Protein	8g	Fat	3g
Carbohydrate	46g	Saturates	1g

2 hrs 40 mins | 30 mins

1 LOAF

INGREDIENTS

- butter, for greasing
- 3½ cups white bread flour
- ¼ cup unsweetened cocoa
- 1 tsp salt
- 1 sachet active dry yeast
- 2 tbsp brown sugar
- 1 tbsp oil
- 1¼ cups lukewarm water

1 Lightly grease a 2-lb/900-g loaf pan with a little butter.

2 Strain the flour and unsweetened cocoa into a large mixing bowl.

3 Stir in the salt, dried yeast, and brown sugar, mixing well.

4 Pour in the oil along with the lukewarm water and mix the ingredients together to make a dough.

5 Place the dough on a lightly floured counter and knead for 5 minutes.

6 Place the dough in a greased bowl, cover, and let rise in a warm place for about 1 hour or until the dough has doubled in size.

7 Punch down the dough and shape it into a loaf. Place the dough in the prepared pan, cover, and let rise in a warm place for a further 30 minutes.

8 Bake in a preheated oven, 400°F/200°C, for 25–30 minutes or until a hollow sound is heard when the bottom of the bread is tapped. Transfer the bread to a wire rack and to cool completely. Cut into slices to serve.

2

4

7
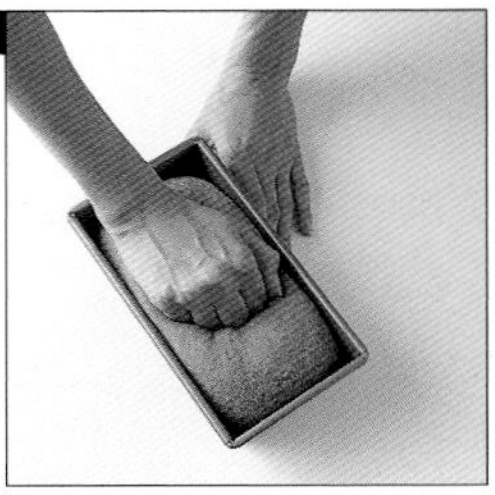

COOK'S TIP

This bread can be sliced and spread with butter or it can be lightly toasted.

Mango Twist Bread

This is a sweet bread which has mango paste mixed into the dough, resulting in a moist loaf with an exotic flavor.

NUTRITIONAL INFORMATION

Calories	228	Sugars	18g
Protein	6g	Fat	4g
Carbohydrate	46g	Saturates	2g

2 hrs 50 mins | 30 mins

1 LOAF

INGREDIENTS

- 3 tbsp butter, cut into small pieces, plus extra for greasing
- 3½ cups white bread flour
- 1 tsp salt
- 1 sachet active dry yeast
- 1 tsp ground ginger
- ¼ cup brown sugar
- 1 small mango, peeled, pitted, and blended to a paste
- 1 cup lukewarm water
- 2 tbsp clear honey
- ⅔ cup golden raisins
- 1 egg, lightly beaten
- confectioners' sugar, for dusting

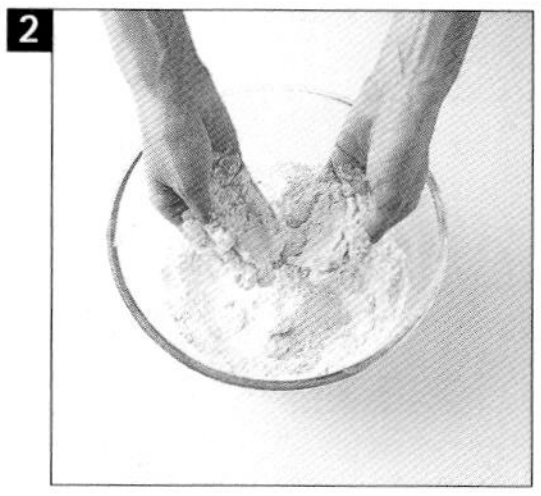

1 Grease a cookie sheet with a little butter and set aside.

2 Strain the flour and salt into a large mixing bowl. Stir in the dried yeast, ground ginger, and brown sugar. Rub in the butter with your fingertips until the mixture resembles bread crumbs.

3 Stir in the mango paste, lukewarm water, and honey and mix together to form a dough.

4 Place the dough on a lightly floured counter and knead for about 5 minutes until smooth. Alternatively, use an electric mixer with a dough hook. Place the dough in a greased bowl, cover, and let rise in a warm place for about 1 hour until it has doubled in size.

5 Knead in the golden raisins and shape the dough into 2 sausage shapes, each 10 inches/25 cm long. Carefully twist the 2 pieces together and pinch the ends to seal. Place the dough on the cookie sheet, cover, and leave in a warm place for a further 40 minutes.

6 Brush the loaf with the egg and bake in a preheated oven, 425°F/220°C, for 30 minutes or until golden brown. Let cool on a wire rack. Dust with confectioners' sugar before serving.

COOK'S TIP

You can tell when the bread is cooked as it will sound hollow when tapped on the bottom.

Olive Oil, Fruit, & Nut Cake

It is worth using a good quality olive oil for this cake as this will determine its flavor. The cake will keep well in an airtight tin.

NUTRITIONAL INFORMATION

Calories	309	Sugars	17g
Protein	4g	Fat	17g
Carbohydrate	38g	Saturates	3g

10 mins   45 mins

SERVES 8

INGREDIENTS

- butter, for greasing
- generous 1½ cups self-rising flour
- ¼ cup superfine sugar
- ½ cup milk
- 4 tbsp orange juice
- ⅔ cup olive oil
- ½ cup mixed dried fruit
- ¼ cup pine nuts

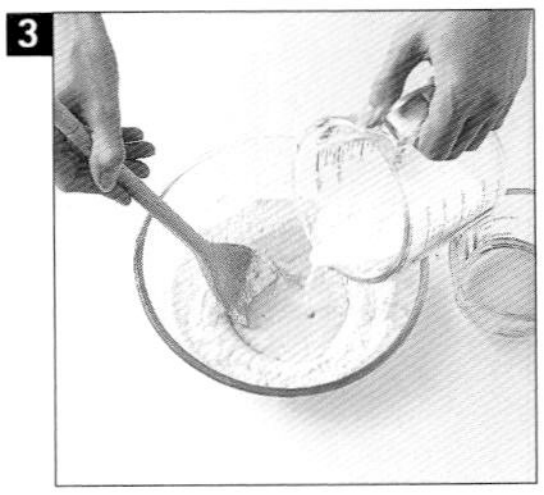

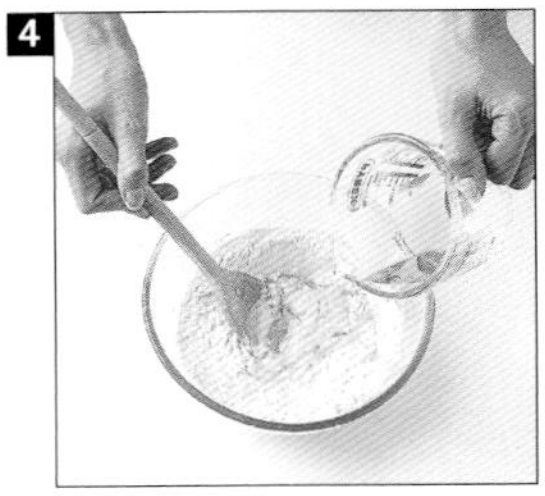

1 Grease a 7-inch/18-cm cake pan with a little butter and then line with baking parchment.

2 Strain the flour into a mixing bowl and stir in the superfine sugar.

3 Make a well in the center of the dry ingredients and pour in the milk and orange juice. Stir the mixture with a wooden spoon, gradually beating in the flour and sugar.

4 Pour in the olive oil, stirring well so that all of the ingredients are evenly and thoroughly mixed.

5 Stir the mixed dried fruit and pine nuts into the mixture and spoon it into the prepared pan, spreading it out evenly and smoothing the surface.

6 Bake in a preheated oven, 350°F/180°C, for about 45 minutes until the cake is golden and firm to the touch.

7 Let the cake cool in the pan for a few minutes before transferring to a wire rack to cool. Serve the cake warm or cold and cut into slices.

COOK'S TIP

Pine nuts are best known as the flavoring ingredient in the classic Italian pesto, but here they give a delicate, slightly resinous flavor to this cake.

Caraway Madeira

This is a classic Madeira cake made in the traditional way with caraway seeds. If you do not like their flavor, they can be omitted.

NUTRITIONAL INFORMATION

Calories	479	Sugars	24g
Protein	7g	Fat	26g
Carbohydrate	57g	Saturates	16g

1¼ hrs

1 hr

SERVES 8

INGREDIENTS

- 1 cup butter, softened, plus extra for greasing
- scant 1 cup brown sugar
- 3 eggs, lightly beaten
- 2½ cups self-rising flour
- 1 tbsp caraway seeds
- grated zest of 1 lemon
- 6 tbsp milk
- 1 or 2 strips of citron peel

1 Grease and line a 2-lb/900-g loaf pan with a little butter.

2 In a bowl, cream together the butter and brown sugar until pale and fluffy.

3 Gradually add the beaten eggs to the creamed mixture, beating well after each addition.

4 Strain the flour into the bowl and gently fold into the creamed mixture with a figure-eight movement.

5 Add the caraway seeds, lemon zest, and milk, and gently fold in until thoroughly blended.

6 Spoon the mixture into the prepared pan and level the surface.

7 Bake in a preheated oven, 325°F/160°C, for 20 minutes.

8 Remove the cake from the oven and gently place the pieces of citron peel on top of the cake. Return it to the oven and bake for a further 40 minutes or until the cake is well risen, golden brown and a fine skewer inserted into the center comes out clean.

9 Let the cake cool in the pan before turning out and transferring to a wire rack to cool completely.

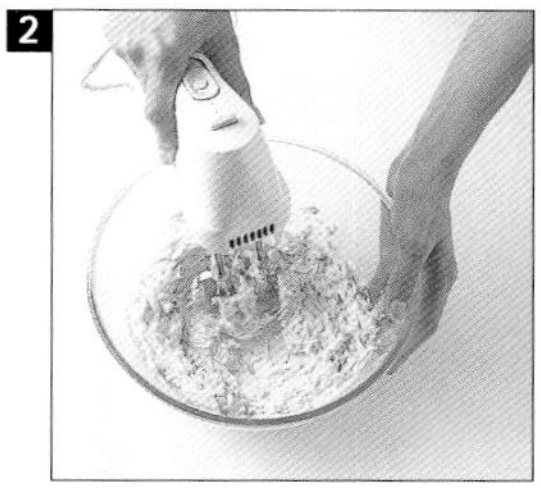

COOK'S TIP

Citron peel is available in the baking section of large stores. If it is unavailable, you can substitute chopped mixed peel.

Clementine Cake

This cake is flavored with clementine rind and juice, creating a rich buttery cake but one full of fresh fruit flavor.

NUTRITIONAL INFORMATION

Calories	427	Sugars	32g
Protein	6g	Fat	25g
Carbohydrate	48g	Saturates	13g

5 mins — 1 hr

SERVES 8

INGREDIENTS

- ¾ cup butter, softened, plus extra for greasing
- 2 clementines
- ¾ cup superfine sugar
- 3 eggs, lightly beaten
- 1¼ cups self-rising flour
- 3 tbsp ground almonds
- 3 tbsp light cream

GLAZE AND TOPPING

- 6 tbsp clementine juice
- 2 tbsp superfine sugar
- 3 white sugar lumps, crushed

2

4

7

1 Grease a 7-inch/18-cm round pan with butter and line the bottom with baking parchment.

2 Pare the zest from the clementines and chop it finely. In a bowl, cream together the butter, sugar, and clementine zest until pale and fluffy.

3 Gradually add the beaten eggs to the mixture, beating thoroughly after each addition.

4 Gently fold in the flour, ground almonds, and light cream. Spoon the mixture into the prepared pan.

5 Bake in a preheated oven, 350°F/ 180°C, for about 55–60 minutes or until a fine skewer inserted into the center comes out clean. Let cool slightly.

6 Meanwhile, make the glaze. Put the clementine juice into a small pan with the superfine sugar. Bring to a boil over a low heat and simmer for 5 minutes.

7 Turn out the cake onto a wire rack. Drizzle the glaze over the cake until it has been absorbed and sprinkle with the crushed sugar lumps. Let cool completely before serving.

COOK'S TIP

If you prefer, chop the zest from the clementines in a food processor or blender along with the sugar in step 2. Tip the mixture into a bowl with the butter and begin to cream the mixture.

Candied Fruit Cake

This cake is extremely colorful; you can choose any mixture of candied fruits, or stick to just one type if you prefer.

NUTRITIONAL INFORMATION

Calories	398	Sugars	34g
Protein	5g	Fat	20g
Carbohydrate	53g	Saturates	12g

1 hr — 1 hr 10 mins

SERVES 8

INGREDIENTS

- ¾ cup butter, softened, plus extra for greasing
- ¾ cup superfine sugar
- 3 eggs, lightly beaten
- 1¼ cups self-rising flour, strained
- 2½ tbsp ground rice
- finely grated zest of 1 lemon
- 4 tbsp lemon juice
- ⅔ cup candied fruits, chopped
- confectioners' sugar, for dusting (optional)

COOK'S TIP

Wash and dry the candied fruits before chopping them. This will prevent them from sinking to the bottom of the cake during cooking.

1 Lightly grease a 7-inch/18-cm cake pan with a little butter and line with baking parchment.

2 In a bowl, whisk together the butter and superfine sugar until the mixture is light and fluffy.

3 Add the beaten eggs, a little at a time. Using a metal spoon, gently fold in the flour and ground rice.

4 Add the grated lemon zest and lemon juice, followed by the chopped candied fruits. Lightly mix all the ingredients together.

5 Spoon the mixture into the prepared pan and level the surface with the back of a spoon or a knife.

6 Bake in a preheated oven, 350°F/180°C, for 1–1 hour 10 minutes until well risen or until a fine skewer inserted into the center of the cake comes out clean.

7 Let the cake cool in the pan for 5 minutes, then turn out onto a wire rack to cool completely.

8 Dust well with confectioners' sugar, if using, before serving.

2
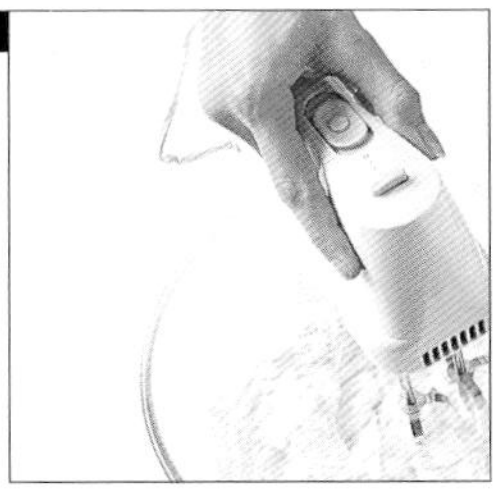

3
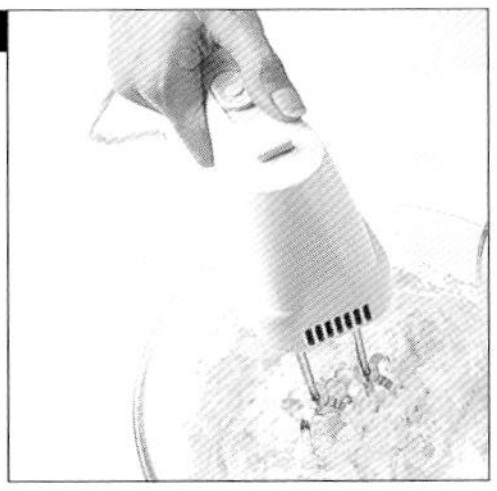

4

Crunchy Fruit Cake

Cornmeal adds texture to this fruit cake, as well a golden yellow color. It also acts as a flour, binding the ingredients together.

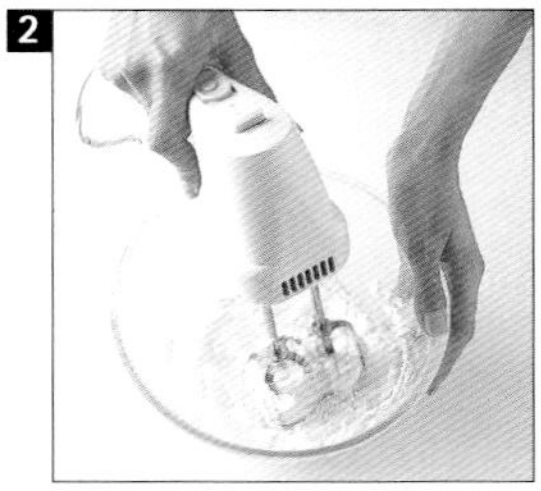

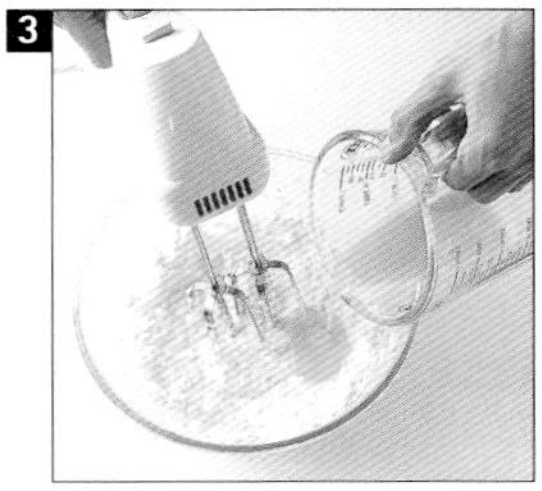

NUTRITIONAL INFORMATION

Calories	328	Sugars	33g
Protein	59g	Fat	15g
Carbohydrate	47g	Saturates	7g

5–10 mins

1 hr

SERVES 8

INGREDIENTS

⅓ cup butter, softened, plus extra for greasing
½ cup superfine sugar
2 eggs, lightly beaten
generous ⅓ cup self-rising flour, strained
1 tsp baking powder
⅔ cup cornmeal
1⅓ cups mixed dried fruit
¼ cup pine nuts
grated zest of 1 lemon
4 tbsp lemon juice
2 tbsp milk

1 Grease a 7-inch/18-cm cake pan with a little butter and line the bottom with baking parchment.

2 In a bowl, whisk together the butter and sugar until light and fluffy.

3 Whisk in the beaten eggs, a little at a time, whisking thoroughly after each addition.

4 Gently fold the flour, baking powder, and cornmeal into the mixture until well blended.

5 Stir in the mixed dried fruit, pine nuts, grated lemon zest, lemon juice, and milk.

6 Spoon the mixture into the prepared pan and level the surface.

7 Bake in a preheated oven, 350°F/180°C, for about 1 hour or until a fine skewer inserted into the center of the cake comes out clean.

8 Let the cake cool in the pan before turning out.

VARIATION

To give a crumblier and lighter fruit cake, omit the cornmeal and use generous 1 cup self-rising flour instead.

Carrot Cake

This classic favorite is always popular with children and adults alike when it is served for afternoon tea.

NUTRITIONAL INFORMATION

Calories	294	Sugars	32g
Protein	3g	Fat	15g
Carbohydrate	409g	Saturates	5g

5–10 mins 25 mins

12 BARS

INGREDIENTS

- butter, for greasing
- scant 1 cup self-rising flour
- pinch of salt
- 1 tsp ground cinnamon
- ⅔ cup brown sugar
- 2 eggs
- scant ½ cup sunflower oil
- scant 1 cup finely grated carrots
- scant ⅓ cup shredded coconut
- 2 tbsp chopped walnuts
- walnut pieces, to decorate

FROSTING

- 4 tbsp butter, softened
- ¼ cup full-fat soft cheese
- 2¼ cups confectioners' sugar, strained
- 1 tsp lemon juice

1 Lightly grease an 8-inch/20-cm square cake pan with a little butter and line with baking parchment.

2 Strain the flour, salt, and ground cinnamon into a large bowl and stir in the brown sugar. Add the eggs and oil to the dry ingredients and mix well.

3 Stir in the grated carrot, shredded coconut, and chopped walnuts.

4 Pour the mixture into the prepared pan and bake in a preheated oven, 350°F/180°C, for 20–25 minutes or until just firm to the touch. Let cool in the pan.

5 Meanwhile, make the cheese frosting. In a bowl, beat together the butter, full-fat soft cheese, confectioners' sugar, and lemon juice until the mixture is light, fluffy, and creamy.

6 Turn the cake out of the pan and cut into 12 bars or slices. Spread with the frosting and then decorate with walnut pieces.

2

3

5

VARIATION

For a moister cake, replace the coconut with 1 coarsely mashed banana.

Lemon Syrup Cake

The lovely light and tangy flavor of the sponge cake is balanced by the lemony syrup poured over the top.

NUTRITIONAL INFORMATION

Calories	424	Sugars	38g
Protein	6g	Fat	21g
Carbohydrate	58g	Saturates	5g

1 hr 5 mins

1 hr

SERVES 8

INGREDIENTS

- butter, for greasing
- scant 1½ cups all-purpose flour
- 2 tsp baking powder
- 1 cup superfine sugar
- 4 eggs
- ⅔ cup sour cream
- grated zest of 1 large lemon
- 4 tbsp lemon juice
- ⅔ cup sunflower oil

SYRUP

- 4 tbsp confectioners' sugar
- 3 tbsp lemon juice

3

3

6

1 Lightly grease an 8-inch/20-cm loose-bottomed round cake pan and line the bottom with baking parchment.

2 Strain the flour and baking powder together into a mixing bowl and stir in the sugar.

3 In a separate bowl, whisk the eggs, sour cream, lemon zest, lemon juice, and oil together. Pour the egg mixture into the dry ingredients and mix well until evenly combined.

4 Pour the mixture into the prepared pan and bake in a preheated oven, 350°F/180°C, for 45–60 minutes until risen and golden brown.

5 Meanwhile, to make the syrup, combine the confectioners' sugar and lemon juice in a small pan. Stir over low heat until just beginning to bubble and turn syrupy.

6 As soon as the cake comes out of the oven prick the surface with a fine skewer, then brush the syrup over the top. Let the cake cool completely in the pan before turning out and serving.

COOK'S TIP

Pricking the surface of the hot cake with a skewer ensures that the syrup seeps right into the cake and the full flavor is absorbed.

Orange Kugelhopf Cake

Baking in a deep, fluted kugelhopf pan ensures that you create a cake with a stunning shape. The moist cake is full of fresh orange flavor.

NUTRITIONAL INFORMATION

Calories	877	Sugars	82g
Protein	12g	Fat	35g
Carbohydrate	137g	Saturates	21g

25 mins | 55 mins

SERVES 4

INGREDIENTS

- 1 cup butter, softened, plus extra for greasing
- generous 1 cup superfine sugar
- 4 eggs, separated
- scant 3½ cups all-purpose flour
- 3 tsp baking powder
- 1¼ cups fresh orange juice
- 1 tbsp orange flower water
- 1 tsp grated orange zest
- salt

SYRUP

- ¾ cup orange juice
- 1 cup granulated sugar

1 Grease and flour a 10-inch/25-cm kugelhopf pan or deep ring mold.

2 In a bowl, cream together the butter and superfine sugar until light and fluffy. Add the egg yolks, 1 at a time, whisking well after each addition.

3 Strain together the flour, a pinch of salt, and the baking powder into a separate bowl. Fold the dry ingredients and the orange juice alternately into the creamed mixture with a metal spoon, working as lightly as possible. Stir in the orange flower water and orange zest.

4 Whisk the egg whites until they form soft peaks and gently fold them into the mixture.

5 Pour into the prepared pan or mold and bake in a preheated oven, 350°F/180°C, for 50–55 minutes or until a metal skewer inserted into the center of the cake comes out clean.

6 Bring the orange juice and sugar to a boil in a small pan over low heat, then simmer gently for 5 minutes until the sugar has dissolved.

7 Remove the cake from the oven and let cool in the pan for 10 minutes.

8 Prick the top of the cake with a fine skewer and brush over half of the syrup. Let the cake cool, still in the pan, for another 10 minutes.

9 Invert the cake onto a wire rack placed over a deep plate and brush the syrup over the cake until it is entirely covered. Serve warm or cold.

3

4
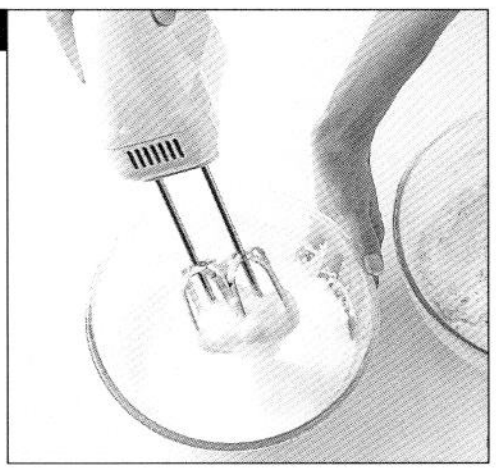

9

Apple Cake with Cider

This can be eaten as a cake at tea time or with a cup of coffee, or it can be warmed through and served with cream for a dessert.

NUTRITIONAL INFORMATION

Calories 263	Sugars 22g
Protein 4g	Fat 9g
Carbohydrate ...43g	Saturates 5g

1 hr 5 mins 40 mins

SERVES 8

INGREDIENTS

- 6 tbsp butter, cut into small pieces, plus extra for greasing
- generous 1½ cups self-rising flour
- 1 tsp baking powder
- ⅓ cup superfine sugar
- 3½ cups chopped dried apple
- generous ½ cup raisins
- ⅔ cup sweet cider
- 1 egg, lightly beaten
- 1 cup raspberries

1 Grease an 8-inch/20-cm cake pan and line with baking parchment.

2 Strain the flour and baking powder into a mixing bowl and rub in the butter with your fingertips until the mixture resembles fine bread crumbs.

3

4

4

3 Stir in the superfine sugar, chopped dried apple, and raisins.

4 Pour in the sweet cider and egg and mix together until thoroughly blended. Stir in the raspberries very gently so they do not break up.

5 Pour the mixture into the prepared cake pan.

6 Bake in a preheated oven, 375°F/190°C, for about 40 minutes until risen and lightly golden.

7 Let the cake cool in the pan, then turn out onto a wire rack. Leave until completely cold before serving.

VARIATION

If you don't want to use cider, replace it with clear apple juice, if you prefer.

Spiced Apple Ring

The addition of pieces of fresh apple and crunchy almonds to the cake mixture makes this beautifully moist yet with a crunch to it.

NUTRITIONAL INFORMATION

Calories	379	Sugars	27g
Protein	5g	Fat	22g
Carbohydrate	43g	Saturates	13g

1 hr 5 mins 30 mins

SERVES 8

INGREDIENTS

- ¾ cup butter, softened, plus extra for greasing
- ¾ cup superfine sugar
- 3 eggs, lightly beaten
- 1¼ cups self-rising flour
- 1 tsp ground cinnamon
- 1 tsp ground allspice
- 2 eating apples, cored and grated
- 2 tbsp apple juice or milk
- ¼ cup slivered almonds

1 Lightly grease a 10-inch/25-cm ovenproof ring mold.

2 In a mixing bowl, cream together the butter and sugar until light and fluffy. Gradually add the beaten eggs, beating well after each addition.

3 Strain the flour and spices, then carefully fold them into the creamed mixture with a figure-eight movement.

4 Stir in the grated apples and the apple juice or milk and mix to a soft dropping consistency.

5 Sprinkle the slivered almonds around the base of the mold and spoon the cake mixture on top. Level the surface with the back of the spoon.

6 Bake in a preheated oven, 350°F/180°C, for about 30 minutes until well risen and a fine skewer inserted into the center comes out clean.

7 Let the cake cool in the pan before turning out and transferring to a wire rack to cool completely. Serve the apple ring cut into slices.

COOK'S TIP

This cake can also be made in a 7-inch/18-cm round cake pan if you do not have an ovenproof ring mold.

Coffee Streusel Cake

This cake has a moist coffee sponge cake on the bottom, covered with a crisp crunchy, spicy topping.

NUTRITIONAL INFORMATION

Calories	409	Sugars	21g
Protein	8g	Fat	19g
Carbohydrate	55g	Saturates	10g

10 mins   1 hr

SERVES 8

INGREDIENTS

butter, for greasing
2 cups all-purpose flour
1 tbsp baking powder
⅓ cup superfine sugar
⅔ cup milk
2 eggs
½ cup butter, melted and cooled
2 tbsp instant coffee mixed with 1 tbsp boiling water
⅓ cup chopped almonds
confectioners' sugar, for dusting

TOPPING

½ cup self-rising flour
⅓ cup raw brown sugar
2 tbsp butter, cut into small pieces
1 tsp ground allspice
1 tbsp water

1 Grease a 9-inch/23-cm loose-bottomed round cake pan with butter and line with baking parchment.

2 Strain together the flour and baking powder into a mixing bowl, then stir in the superfine sugar.

3 Whisk the milk, eggs, melted butter, and coffee mixture together and pour onto the dry ingredients. Add the chopped almonds and mix lightly together. Spoon the mixture into the prepared pan.

4 To make the topping, mix the flour and raw brown sugar together in a separate bowl.

5 Rub in the butter with your fingertips until the mixture is crumbly. Sprinkle in the ground allspice and water and bring the mixture together in loose crumbs. Sprinkle the topping evenly over the cake.

6 Bake in a preheated oven, 375°F/190°C, for 50 minutes–1 hour. Cover loosely with foil if the topping starts to brown too quickly.

7 Let cool in the pan, then turn out. Dust with confectioners' sugar just before serving.

Sugar-free Fruit Cake

This cake is full of flavor from the mixed fruits. The fruit gives the cake its sweetness so there is no need for extra sugar.

NUTRITIONAL INFORMATION

Calories	423	Sugars	34g
Protein	8g	Fat	16g
Carbohydrate	68g	Saturates	9g

1 hr 5 mins

1 hr

SERVES 8

INGREDIENTS

- ½ cup butter, cut into small pieces, plus extra for greasing
- 2½ cups all-purpose flour
- 2 tsp baking powder
- 1 tsp ground allspice
- ⅓ cup no-soak dried apricots, chopped
- ½ cup chopped pitted dates
- ⅓ cup candied cherries, chopped
- ⅔ cup raisins
- ½ cup milk
- 2 eggs, lightly beaten
- grated zest of 1 orange
- 5–6 tbsp orange juice
- 3 tbsp clear honey

3

4

5

1 Grease an 8-inch/20-cm round cake pan with a little butter and line the bottom with baking parchment.

2 Strain the flour, baking powder, and ground allspice together into a large mixing bowl.

3 Add the butter and rub it in with your fingertips until the mixture resembles fine bread crumbs.

4 Carefully stir in the apricots, dates, candied cherries, and raisins, with the milk, beaten eggs, grated orange zest, and orange juice.

5 Stir in the honey and mix everything together to form a soft dropping consistency. Spoon into the prepared cake pan and level the surface.

6 Bake in a preheated oven, 350°F/180°C, for 1 hour until a fine skewer inserted into the center of the cake comes out clean.

7 Leave the cake to cool in the pan before turning out.

VARIATION

For a fruity alternative, replace the honey with 1 mashed ripe banana, if you prefer.

Almond Cake

Being glazed with a honey syrup after baking gives this cake a lovely moist texture, but it can be eaten without the glaze, if preferred.

NUTRITIONAL INFORMATION

Calories	324	Sugars	27g
Protein	5g	Fat	16g
Carbohydrate	43g	Saturates	4g

2 hrs 5 mins — 50 mins

SERVES 8

INGREDIENTS

- ⅓ cup soft margarine, plus extra for greasing
- ¼ cup brown sugar
- 2 eggs
- 1¼ cups self-rising flour
- 1 tsp baking powder
- 4 tbsp milk
- 2 tbsp clear honey
- ½ cup slivered almonds

SYRUP

- ⅔ cup clear honey
- 2 tbsp lemon juice

1 Grease a 7-inch/18-cm round cake pan and line with baking parchment.

2 Place the margarine, brown sugar, eggs, flour, baking powder, milk, and honey in a large mixing bowl and beat well with a wooden spoon for about 1 minute until all of the ingredients are thoroughly mixed together.

3 Spoon into the prepared pan, level the surface with the back of a spoon or a knife and sprinkle with the almonds.

4 Bake in a preheated oven, 350°F/180°C, for about 50 minutes or until the cake is well risen and a fine skewer inserted into the center of the cake comes out clean.

5 Meanwhile, make the syrup. Combine the honey and lemon juice in a small pan and simmer over low heat for about 5 minutes or until the syrup starts to coat the back of a spoon.

6 As soon as the cake comes out of the oven, pour the syrup over it, allowing it to seep into the middle of the cake.

7 Let the cake cool for at least 2 hours before slicing.

2

3

6

COOK'S TIP

Experiment with different flavored honeys for the syrup glaze until you find one that you think tastes best.

Gingerbread

This spicy gingerbread is made even moister and more delicious by the addition of chopped fresh apples.

NUTRITIONAL INFORMATION

Calories	248	Sugars	21g
Protein	3g	Fat	11g
Carbohydrate	36g	Saturates	7g

1¼ hrs

35 mins

12 BARS

INGREDIENTS

- ⅔ cup butter, plus extra for greasing
- scant 1 cup brown sugar
- 2 tbsp molasses
- generous 1½ cups all-purpose flour
- 1 tsp baking powder
- 2 tsp baking soda
- 2 tsp ground ginger
- ⅔ cup milk
- 1 egg, lightly beaten
- 2 eating apples, peeled, chopped, and coated with 1 tbsp lemon juice

2

4

5

1 Grease a 9-inch/23-cm square cake pan and line with baking parchment.

2 Melt the butter, sugar, and molasses in a pan over low heat. Remove the pan from the heat and let cool.

3 Strain the flour, baking powder, baking soda, and ginger together into a mixing bowl.

4 Stir in the milk, beaten egg, and cooled buttery liquid, followed by the chopped apples coated with the lemon juice.

5 Mix together gently, then pour the mixture into the prepared pan.

6 Bake in a preheated oven, 325°F/170°C, for 30–35 minutes until the cake has risen and a fine skewer inserted into the center comes out clean.

7 Let the cake cool in the pan before turning out and cutting into 12 bars.

VARIATION

If you enjoy the flavor of ginger, try adding 1 tablespoon finely chopped preserved ginger to the mixture in step 3.

Apple Shortcakes

This dessert is a freshly baked sweet biscuit, split and filled with sliced apples and whipped cream. The shortcakes can be eaten warm or cold.

NUTRITIONAL INFORMATION

Calories	511	Sugars	44g
Protein	5g	Fat	24g
Carbohydrate	73g	Saturates	15g

25 mins | 15 mins

MAKES 4

INGREDIENTS

- 2 tbsp butter, cut into small pieces, plus extra for greasing
- 1¼ cups all-purpose flour
- ½ tsp salt
- 1 tsp baking powder
- 1 tbsp superfine sugar
- ¼ cup milk
- confectioners' sugar, for dusting

FILLING

- 3 dessert apples, peeled, cored, and sliced
- ½ cup superfine sugar
- 1 tbsp lemon juice
- 1 tsp ground cinnamon
- 1¼ cups water
- ⅔ cup heavy cream, lightly whipped

3

3

5

1 Lightly grease a cookie sheet with a little butter.

2 Strain the flour, salt and baking powder into a mixing bowl. Stir in the sugar, then rub in the butter with your fingertips until the mixture resembles fine bread crumbs.

3 Pour in the milk and mix to a soft dough. On a lightly floured counter, knead the dough lightly, then roll out to ½ inch/1 cm thick. Stamp out 4 rounds, using a 5 cm/2 inch cutter. Transfer the rounds to the prepared cookie sheet.

4 Bake in a preheated oven, 425°F/220°C, for about 15 minutes until risen and lightly browned. Let cool.

5 To make the filling, place the apple slices, sugar, lemon juice, and cinnamon in a saucepan. Add the water, bring to a boil, and simmer, uncovered, for 5-10 minutes until the apples are tender. Let cool a little, then remove the apples.

6 Split the shortcakes in half. Place each bottom half on an individual serving plate and spoon on a quarter of the apple slices, then the cream. Place the other half of the shortcake on top. Serve dusted with confectioners' sugar.

Molasses Biscuits

These biscuits are light and buttery like traditional biscuits, but they have a deliciously rich flavor which comes from the molasses.

NUTRITIONAL INFORMATION

Calories	208	Sugars	9g
Protein	4g	Fat	9g
Carbohydrate	30g	Saturates	6g

15 mins

10 mins

SERVES 8

INGREDIENTS

- 6 tbsp butter, cut into small pieces, plus extra for greasing
- generous 1½ cups self-rising flour
- 1 tbsp superfine sugar
- 1 dessert apple, peeled, cored, and chopped
- 1 egg, lightly beaten
- 2 tbsp molasses
- 5 tbsp milk
- salt

1 Lightly grease a cookie sheet with a little butter.

2 Strain the flour, sugar, and a pinch of salt into a mixing bowl.

3 Add the butter and rub it in with your fingertips until the mixture resembles fine bread crumbs.

4 Add the chopped apple to the mixture and stir until thoroughly combined.

5 Mix the beaten egg, molasses, and milk together in a pitcher. Add to the dry ingredients and mix to form a soft dough.

6 On a lightly floured counter, roll out the dough to a thickness of ¾ inch/2 cm and cut out 8 circles, using a 2-inch/5-cm cutter.

7 Arrange the biscuits on the prepared cookie sheet and bake in a preheated oven, 425°F/220°C, for about 8–10 minutes.

8 Transfer the biscuits to a wire rack and let cool slightly. Serve split in half and spread with butter.

4

5

6

COOK'S TIP

These biscuits can be frozen, but are best thawed and eaten within 1 month.

Cherry Biscuits

These are an alternative to traditional biscuits, using sweet candied cherries which not only create color but add a distinct flavor.

NUTRITIONAL INFORMATION

Calories	211	Sugars	10g
Protein	4g	Fat	9g
Carbohydrate	31g	Saturates	6g

10 mins | 30 mins

MAKES 8

INGREDIENTS

- 6 tbsp butter, cut into small pieces, plus extra for greasing
- generous 1½ cups self-rising flour
- 1 tbsp superfine sugar
- 3 tbsp candied cherries, chopped
- 3 tbsp golden raisins
- 1 egg, lightly beaten
- scant ¼ cup milk
- salt

1 Lightly grease a cookie sheet with a little butter.

2 Strain the flour, sugar, and salt into a mixing bowl and rub in the butter with your fingertips until the mixture resembles bread crumbs.

3 Stir in the candied cherries and golden raisins. Add the beaten egg.

4 Reserve 1 tablespoon of the milk for glazing, then add the remainder to the mixture. Mix well together to form a soft dough.

5 On a lightly floured counter, roll out the dough to a thickness of ¾ inch/2 cm and cut out 8 circles, using a 2-inch/5-cm cutter.

6 Place the biscuits on the prepared cookie sheet and brush the tops with the reserved milk.

7 Bake in a preheated oven, 425°F/220°C, for 8–10 minutes or until the biscuits are golden brown.

8 Transfer the biscuits to a wire rack to cool completely, then serve them split and buttered.

3

4

5

COOK'S TIP

These biscuits will freeze very successfully, but they are best thawed and eaten within 1 month.

Cranberry Muffins

These savory muffins are an ideal accompaniment to soup, or they make a nice change from sweet cakes for serving with coffee.

NUTRITIONAL INFORMATION

Calories	96	Sugars	4g
Protein	3g	Fat	4g
Carbohydrate	14g	Saturates	2g

1 hr 5 mins

30 mins

MAKES 18

INGREDIENTS

- butter, for greasing
- generous 1½ cups all-purpose flour
- 2 tsp baking powder
- ½ tsp salt
- ¼ cup superfine sugar
- 4 tbsp butter, melted
- 2 eggs, lightly beaten
- generous ¾ cup milk
- 1 cup fresh cranberries
- scant ½ cup freshly grated Parmesan cheese

2

3

4

1 Lightly grease 2 muffin pans with a little butter.

2 Strain the flour, baking powder, and salt into a mixing bowl. Stir in the superfine sugar.

3 In a separate bowl, combine the butter, beaten eggs, and milk, then pour into the bowl of dry ingredients. Mix lightly together until all of the ingredients are evenly combined, then stir in the fresh cranberries.

4 Divide the mixture among the prepared pans. Sprinkle the grated Parmesan cheese over the top.

5 Bake in a preheated oven, 400°F/200°C, for about 20 minutes or until the muffins are well risen and a golden brown color.

6 Let the muffins cool slightly in the pans. Transfer the muffins to a wire rack and to cool completely.

VARIATION

For a sweet alternative to this recipe, replace the Parmesan cheese with raw brown sugar in step 6, if you prefer.

Fruit Loaf with Apple Spread

This sweet, fruity loaf is ideal served for tea or as a healthy snack. The fruit spread can be made quickly while the cake is in the oven.

NUTRITIONAL INFORMATION

Calories	733	Sugars	110g
Protein	12g	Fat	5g
Carbohydrate	171g	Saturates	1g

1¼ hrs   2 hrs

SERVES 4

INGREDIENTS

- butter, for greasing
- 2 cups rolled oats
- ½ cup light brown sugar
- 1 tsp ground cinnamon
- ⅔ cup golden raisins
- 1 cup seedless raisins
- 2 tbsp malt extract
- 1¼ cups unsweetened apple juice
- 1¼ cups whole-wheat self-rising flour
- 1½ tsp baking powder
- strawberries and apple wedges, to serve

FRUIT SPREAD

- 1½ cups strawberries, washed and hulled
- 2 eating apples, cored, chopped, and mixed with 1 tbsp lemon juice to prevent browning
- 1¼ cups unsweetened apple juice

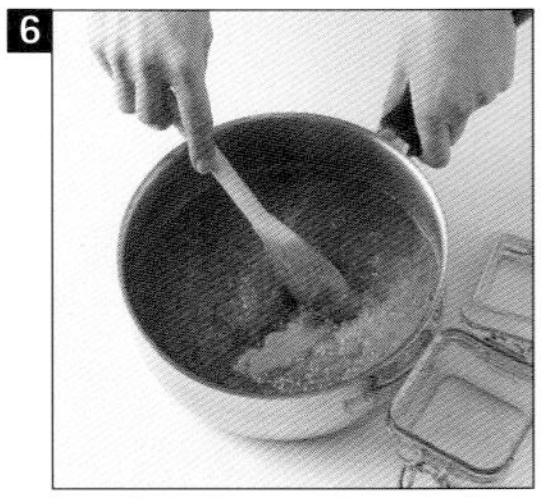

1 Grease a 2-lb/900-g loaf pan with butter and line with baking parchment. Set aside

2 Place the oats, sugar, cinnamon, golden raisins, seedless raisins, and malt extract in a mixing bowl. Pour in the apple juice, stir well and set aside to soak for 30 minutes.

3 Strain in the flour and baking powder, adding any brain that remains in the strainer, and fold in using a metal spoon.

4 Spoon the mixture into the pan and bake in a preheated oven, 350°F/180°C, for 1½ hours until until a skewer inserted into the center comes out clean.

5 Let stand for 10 minutes, then turn onto a rack and to cool.

6 Meanwhile, make the fruit spread. Place the strawberries and apples in a pan and pour in the apple juice. Bring to a boil, cover, and simmer gently for 30 minutes. Beat the sauce well and spoon into a sterilized, warm jar. Let cool, then seal, and label.

7 Serve the loaf with 1–2 tablespoons of the fruit spread and an assortment of strawberries and apple wedges.

Banana & Lime Cake

A substantial cake that is ideal served for tea. The mashed bananas help to keep the cake moist, and the lime frosting gives it extra zing and zest.

NUTRITIONAL INFORMATION

Calories	235	Sugars	31g
Protein	5g	Fat	1g
Carbohydrate	55g	Saturates	0.3g

35 mins

45 mins

SERVES 10

INGREDIENTS

- butter, for greasing
- generous 2 cups all-purpose flour
- 1 tsp salt
- 1½ tsp baking powder
- scant 1 cup light brown sugar
- 1 tsp lime zest, grated
- 1 egg, lightly beaten
- 1 banana, mashed with 1 tbsp lime juice
- ⅔ cup low-fat plain yogurt
- ⅔ cup golden raisins

TOPPING

- generous 1 cup confectioners' sugar
- 1–2 tsp lime juice
- ½ tsp finely grated lime zest

TO DECORATE

- banana chips
- finely grated lime zest

1 Grease a deep round 7-inch/18-cm cake pan with butter and line with baking parchment.

2 Sift the flour, salt, and baking powder into a mixing bowl and stir in the sugar and lime zest.

3 Make a well in the center of the dry ingredients and add the egg, banana, yogurt, and golden raisins. Mix well until thoroughly incorporated.

4 Spoon the mixture into the pan and smooth the surface. Bake in a preheated oven, 350°F/180°C, for 40–45 minutes until firm to the touch or until a skewer inserted in the center comes out clean. Let cool in the pan for 10 minutes, then turn out onto a wire rack.

5 To make the topping, sift the confectioners' sugar into a small bowl and mix with the lime juice to form a soft, but not too runny frosting. Stir in the grated lime zest. Drizzle the lime frosting over the cake, letting it run down the sides.

6 Decorate the cake with banana chips and lime zest. Before serving, let the cake stand for 15 minutes so that the frosting sets.

1

3

4

VARIATION

For a delicious alternative, replace the lime zest and juice with orange, and the golden raisins with chopped apricots.

Crispy-Topped Fruit Bake

The sugar lumps give a lovely crunchy tasted to this easy-to-make, light cake, which is ideal to serve with cream for a dessert.

NUTRITIONAL INFORMATION

Calories	227	Sugars	30g
Protein	5g	Fat	1g
Carbohydrate	53g	Saturates	0.2g

15 mins 1 hr

SERVES 10

INGREDIENTS

- butter, for greasing
- 12 oz/350 g cooking apples
- 3 tbsp lemon juice
- generous 2 cups whole-wheat self-rising flour
- ½ tsp baking powder
- 1 tsp ground cinnamon, plus extra for dusting
- 1 cup prepared blackberries, thawed if frozen, plus extra to decorate
- scant 1 cup light brown sugar
- 1 egg, lightly beaten
- ¾ cup low-fat plain yogurt
- 2 oz/60 g white or brown sugar lumps, lightly crushed
- sliced eating apple, to decorate

1 Grease a 2-lb/900-g loaf pan with a little butter and line with baking parchment.

2 Core, peel, and finely dice the cooking apples. Place them in a pan with the lemon juice, bring to a boil, cover, and simmer for 10 minutes until soft and pulpy. Beat well and set aside to cool.

2

3 Strain the flour, baking powder, and 1 teaspoon of cinnamon into a bowl, adding any bran that remains in the strainer. Stir in ⅔ cup of the blackberries and the sugar.

3

4 Make a well in the center of the ingredients and add the egg, yogurt, and cooled apple paste. Mix well to incorporate thoroughly. Spoon the mixture into the prepared loaf pan and smooth over the top.

5 Sprinkle with the remaining blackberries, pressing them down into the cake mixture, and top with the crushed sugar lumps. Bake in a preheated oven, 375°F/190°C, for 40–45 minutes. Let cool in the pan.

5

6 Remove the cake from the pan and peel away the baking parchment. Serve dusted with cinnamon and decorated with extra blackberries and apple slices.

VARIATION

Try replacing the blackberries with blueberries. Use the canned or frozen variety if fresh blueberries are unavailable.

Rich Fruit Cake

Serve this moist, fruit-laden cake for a special occasion. It would also make an excellent Thanksgiving cake.

NUTRITIONAL INFORMATION

Calories	772	Sugars	137g
Protein	14g	Fat	5g
Carbohydrate	179g	Saturates	1g

35 mins

1¾ hrs

SERVES 4

INGREDIENTS

- butter, for greasing
- generous ½ cup no-soak dried prunes
- 1 cup chopped pitted dates
- generous ¾ cup unsweetened orange juice
- 2 tbsp molasses
- 1 tsp finely grated lemon zest
- 1 tsp finely grated orange zest
- generous 1½ cups whole-wheat self-rising flour
- 1 tsp mixed spice
- ⅔ cup seedless raisins
- ⅔ cup golden raisins
- ⅔ cup currants
- ⅔ cup dried cranberries
- 3 large eggs, separated

TO DECORATE

- 1 tbsp apricot jelly, warmed
- confectioners' sugar, for dusting
- generous 1 cup sugarpaste
- strips of orange zest
- strips of lemon zest

1

2

3

1 Grease and line a deep round 8-inch/20-cm cake pan. Chop the prunes, place in a pan with the dates, pour over the orange juice and simmer over low heat for 10 minutes. Remove the pan from the heat and beat the fruit mixture to a paste. Add the molasses and lemon and orange zest. Let cool.

2 Strain the flour and spice into a bowl, adding any bran that remains in the strainer. Add the dried fruits. When the prune mixture is cool, whisk in the egg yolks. In a clean bowl, whisk the egg whites until stiff. Spoon the fruit mixture into the dry ingredients and mix together.

3 Gently fold in the egg whites using a metal spoon. Transfer to the prepared cake pan and bake in a preheated oven, 325°F/170°C, for 1½ hours. Let cool.

4 Remove the cake from the pan and brush the top with jelly. Dust the counter with confectioners' sugar and roll out the sugarpaste thinly. Lay the sugarpaste over the top of the cake and trim the edges. Decorate with citrus zest.

Carrot & Ginger Cake

This melt-in-the-mouth version of a favorite cake has a fraction of the fat of the traditional cake, making it a wonderfully healthy treat.

NUTRITIONAL INFORMATION

Calories	249	Sugars	28g
Protein	7g	Fat	6g
Carbohydrate	46g	Saturates	1g

15 mins · 1¼ hrs

SERVES 10

INGREDIENTS

- butter or low-fat spread, for greasing
- generous 1½ cups all-purpose flour
- 1 tsp baking powder
- 1 tsp baking soda
- 2 tsp ground ginger
- ½ tsp salt
- scant 1 cup light brown sugar
- generous 1 cup grated carrots
- 2 pieces preserved ginger, chopped
- 1 tablespoon grated fresh ginger root
- ⅓ cup seedless raisins
- 2 eggs, lightly beaten
- 3 tbsp corn oil
- juice of 1 orange

FROSTING

- 1 cup low-fat soft cheese
- 4 tbsp confectioners' sugar
- 1 tsp vanilla extract

TO DECORATE

- grated carrot
- finely chopped preserved ginger
- ground ginger

1 Grease an 8-inch/20-cm round cake tin with butter or low-fat spread and line with baking parchment.

2

2

4

2 Strain the flour, baking powder, baking soda, ground ginger, and salt into a bowl. Stir in the sugar, carrots, preserved ginger, fresh ginger, and raisins. Beat together the eggs, oil, and orange juice, then pour into the bowl. Mix the ingredients together well.

3 Spoon the mixture into the tin and bake in a preheated oven, 350°F/180°C, for 1–1¼ hours until firm to the touch, or until a skewer inserted into the center of the cake comes out clean.

4 To make the frosting, place the soft cheese in a bowl and beat to soften. Sift in the confectioners' sugar and add the vanilla extract. Mix well.

5 Remove the cooled cake from the pan and smooth the frosting over the top. Decorate the cake and serve.

Strawberry Roulade

Serve this moist, light sponge cake rolled up with a creamy almond and strawberry filling for a delicious tea-time treat.

NUTRITIONAL INFORMATION

Calories	166	Sugars	19g
Protein	6g	Fat	3g
Carbohydrate	30g	Saturates	1g

30 mins

10 mins

SERVES 8

INGREDIENTS

3 large eggs

⅔ cup superfine sugar

scant 1 cup all-purpose flour

1 tbsp hot water

FILLING

¾ cup low-fat mascarpone

1 tsp almond extract

1½ cups small strawberries

TO DECORATE

1 tbsp slivered almonds, toasted

1 tsp confectioners' sugar

a few strawberries

1 Line a 14 x 10 inch/35 x 25 cm jelly roll pan with baking parchment.

2 Place the eggs in a heatproof bowl with the superfine sugar. Place the bowl over a pan of hot water and whisk until pale and thick.

3 Remove the bowl from the pan. Strain in the flour and fold into the eggs along with the hot water. Pour the mixture into the pan and bake in a preheated oven, 425°F/220°C, for 8–10 minutes until golden and set.

3 Turn out the cake onto a sheet of baking parchment. Peel off the lining paper and roll up the sponge cake tightly along with the baking parchment. Wrap in a dish cloth and let cool.

4 Mix together the mascarpone and the almond extract. Reserving a few strawberries for decoration, wash, hull, and slice the rest. Chill mascarpone mixture and the strawberries in the refrigerator until required.

5 Unroll the cake, spread the mascarpone mixture over the surface, and sprinkle with sliced strawberries. Roll the cake up again and transfer to a serving plate. Sprinkle with almonds and lightly dust with confectioners' sugar. Decorate with the reserved strawberries.

1

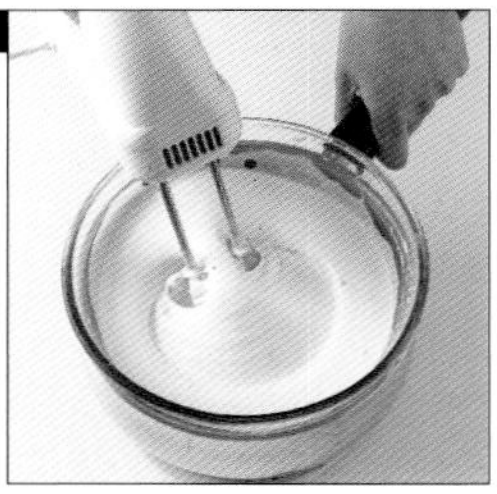

3

5

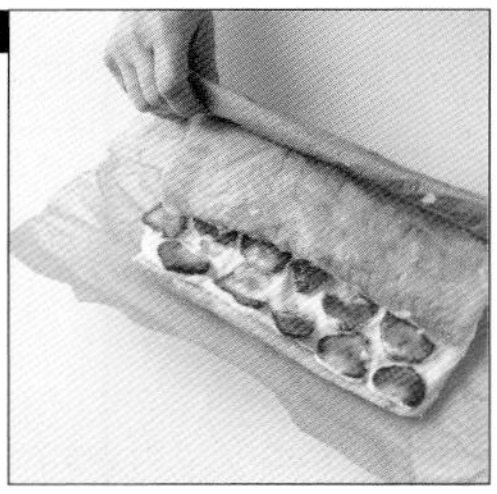

Fruity Muffins

Perfect for those on a low-fat diet or watching their weight, these little cakes contain no butter, just a little corn oil.

NUTRITIONAL INFORMATION

Calories	162	Sugars	11g
Protein	4g	Fat	4g
Carbohydrate	28g	Saturates	1g

10 mins | 30 mins

MAKES 10

INGREDIENTS

- generous 1½ cups whole-wheat self-rising flour
- 2 tsp baking powder
- 2 tbsp light brown sugar
- ¾ cup no-soak dried apricots, finely chopped
- 1 medium banana, mashed with 1 tbsp orange juice
- 1 tsp orange zest, finely grated
- 1¼ cups skim milk
- 1 egg, lightly beaten
- 3 tbsp corn oil
- 2 tbsp rolled oats
- fruit spread, honey, or maple syrup, to serve

1 Place 10 paper muffin cases in a deep muffin pan. Strain the flour and baking powder into a mixing bowl, adding any bran that remains in the strainer. Stir in the sugar and chopped apricots.

2 Make a well in the center of the dry ingredients and add the banana, orange zest, milk, beaten egg, and oil. Mix well to form a thick batter. Divide the batter evenly among the 10 paper cases.

3 Sprinkle with a few oats and bake in a preheated oven, 400°F/200°C, for 25–30 minutes until well risen and firm to the touch, or until a skewer inserted into the center comes out clean.

4 Transfer the muffins to a wire rack to cool slightly. Serve the muffins warm, in their paper cases, with a little fruit spread, honey, or maple syrup.

VARIATION

If you like dried figs, they make a deliciously crunchy alternative to the apricots; they also go very well with the orange flavor. Other no-soak dried fruits, chopped up finely, can be used as well.

2

2

3

Orange & Almond Cake

This light and tangy citrus cake from Sicily is better eaten as a dessert than as a cake. It is especially good served after a large meal.

NUTRITIONAL INFORMATION

Calories	399	Sugars	20g
Protein	8g	Fat	31g
Carbohydrate	23g	Saturates	13g

30 mins | 40 mins

SERVES 8

INGREDIENTS

- butter, for greasing
- 4 eggs, separated
- scant ¾ cup superfine sugar, plus 2 tsp for the cream
- finely grated zest and juice of 2 oranges
- finely grated zest and juice of 1 lemon
- generous 1 cup ground almonds
- 3 tbsp self-rising flour
- generous ¾ cup light whipping cream
- 1 tsp cinnamon
- 1 tbsp slivered almonds, toasted, to decorate
- confectioners' sugar, for dusting

1 Grease a deep 7-inch/18-cm round cake pan with butter and line the base with baking parchment.

1

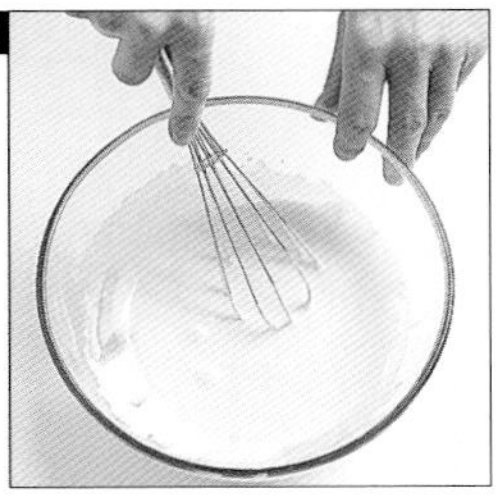
2

3

2 Blend the egg yolks with the sugar until thick and creamy. Whisk half of the orange zest and all of the lemon zest into the egg yolks.

3 Mix the juice from the oranges and lemon with the ground almonds and stir into the egg yolk mixture. Gently fold in the flour.

4 Whisk the egg whites until stiff and gently fold into the egg yolk mixture.

5 Pour the mixture into the pan and bake in a preheated oven, 350°F/180°C, for 35–40 minutes, or until golden and springy to the touch. Let cool in the pan for 10 minutes and then turn out.

6 Whip the cream to form soft peaks. Stir in the remaining orange zest, cinnamon and sugar. Cover the cooled cake with the slivered almonds, dust with confectioners' sugar, and serve with the orange and cinnamon cream.

VARIATION

You could serve this cake with a syrup. Boil the juice and finely grated zest of 2 oranges, scant ⅓ cup superfine sugar, and 2 tablespoons of water for 5–6 minutes until slightly thickened. Stir in 1 tablespoon of orange liqueur just before serving.

Coconut Cake

This is a great family favorite. I was always delighted to find it included in my lunch box and considered it a real treat!

NUTRITIONAL INFORMATION

Calories	464	Sugars	20g
Protein	8g	Fat	26g
Carbohydrate	54g	Saturates	18g

10 mins | 30 mins

SERVES 6-8

INGREDIENTS

- ½ cup butter, cut into small pieces, plus extra for greasing
- generous 1½ cups self-rising flour
- ½ cup raw brown sugar
- 1 cup shredded coconut, plus extra for sprinkling
- 2 eggs, lightly beaten
- 4 tbsp milk
- salt

1. Grease a 2-lb/900-g loaf pan and line the bottom with baking parchment.

2. Strain the flour and a pinch of salt into a mixing bowl and rub in the butter with your fingertips until the mixture resembles fine bread crumbs.

3. Stir in the sugar, shredded coconut, eggs, and milk and mix to a soft dropping consistency.

4. Spoon the mixture into the prepared pan and level the surface with a spatula. Bake in a preheated oven, 325°F/160°C, for 30 minutes.

5. Remove the cake from the oven and sprinkle with the extra coconut. Return the cake to the oven and bake for a further 30 minutes until well risen and golden and a fine skewer inserted into the center comes out clean.

6. Let the cake cool slightly in the pan before turning out and transferring to a wire rack to cool completely. Serve cut into slices.

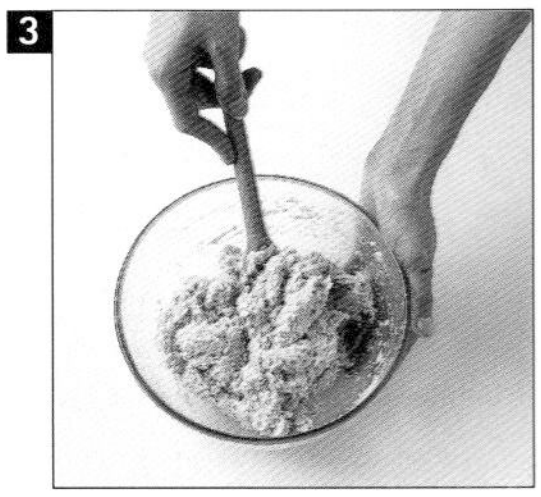

COOK'S TIP

The flavor of this cake is enhanced by storing it in a cool dry place for a few days before eating.

Pear & Ginger Cake

This deliciously buttery pear and ginger cake is ideal with a cup of coffee, or you can serve it with cream for a delicious dessert.

NUTRITIONAL INFORMATION

Calories 531	Sugars 41g
Protein 6g	Fat 30g
Carbohydrate . . .62g	Saturates 19g

15 mins — 40 mins

SERVES 6

INGREDIENTS

- scant 1 cup sweet butter, softened, plus extra for greasing
- generous ¾ cup superfine sugar
- 1¼ cups self-rising flour, strained
- 1 tbsp ground ginger
- 3 eggs, lightly beaten
- 1 lb/450 g dessert pears, peeled, cored, and thinly sliced
- 1 tbsp brown sugar
- ice cream or cream, to serve

2 

3 

4 

1 Lightly grease a deep 8-inch/20.5-cm cake pan with butter and line the base with baking parchment.

2 Using a whisk, combine all but 2 tablespoons of the butter with the sugar, flour, ginger, and eggs, and mix to form a smooth consistency.

3 Spoon the cake mixture into the prepared pan, leveling out the surface.

4 Arrange the pear slices over the cake mixture. Sprinkle with the brown sugar and dot with the remaining butter.

5 Bake in a preheated oven, 350°F/ 180°C, for 35–40 minutes or until the cake is golden on top and feels springy to the touch.

6 Serve the pear and ginger cake warm, with ice cream or cream, if you wish.

COOK'S TIP

Store ground ginger in an airtight jar, preferably made of colored glass, or store in a clear glass jar in a cool, dark place.

Almond Slices

A mouthwatering dessert that is sure to impress your guests, especially if it is served with whipped cream.

NUTRITIONAL INFORMATION

Calories	416	Sugars	37g
Protein	11g	Fat	26g
Carbohydrate	38g	Saturates	12g

5 mins — 45 mins

SERVES 8

INGREDIENTS

- 3 eggs
- ⅔ cup ground almonds
- 1½ cups milk powder
- 1 cup granulated sugar
- ½ tsp saffron strands
- scant ½ cup sweet butter
- 1 tbsp slivered almonds, to decorate

1 Beat the eggs together in a bowl and set aside.

2 Place the ground almonds, milk powder, sugar, and saffron in a large mixing bowl and stir to mix well.

3 Melt the butter in a small pan over low heat. Pour the melted butter over the dry ingredients and mix well until thoroughly combined.

4 Add the reserved beaten eggs to the mixture and stir to blend well.

5 Spread the cake mixture evenly in a shallow 7–9-inch/15–20-cm ovenproof dish and bake in a preheated oven, 325°F/160°C, for 45 minutes. Test whether the cake is cooked through by piercing with the tip of a sharp knife or a skewer—it will come out clean if it is cooked thoroughly.

6 Cut the almond cake into slices. Decorate the almond slices with slivered almonds, and transfer to serving plates. Serve hot or cold.

COOK'S TIP

These almond slices are best eaten hot, but they may also be served cold. They can be made a day or even a week in advance and reheated. They also freeze beautifully.

Soda Bread

This variation of traditional Irish soda bread is best eaten the same day it has been baked, still warm from the oven.

NUTRITIONAL INFORMATION

Calories	203	Sugars	7g
Protein	8g	Fat	2g
Carbohydrate	42g	Saturates	0g

1 hr 10 mins   40 mins

1 LOAF

INGREDIENTS

- butter, for greasing
- generous 2 cups all-purpose flour, plus extra for dusting
- generous 2 cups whole-wheat flour
- 2 tsp baking powder
- 1 tsp baking soda
- 2 tbsp superfine sugar
- 1 tsp salt
- 1 egg, lightly beaten
- generous 1¾ cups unsweetened yogurt

1 Grease a cookie sheet with butter and dust lightly with flour.

2 Strain both types of flour, the baking powder, baking soda, sugar, and salt into a large bowl. Tip any bran remaining in the strainer into the bowl.

3 In a pitcher, beat together the egg and yogurt and pour the mixture into the dry ingredients. Mix everything together to make a soft and sticky dough.

4 On a lightly floured counter, knead the dough for a few minutes until it is smooth, then shape the dough into a round about 2 inches/5 cm deep.

5 Transfer the dough to the prepared cookie sheet. Mark a cross shape in the center of the top of the dough.

6 Bake in a preheated oven, 375°F/190°C, for about 40 minutes or until the bread is golden brown.

7 Transfer the loaf to a wire rack and let cool. Cut into slices to serve.

3

3

5

VARIATION

For a fruity version of this soda bread, add ¾ cup of raisins to the dry ingredients in step 2.

Spicy Bread

Serve this spicy bread fresh from the oven with your favorite soup or a tomato and onion salad for a light lunch or supper.

3

4

6

NUTRITIONAL INFORMATION

Calories	122	Sugars	1g
Protein	4g	Fat	3g
Carbohydrate	22g	Saturates	2g

1 hr 10 mins — 45 mins

1 LOAF

INGREDIENTS

- 2 tbsp butter, cut into small pieces, plus extra for greasing
- generous 1½ cups self-rising flour
- ¾ cup all-purpose flour
- 1 tsp baking powder
- ¼ tsp salt
- ¼ tsp cayenne pepper
- 2 tsp curry powder
- 2 tsp poppy seeds
- ⅔ cup milk
- 1 egg, lightly beaten

1 Grease a cookie sheet with a little butter.

2 Strain the self-raising flour and the all-purpose flour into a mixing bowl along with the baking powder, salt, cayenne, curry powder, and poppy seeds.

3 Rub in the butter with your fingertips until everything is well mixed together.

4 Add the milk and the beaten egg and mix to a soft dough.

5 Turn the dough out onto a lightly floured counter, then knead lightly for a few minutes.

6 Shape the dough into a round about 2 inches/5 cm deep and mark it with a cross shape in the center of the top with the blade of a knife.

7 Bake in a preheated oven, 375°F/190°C, for 45 minutes.

8 Transfer the bread to a wire rack and let cool. Serve in chunks or slices.

COOK'S TIP

If the bread looks as though it is browning too much, cover it with a piece of foil for the remainder of the cooking time.

Chili Corn Bread

This Mexican-style corn bread makes a great accompaniment to chili con carne or it can be eaten on its own as a tasty snack.

NUTRITIONAL INFORMATION

Calories	179	Sugars	1g
Protein	3g	Fat	14g
Carbohydrate	10g	Saturates	3g

5 mins — 25 mins

SERVES 12

INGREDIENTS

- butter, for greasing
- generous 1½ cups all-purpose flour
- 1 cup cornmeal
- 1 tbsp baking powder
- ½ tsp salt
- 1 green chili, seeded and finely chopped
- 5 scallions, finely chopped
- 2 eggs
- generous ½ cup sour cream
- ½ cup sunflower oil

1 Grease an 8-inch/20-cm square cake pan with butter and line the bottom with baking parchment.

VARIATION

Add ¾ cup of corn kernels to the mixture in step 3, if you prefer.

2 Strain the flour, cornmeal, baking powder, and salt together into a large mixing bowl.

3 Add the finely chopped green chili and the scallions to the dry ingredients and mix well.

4 In a pitcher, beat the eggs together with the sour cream and sunflower oil. Pour the mixture into the bowl of dry ingredients. Mix everything together quickly and thoroughly.

5 Pour the mixture into the prepared cake pan.

6 Bake in a preheated oven, 400°F/200°C, for 20–25 minutes or until the loaf has risen and is lightly browned.

7 Let the bread cool slightly before turning out of the pan. Cut into bars or squares to serve.

3

4

4

Cheese & Ham Loaf

This recipe is a quick way to make tasty bread, using self-rising flour and baking powder to ensure a good rising.

NUTRITIONAL INFORMATION

Calories	360	Sugars	2g
Protein	14g	Fat	21g
Carbohydrate	31g	Saturates	13g

25–30 mins 1 hr

SERVES 6

INGREDIENTS

- 6 tbsp butter, cut into small pieces, plus extra for greasing
- generous 1½ cups self-rising flour
- 1 tsp salt
- 2 tsp baking powder
- 1 tsp paprika
- 1¼ cups grated sharp cheese
- scant ½ cup chopped smoked ham
- 2 eggs, lightly beaten
- ⅔ cup milk

1 Grease a 1-lb/450-g loaf pan with butter and line the bottom with baking parchment.

2 Strain the flour, salt, baking powder, and paprika together into a mixing bowl.

3 Rub in the butter with your fingertips until the mixture resembles fine bread crumbs. Stir in the cheese and ham.

4 Add the beaten eggs and milk to the dry ingredients in the bowl and combine well.

5 Spoon the cheese and ham mixture into the prepared loaf pan.

6 Bake in a preheated oven, 350°F/180°C, for about 1 hour or until the loaf is well risen.

7 Let the bread cool in the pan, then turn out and transfer to a wire rack to cool completely.

8 Serve the bread cut into thick slices.

3

4

4

COOK'S TIP

This tasty bread is best eaten on the day it is made, as it does not keep for very long.

Cheese & Chive Bread

This is a quick bread to make. It is full of cheesy flavor and, to enjoy it at its best, it should be eaten as fresh as possible.

4

5

6

NUTRITIONAL INFORMATION

Calories	190	Sugars	1g
Protein	7g	Fat	9g
Carbohydrate	22g	Saturates	5g

25 mins 30 mins

SERVES 8

INGREDIENTS

- butter, for greasing
- generous 1½ cups self-rising flour
- 1 tsp salt
- 1 tsp mustard powder
- 1 cup grated sharp cheese
- 2 tbsp chopped fresh chives
- 1 egg, lightly beaten
- 2 tbsp butter, melted
- ⅔ cup milk

1 Grease a 9-inch/23-cm square cake pan with butter and line the base with baking parchment.

2 Strain the self-rising flour, salt, and mustard powder together into a large mixing bowl.

3 Reserve 3 tablespoons of the grated sharp cheese for sprinkling over the top of the loaf before baking in the oven.

4 Stir the remaining cheese into the bowl along with the chopped fresh chives. Mix well together.

5 Add the beaten egg, melted butter, and milk and stir the mixture thoroughly to combine.

6 Pour the mixture into the prepared pan and spread out evenly with a knife or spatula. Sprinkle over the reserved grated cheese.

7 Bake in a preheated oven, 375°F/190°C, for about 30 minutes.

8 Let the bread cool slightly in the pan., then turn out onto a wire rack to cool completely. Cut into triangles to serve.

COOK'S TIP

You can use any hard, sharp cheese of your choice for this recipe.

Garlic Bread Rolls

This bread is not at all like the store-bought, ready-made garlic bread. Instead it has a subtle flavor and a soft texture.

NUTRITIONAL INFORMATION

Calories	265	Sugars	3g
Protein	10g	Fat	6g
Carbohydrate	46g	Saturates	2g

1¾ hrs   35 mins

SERVES 8

INGREDIENTS

- butter, for greasing
- 12 cloves garlic, peeled
- 1½ cups milk
- 3½ cups white bread flour
- 1 tsp salt
- 1 sachet active dry yeast
- 1 tbsp dried mixed herbs
- 2 tbsp sunflower oil
- 1 egg, lightly beaten
- milk, for brushing
- rock salt, for sprinkling

1 Grease a cookie sheet with a little butter and set aside.

2 Place the garlic cloves and milk in a pan, bring to a boil, and simmer gently for 15 minutes. Let cool slightly, then process in a blender or food processor to blend in the garlic.

3 Strain the flour and salt into a large mixing bowl and stir in the dried yeast and mixed herbs.

4 Add the garlic-flavored milk, sunflower oil, and beaten egg to the dry ingredients and mix everything to form a dough.

5 Place the dough on a lightly floured counter and knead lightly for a few minutes until smooth and soft.

6 Place the dough in a greased bowl, cover, and let rise in a warm place for about 1 hour or until doubled in size.

7 Punch down the dough by kneading it for 2 minutes. Divide the dough into 8 pieces and shape into rolls. Place the rolls on the prepared cookie sheet. Score the top of each roll with a knife, cover, and leave for 15 minutes.

8 Brush the rolls with milk and sprinkle rock salt over the top. Bake in a preheated oven, 425°F/220°C, for 15–20 minutes.

9 Transfer the rolls to a wire rack and let cool before serving.

2

4

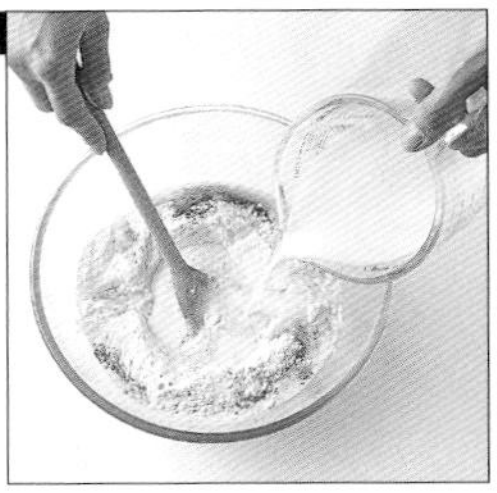

5

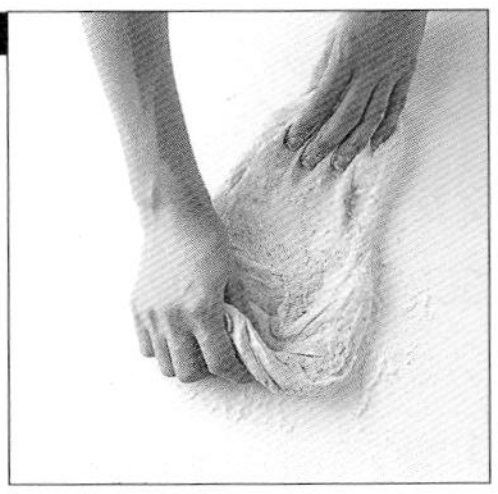

Mini Focaccia

This is a delicious Italian bread made with olive oil. The topping of red onions and thyme is particularly flavorsome.

NUTRITIONAL INFORMATION

Calories	439	Sugars	3g
Protein	9g	Fat	15g
Carbohydrate	71g	Saturates	2g

2¼ hrs

25 mins

SERVES 4

INGREDIENTS

- 2 tbsp olive oil, plus extra for greasing
- 350 g/12 oz strong white flour
- ½ tsp salt
- 1 sachet easy-blend dried yeast
- 250 ml/9 fl oz hand-hot water
- 100 g/3½ oz stoned green or black olives, halved

TOPPING

- 2 red onions, sliced
- 2 tbsp olive oil
- 1 tsp sea salt
- 1 tbsp thyme leaves

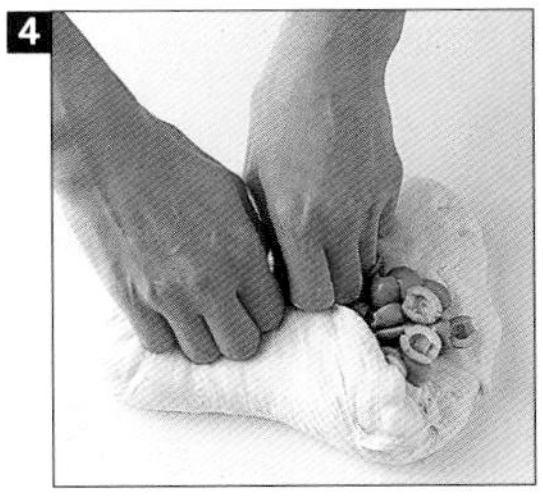

1 Lightly oil several baking trays. Sieve the flour and salt into a large mixing bowl, then stir in the yeast. Pour in the olive oil and hand-hot water and mix everything together to form a dough.

2 Turn the dough out on to a lightly floured surface and knead it for about 5 minutes. Alternatively, use an electric mixer with a dough hook.

3 Place the dough in a greased bowl, cover and leave in a warm place for about 1–1½ hours or until it has doubled in size. Knock back the dough by kneading it again for 1–2 minutes.

4 Knead half of the olives into the dough. Divide the dough into quarters and then shape the quarters into rounds. Place them on the baking trays and push your fingers into the dough to create a dimpled effect.

5 To make the topping, sprinkle the red onions and remaining olives over the rounds. Drizzle the oil over the top and sprinkle with the sea salt and thyme leaves. Cover and leave to rise for 30 minutes.

6 Bake in a preheated oven, 190°C/375°F/Gas Mark 5, for 20–25 minutes or until the focaccia are golden.

7 Transfer to a wire rack and leave to cool before serving.

VARIATION

Use this quantity of dough to make 1 large focaccia, if you prefer.

Sun-dried Tomato Rolls

These white rolls have the addition of finely chopped sun-dried tomatoes. The tomatoes are sold in jars and are available at most large stores.

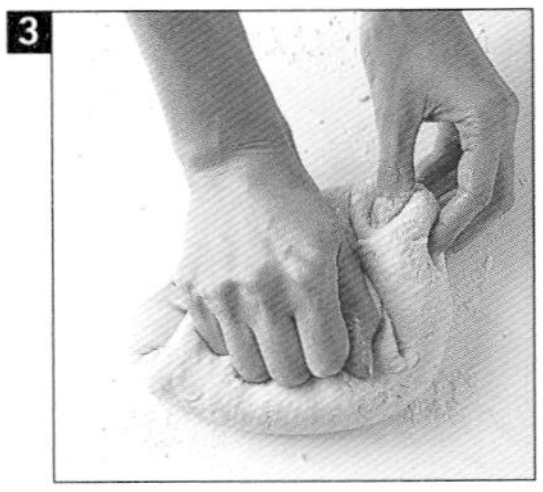

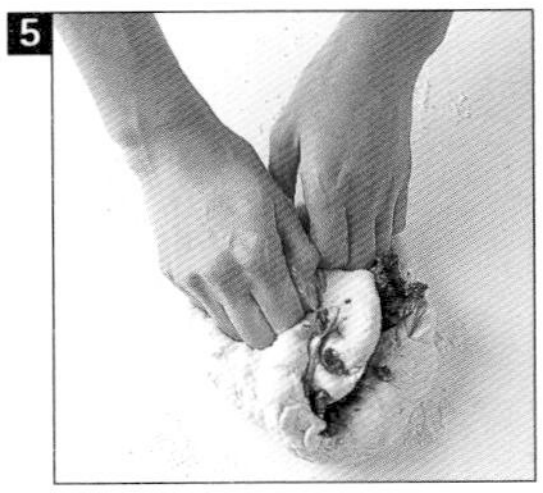

NUTRITIONAL INFORMATION

Calories	214	Sugars	1g
Protein	5g	Fat	12g
Carbohydrate	22g	Saturates	7g

2¼ hrs   15 mins

SERVES 8

INGREDIENTS

- butter, for greasing
- generous 1½ cups white bread flour
- ½ tsp salt
- 1 sachet active dry yeast
- ⅓ cup butter, melted and cooled slightly
- 3 tbsp lukewarm milk
- 2 eggs, lightly beaten
- 1¾ oz/50 g sun-dried tomatoes, well drained and finely chopped
- milk, for brushing

1 Lightly grease a cookie sheet with a little butter and set aside.

2 Strain the flour and salt into a large mixing bowl. Stir in the yeast, then pour in the butter, milk, and eggs. Mix together to form a dough.

3 Turn the dough onto a lightly floured counter and knead for about 5 minutes. Alternatively, use an electric mixer with a dough hook.

4 Place the dough in a greased bowl, cover, and let rise in a warm place for 1–1½ hours or until the dough has doubled in size.

5 Punch down the dough for 2–3 minutes. Knead the sun-dried tomatoes into the dough, sprinkling the counter with extra flour, as the tomatoes are quite oily.

6 Divide the dough into 8 balls and place them on the cookie sheet. Cover and let rise for about 30 minutes or until the rolls have doubled in size.

7 Brush the rolls with milk and bake in a preheated oven, 450°F/230°C, for 10–15 minutes or until the rolls are golden brown.

8 Transfer the rolls to a wire rack and let cool slightly before serving.

VARIATION

Add some finely chopped anchovies or olives to the dough in step 5 for extra flavor, if wished.

Thyme Crescents

These savory crescent snacks are perfect for a quick and tasty bite to eat. They can also be shaped into twists, if preferred.

NUTRITIONAL INFORMATION

Calories 209	Sugars 0g
Protein 2g	Fat 18g
Carbohydrate ...12g	Saturates 7g

10 mins | 15 mins

SERVES 8

INGREDIENTS

scant ½ cup butter, softened, plus extra for greasing

9 oz/250 g fresh ready-made puff pie dough, thawed if frozen

1 clove garlic, crushed

1 tsp lemon juice

1 tsp dried thyme

salt and pepper

1 Lightly grease a cookie sheet with a little butter.

2 On a lightly floured surface, roll out the pie dough to form a 10-inch/25 cm circle and cut into 8 wedges.

3 In a small bowl, mix the softened butter, garlic clove, lemon juice, and dried thyme together until soft. Season with salt and pepper to taste.

4 Spread a little of the butter and thyme mixture onto each wedge of pie dough, dividing it equally among them. Carefully roll up each wedge, starting from the wide end.

5 Arrange the crescents on the prepared cookie sheet and chill for 30 minutes.

6 Dampen the cookie sheet with cold water. This will create a steamy atmosphere in the oven while the crescents are baking which will help the pastries to rise.

7 Bake in a preheated oven, 400°F/200°C, for 10–15 minutes, until the crescents are well risen and golden. Transfer the crescents to a wire rack and serve warm or cold.

2

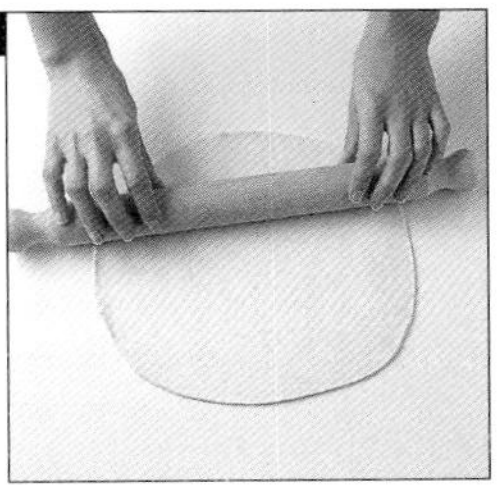

2

4

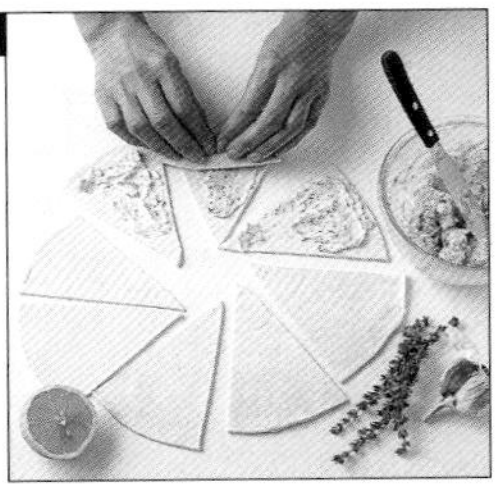

COOK'S TIP

Dried herbs have a stronger flavor than fresh ones, which makes them perfect for this recipe. The crescents can be made with other dried herbs of your choice, such as rosemary and sage, or mixed herbs.

Cheese & Mustard Biscuits

These homemade biscuits are given an interesting flavor by adding grated sharp cheese and mustard to the mixture.

NUTRITIONAL INFORMATION

Calories	218	Sugars	1g
Protein	7g	Fat	12g
Carbohydrate	22g	Saturates	7g

15 mins   15 mins

MAKES 8

INGREDIENTS

- 4 tbsp butter, cut into small pieces, plus extra for greasing
- generous 1½ cups self-rising flour
- 1 tsp baking powder
- 1¼ cups grated sharp cheese
- 1 tsp mustard powder
- ⅔ cup milk
- salt and pepper

1 Lightly grease a cookie sheet with a little butter.

2 Strain the flour, baking powder, and a pinch of salt into a mixing bowl. Rub in the butter with your fingertips until the mixture resembles bread crumbs.

3 Stir in the grated cheese, mustard, and enough milk to form a soft dough.

4 On a lightly floured counter, knead the dough very lightly, then flatten it out with the palm of your hand to a depth of about 1 inch/2.5 cm.

5 Cut the dough into 8 wedges with a knife. Brush each one with a little milk and sprinkle with pepper to taste.

2

3

5

6 Bake in a preheated oven, 425°F/220°C, for 10–15 minutes until the biscuits are golden brown.

7 Transfer the biscuits to a wire rack and let cool slightly before serving.

COOK'S TIP

Biscuits should be eaten on the day they are made, as they quickly go stale. Serve them split in half and spread with butter.

Cheese & Chive Biscuits

These tea-time classics have been given a healthy twist by the use of low-fat soft cheese and reduced-fat Cheddar cheese.

NUTRITIONAL INFORMATION

Calories	297	Sugars	3g
Protein	13g	Fat	7g
Carbohydrate	49g	Saturates	4g

10 mins 20 mins

MAKES 10

INGREDIENTS

- generous 1½ cups self-rising flour
- 1 tsp powdered mustard
- ½ tsp cayenne pepper
- ½ tsp salt
- ½ cup low-fat soft cheese with added herbs
- 2 tbsp snipped fresh chives, plus extra to garnish
- scant ½ cup skim milk, plus 2 tbsp for brushing
- generous ½ cup grated reduced-fat sharp Cheddar cheese
- low-fat soft cheese, to serve

1. Strain the flour, mustard, cayenne pepper, and salt into a mixing bowl.
2. Add the soft cheese to the mixture and mix together until well incorporated. Stir in the snipped chives.
3. Make a well in the center of the ingredients and gradually pour in the ½ cup of milk, stirring as you pour, until the mixture forms a soft dough.
4. Turn the dough onto a floured counter and knead lightly. Roll out until ¾ inch/2 cm thick, and use a 2-inch/5-cm plain dough cutter to stamp out as many circles as you can. Transfer the circles to a cookie sheet.
5. Re-knead the dough trimmings together and roll out again. Stamp out more circles—you should be able to make 10 biscuits in total.
6. Brush the biscuits with the remaining milk and sprinkle with the grated cheese. Bake in a preheated oven, 400°F/200°C, for 15–20 minutes until risen and golden.
7. Transfer to a wire rack to cool. Serve warm with low-fat soft cheese, garnished with chives.

2

4

6

VARIATION

For sweet biscuits, omit the mustard, cayenne pepper, chives, and grated cheese. Replace the flavored soft cheese with plain low-fat soft cheese. Add ½ cup currants and 2 tablespoons of superfine sugar. Serve with low-fat soft cheese and fruit spread.

Savory Bell Pepper Bread

This flavorsome bread contains only the minimum amount of fat. Serve with a bowl of hot soup for a filling and nutritious light meal.

NUTRITIONAL INFORMATION

Calories	468	Sugars	11g
Protein	16g	Fat	5g
Carbohydrate	97g	Saturates	1g

2 hrs

50 mins

SERVES 4

INGREDIENTS

- butter, for greasing
- 1 small red bell pepper, halved and seeded
- 1 small green bell pepper, halved and seeded
- 1 small yellow bell pepper, halved and seeded
- 2 oz/55 g dry-pack sun-dried tomatoes
- scant ¼ cup boiling water
- 2 tsp dried yeast
- 1 tsp superfine sugar
- ⅔ cup lukewarm water
- 3½ cups white bread flour
- 2 tsp dried rosemary
- 2 tbsp tomato paste
- ⅔ cup low-fat plain yogurt
- 1 tbsp coarse salt
- 1 tbsp olive oil

1 Lightly grease a 9-inch/23-cm round spring-form cake pan. Place the bell pepper halves on a broiler rack and cook under a preheated broiler until the skin is charred. Let cool for 10 minutes, peel off the skin, and chop the flesh. Slice the tomatoes into strips, place in a bowl and pour over the boiling water. Set aside to soak.

2 Combine the yeast, sugar, and lukewarm water and leave for 10–15 minutes until frothy. Sift the flour into a bowl and add 1 teaspoon of dried rosemary. Make a well in the center and pour in the yeast mixture.

3 Add the tomato paste, tomatoes and soaking liquid, bell peppers, yogurt, and half the salt. Mix to form a soft dough. Turn out onto a lightly floured counter and knead for 3–4 minutes until smooth and elastic. Place in a lightly floured bowl, cover, and let stand in a warm room for 40 minutes until doubled in size.

4 Knead the dough again and place in the prepared cake pan. Using a wooden spoon, form "dimples" in the surface. Cover and leave for 30 minutes. Brush with oil and sprinkle with rosemary and salt. Bake in a preheated oven, 425°F/220°C, for 35–40 minutes. Cool the loaf for 10 minutes and then release from the pan. Place on a wire rack to cool completely before serving.

2

3

4

COOK'S TIP

For a quick, filling snack serve the bread with a bowl of hot soup in winter, or crisp salad greens in summer.

Olive Oil Bread with Cheese

This flat cheese bread is similar to focaccia. It is delicious served with antipasto or simply on its own. This recipe makes one loaf.

NUTRITIONAL INFORMATION

Calories	586	Sugars	3g
Protein	22g	Fat	26g
Carbohydrate	69g	Saturates	12g

1 hr | 30 mins

SERVES 4

INGREDIENTS

- ½ oz/15 g dried yeast
- 1 tsp granulated sugar
- 1 cup lukewarm water
- 2½ cups white bread flour
- 1 tsp salt
- 3 tbsp olive oil
- 7 oz/200 g romano cheese, cubed
- ½ tbsp fennel seeds, lightly crushed

1 Mix the yeast with the sugar and a generous ⅓ cup of the lukewarm water. Set aside in a warm place for about 15 minutes until frothy.

2 Mix the flour with the salt. Add 1 tablespoon of the oil, the yeast mixture, and the remaining water, to form a smooth dough. Knead the dough for 4 minutes.

COOK'S TIP

Romano is a hard, quite salty cheese, which is sold in most large food stores and Italian delicatessens. If you cannot obtain romano, use strong Cheddar or Parmesan cheese instead.

3 Divide the dough into 2 equal portions. Roll out each portion to a form a circle ¼ inch/6 mm thick. Place 1 circle on a cookie sheet.

4 Scatter the cheese and half of the fennel seeds evenly over the circle.

5 Place the second circle on top and squeeze the edges together to seal so that the filling does not leak during the cooking time.

6 Using a sharp knife, make a few slashes in the top of the dough and brush with the remaining olive oil.

7 Sprinkle with the remaining fennel seeds and set the loaf aside to rise for 20–30 minutes.

8 Bake in a preheated oven, 400°F/200°C, for 30 minutes or until golden brown. Remove from the oven and serve while still warm.

3

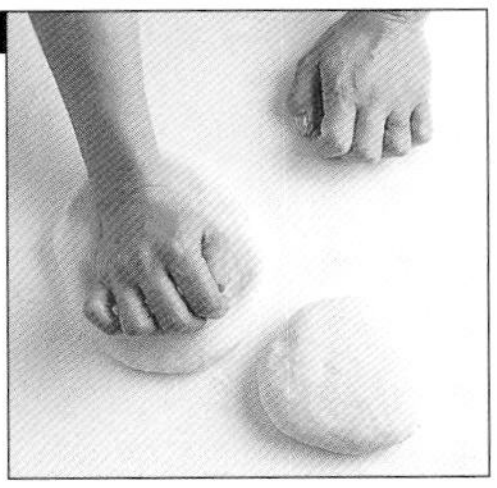

4

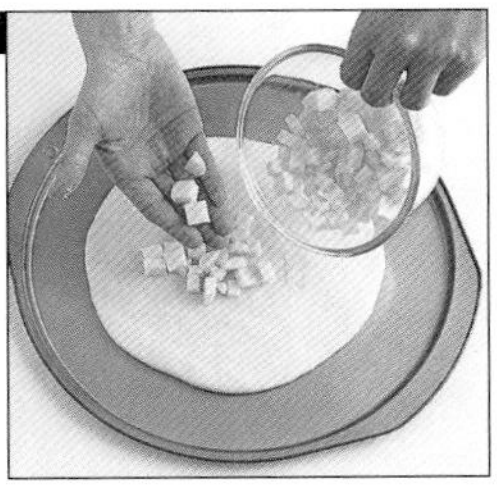

5

Cookies

Nothing can compare with a homemade cookie for bringing a touch of pleasure to a coffee break or tea-time. This selection of delicious cookies and after-dinner treats

will tantalize your tastebuds and keep you coming back for more.

More-ish cookies like Citrus Crescents, Meringues, Rock Drops, and Gingersnaps are quick, easy, and satisfying to make. You can easily vary the ingredients to suit your taste—the possibilities for inventiveness when making cookies are endless and this chapter shows you how.

Cheese Sables

These savory crackers have a delicious buttery flavor. Make sure you use a sharp cheese for the best flavor.

NUTRITIONAL INFORMATION

Calories 278	Sugars 0g
Protein 2g	Fat 5g
Carbohydrate 3g	Saturates 3g

50 mins | 20 mins

MAKES 35

INGREDIENTS

⅔ cup butter, cut into small pieces, plus extra for greasing

generous 1 cup all-purpose flour

1½ cups grated sharp cheese

1 egg yolk

sesame seeds, for sprinkling

1 Lightly grease several cookie sheets with a little butter.

2 Mix the flour and grated cheese together in a bowl.

3 Add the butter to the cheese and flour mixture and mix with your fingertips until combined.

4 Stir in the egg yolk and mix to form a dough. Wrap the dough and chill in the refrigerator for about 30 minutes.

5 On a lightly floured counter, roll out the cheese dough thinly. Cut out 2½-inch/6-cm circles, re-rolling the trimmings to make about 35 circles.

6 Carefully transfer the dough circles onto the prepared cookie sheets and sprinkle the sesame seeds evenly over the top of them.

3

5
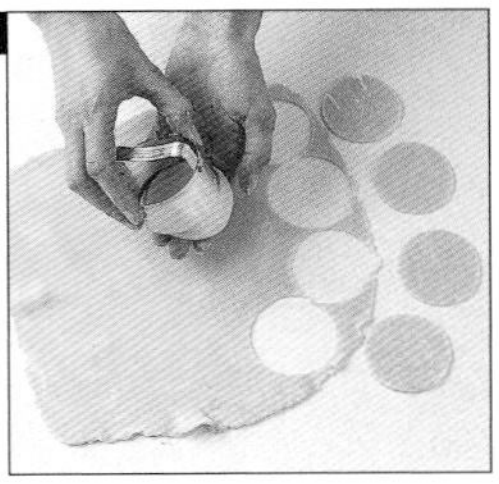

6

7 Bake in a preheated oven, 200°C/400°F, for 20 minutes, until the sables are lightly golden.

8 Transfer the cheese sables to a wire rack with a fish slice or spatula and let cool slightly before serving.

COOK'S TIP

Cut out any shape you like for your savory sables. Children will enjoy them cut into animal or other fun shapes.

Savory Curried Crackers

When making these crackers, try different types of curry powder strengths until you find the one that suits your own tastes.

NUTRITIONAL INFORMATION

Calories	48	Sugars	0g
Protein	2g	Fat	4g
Carbohydrate	2g	Saturates	2g

45 mins 15 mins

MAKES 40

INGREDIENTS

- ⅓ cup butter, softened, plus extra for greasing
- ¾ cup all-purpose flour
- 1 tsp salt
- 2 tsp curry powder
- 1 cup grated mellow hard cheese
- 1 cup freshly grated Parmesan cheese

3

4

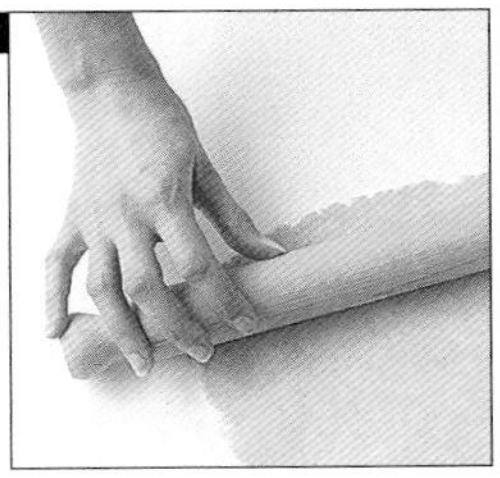

5

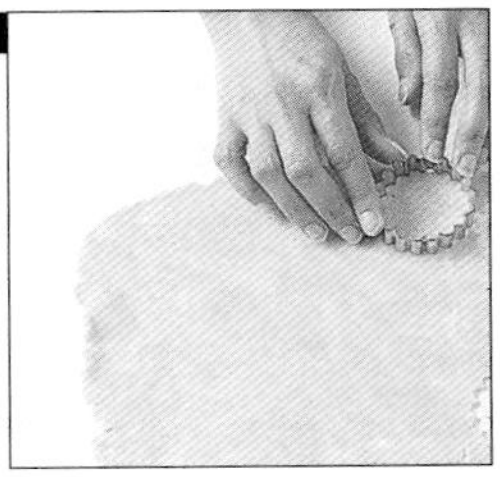

1 Lightly grease about 4 cookie sheets with a little butter.

2 Strain the all-purpose flour and salt into a mixing bowl.

3 Stir in the curry powder and both the grated cheeses. Add the softened butter and rub it in with your fingertips until the mixture comes together to form a soft dough.

4 On a lightly floured counter, roll out the dough thinly to form a rectangle.

5 Using a 2-inch/5-cm cookie cutter, cut out 40 crackers.

6 Arrange the crackers on the cookie sheets.

7 Bake in a preheated oven, 350°F/180°C, for 10–15 minutes.

8 Let the crackers cool slightly on the cookie sheets. Transfer the crackers to a wire rack until completely cold and crisp, then serve.

COOK'S TIP

These crackers can be stored for several days in an airtight container.

Spiced Cookies

These spicy cookies are perfect to serve with fruit salad or ice cream for a very easy instant dessert.

NUTRITIONAL INFORMATION

Calories	117	Sugars	8g
Protein	1g	Fat	6g
Carbohydrate	15g	Saturates	4g

35 mins

12 mins

MAKES 12

INGREDIENTS

¾ cup sweet butter, plus extra for greasing

scant 1 cup dark brown sugar

generous 1½ cups all-purpose flour

pinch of salt

½ tsp baking soda

1 tsp ground cinnamon

½ tsp ground coriander

½ tsp ground nutmeg

¼ tsp ground cloves

2 tbsp dark rum

2

3

5

1 Lightly grease 2 cookie sheets with a little butter.

2 Cream together the butter and sugar and whisk until light and fluffy.

3 Strain the flour, salt, baking soda, cinnamon, coriander, nutmeg, and cloves into the creamed mixture.

4 Add the dark rum and stir it into the creamed mixture.

5 Using 2 teaspoons, place small mounds of the mixture on the prepared cookie sheets, placing them 3 inches/7.5 cm apart to allow for spreading during cooking. Flatten each one slightly with the back of a spoon.

6 Bake in a preheated oven, 350°F/180°C, for 10–12 minutes until golden brown in color.

7 Transfer the cookies to wire racks to cool and crispen before serving.

COOK'S TIP

Use the back of a fork to flatten the cookies slightly before baking.

Cinnamon Squares

These moist, cake-like squares have a lovely spicy flavor. Sunflower seeds give them a nutty texture.

NUTRITIONAL INFORMATION

Calories	397	Sugars	23g
Protein	6g	Fat	25g
Carbohydrate	40g	Saturates	14g

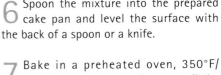

1 hr 10 mins 45 mins

MAKES12

INGREDIENTS

- 1 cup butter, softened, plus extra for greasing
- 1¼ cups superfine sugar
- 3 eggs, lightly beaten
- 1¾ cups self-rising flour
- ½ tsp baking soda
- 1 tbsp ground cinnamon
- ⅔ cup sour cream
- 3½ oz/100 g sunflower seeds

1 Grease a 9-inch/23-cm square cake pan with a little butter and line the bottom with baking parchment.

2 In a large mixing bowl, cream together the butter and superfine sugar until the mixture is light and fluffy.

3 Gradually add the beaten eggs to the mixture, beating thoroughly after each addition.

4 Strain the self-rising flour, baking soda, and ground cinnamon together into the creamed mixture and fold in gently, using a metal spoon in a figure-eight movement.

5 Spoon in the sour cream and sunflower seeds and mix gently until well combined.

6 Spoon the mixture into the prepared cake pan and level the surface with the back of a spoon or a knife.

7 Bake in a preheated oven, 350°F/180°C, for about 45 minutes until the mixture is firm to the touch when pressed with a finger.

8 Loosen the edges with a round-bladed knife, then turn out on to a wire rack to cool completely. Slice into 12 squares before serving.

3

4

5

COOK'S TIP

These moist squares will freeze well and will keep for up to 1 month.

Gingersnaps

Nothing compares with the taste of these freshly baked authentic gingersnaps, which have a lovely hint of orange flavor.

NUTRITIONAL INFORMATION

Calories 106	Sugars 9g
Protein 1g	Fat 4g
Carbohydrate . . .18g	Saturates 2g

10 mins 20 mins

MAKES 30

INGREDIENTS

½ cup butter, plus extra for greasing
2½ cups self-rising flour
pinch of salt
1 cup superfine sugar
1 tbsp ground ginger
1 tsp baking soda
¼ cup light corn syrup
1 egg, lightly beaten
1 tsp grated orange zest
with a little butter

1 Lightly grease several cookie sheets.

2 Strain the flour, salt, sugar, ground ginger, and baking soda into a large mixing bowl.

3 Heat the butter and light corn syrup together in a pan over very low heat until the butter has melted.

4 Let the butter mixture cool slightly, then pour it onto the dry ingredients. Add the egg and orange zest and mix together thoroughly.

5 Using your hands, carefully shape the dough into 30 even-size balls.

6 Place the balls well apart on the prepared cookie sheets, then flatten them slightly with your fingers.

7 Bake in a preheated oven, 325°F/160°C, for 15–20 minutes.

8 Carefully transfer the cookies to a wire rack to cool and crispen.

COOK'S TIP

Store these cookies in an airtight container and eat them within 1 week.

Peanut Butter Cookies

These crunchy cookies will be popular with children of all ages as they contain their favorite food—peanut butter.

NUTRITIONAL INFORMATION

Calories 186	Sugars 13g
Protein 4g	Fat 11g
Carbohydrate ...19g	Saturates 5g

40 mins 15 mins

MAKES20

INGREDIENTS

- ½ cup butter, softened, plus extra for greasing
- ½ cup chunky peanut butter
- generous 1 cup granulated sugar
- 1 egg, lightly beaten
- generous 1 cup all-purpose flour
- ½ tsp baking powder
- pinch of salt
- ½ cup chopped unsalted natural peanuts

1 Lightly grease 2 cookie sheets. with a little butter.

2 In a large mixing bowl, beat together the butter and peanut butter.

3 Gradually add the granulated sugar and beat well.

4 Add the beaten egg, a little at a time, beating after each addition until it is thoroughly combined.

5 Strain the flour, baking powder, and salt into the peanut butter mixture.

6 Add the peanuts and bring all of the ingredients together to form a soft dough. Wrap and chill for 30 minutes.

7 Form the dough into 20 balls and place them on the prepared cookie sheets about 2 inches/5 cm apart to allow for spreading. Flatten them slightly with your hand.

8 Bake in a preheated oven, 375°F/190°C, for 15 minutes until golden brown. Transfer the cookies to a wire rack and let cool.

COOK'S TIP

For a crunchy bite and sparkling appearance, sprinkle the cookies with raw brown sugar before baking.

Hazelnut Squares

These can be made quickly and easily for an afternoon tea treat. The chopped hazelnuts can be replaced by any other nut of your choice.

NUTRITIONAL INFORMATION

Calories	163	Sugars	10g
Protein	2g	Fat	10g
Carbohydrate	18g	Saturates	4g

15 mins — 25 mins

MAKES 16

INGREDIENTS

- ⅓ cup butter, cut into small pieces, plus extra for greasing
- generous 1 cup all-purpose flour
- 1 tsp baking powder
- ¾ cup brown sugar
- 1 egg, lightly beaten
- 4 tbsp milk
- 1 cup halved hazelnuts
- raw brown sugar, for sprinkling (optional)
- salt

3

4

5

1 Grease a 9-inch/23-cm square cake pan with a little butter and line the bottom with baking parchment.

2 Strain the flour, a pinch of salt, and the baking powder into a large bowl.

3 Rub in the butter with your fingertips until the mixture resembles fine bread crumbs. Stir in the brown sugar.

4 Add the beaten egg, milk, and nuts to the mixture and stir well until thoroughly combined.

5 Spoon the mixture into the prepared cake pan, spreading it out evenly, and level the surface. Sprinkle with raw brown sugar, if using.

6 Bake in a preheated oven, 350°F/180°C, for about 25 minutes or until the mixture is firm to the touch when pressed with a finger.

7 Let cool for 10 minutes in the pan, then loosen the edges with a round-bladed knife and turn out onto a wire rack. Cut into squares and let cool completely before serving.

VARIATION

For a coffee time cookie, replace the milk with the same amount of cold strong black coffee—the stronger the better.

Coconut Flapjacks

Ever-popular, these freshly baked, chewy flapjacks are just the thing for a tea-time treat or after-school snack.

NUTRITIONAL INFORMATION

Calories 269	Sugars 19g
Protein 3g	Fat 16g
Carbohydrate ...32g	Saturates 10g

45 mins — 30 mins

MAKES 16

INGREDIENTS

- 1 cup butter, plus extra for greasing
- 1 cup raw brown sugar
- 2 tbsp light corn syrup
- 3½ cups rolled oats
- 1 cup shredded coconut
- ⅓ cup chopped candied cherries

2

3

4

1 Lightly grease a 12 x 9-inch/30 x 23-cm cookie sheet with a little butter and set aside.

2 Heat the butter, raw brown sugar, and light corn syrup in a large pan over low heat until just melted.

3 Stir in the oats, shredded coconut, and candied cherries and mix well until evenly combined.

4 Spread the mixture evenly onto the prepared cookie sheet and gently press down with the back of a spatula to make a smooth surface.

5 Bake the flapjack in a preheated oven, 325°F/170°C, for about 30 minutes until golden.

6 Remove from the oven and let cool on the cookie sheet for 10 minutes.

7 Cut the mixture into squares using a sharp knife.

8 Carefully transfer the flapjack squares to a wire rack and let cool completely.

COOK'S TIP

The flapjacks are best stored in an airtight container and eaten within 1 week. They can also be frozen for up to 1 month.

Oat & Raisin Cookies

These oaty, fruity cookies are delicious with a cup of coffee for a special reward after a busy morning.

NUTRITIONAL INFORMATION

Calories 227	Sugars 22g
Protein 4g	Fat 7g
Carbohydrate ...39g	Saturates 3g

50 mins

15 mins

MAKES 10

INGREDIENTS

- 4 tbsp butter, plus extra for greasing
- generous ½ cup superfine sugar
- 1 egg, lightly beaten
- generous ⅓ cup all-purpose flour
- ½ tsp salt
- ½ tsp baking powder
- 2 cups rolled oats
- ¾ cup raisins
- 2 tbsp sesame seeds

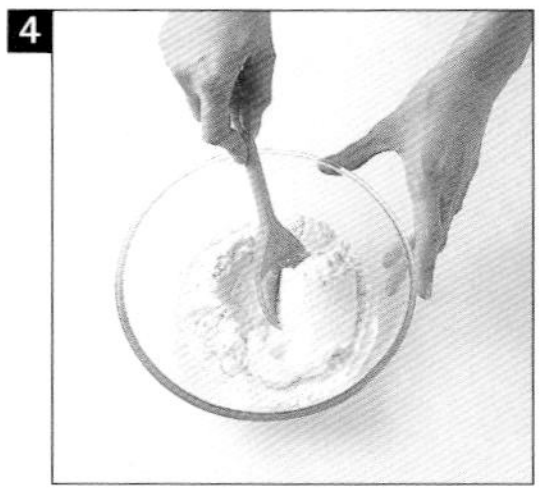

1 Lightly grease 2 cookie sheets with a little butter.

2 In a large mixing bowl, cream together the butter and sugar until light and fluffy.

3 Gradually add the beaten egg, beating well after each addition until thoroughly combined.

4 Strain the flour, salt, and baking powder together into the creamed mixture. Mix well.

5 Add the oats, raisins, and sesame seeds, and mix together thoroughly to form a dough.

6 Place spoonfuls of the mixture spaced well apart on the prepared cookie sheets to allow room to spread during cooking and flatten them slightly with the back of a spoon.

7 Bake in a preheated oven, 350°F/180°C, for 15 minutes.

8 Let the cookies cool slightly on the cookie sheets.

9 Transfer the cookies to a wire rack to cool completely before serving.

COOK'S TIP

To enjoy these cookies at their best, store them in an airtight container.

Rosemary Cookies

Do not be put off by the idea of herbs being used in these crisp cookies—try them and you will be pleasantly surprised.

NUTRITIONAL INFORMATION

Calories	58	Sugars	4g
Protein	1g	Fat	2g
Carbohydrate	10g	Saturates	1g

1 hr 10 mins 15 mins

MAKES 25

INGREDIENTS

- 4 tbsp butter, softened, plus extra for greasing
- 4 tbsp superfine sugar
- grated zest of 1 lemon
- 4 tbsp lemon juice
- 1 egg, separated
- 2 tsp finely chopped fresh rosemary
- scant 1½ cups all-purpose flour, strained
- superfine sugar, for sprinkling (optional)

1 Lightly grease 2 cookie sheets with a little butter.

2 In a large mixing bowl, cream together the butter and sugar until pale and fluffy.

3 Add the lemon zest and juice, then the egg yolk, and beat until they are thoroughly combined. Stir in the chopped fresh rosemary.

4 Add the strained flour, mixing well until a soft dough is formed. Wrap in plastic wrap and chill in the refrigerator for 30 minutes.

5 On a lightly floured counter, roll out the dough thinly and stamp out about 25 circles with a 2½-inch/6-cm cookie cutter. Arrange the dough circles on the prepared cookie sheets.

6 In a bowl, lightly whisk the egg white. Gently brush the egg white over the surface of each cookie, then sprinkle with a little superfine sugar, if liked.

7 Bake in a preheated oven, 350°F/180°C, for about 15 minutes.

8 Transfer the cookies to a wire rack and let cool before serving.

4

5
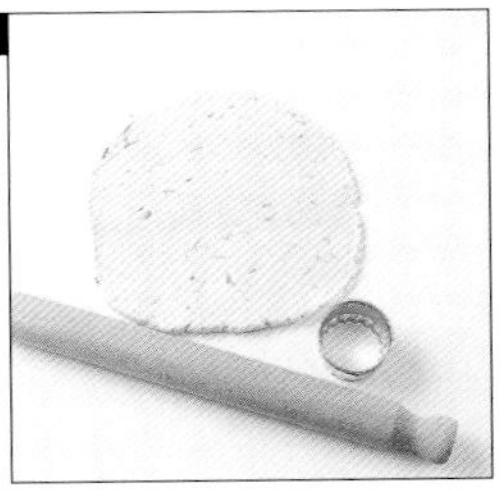

6
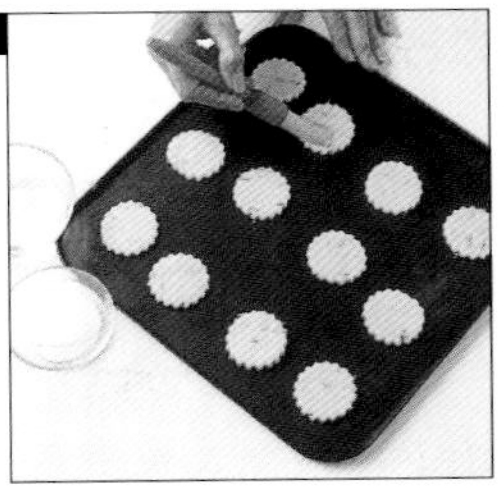

VARIATION

In place of the fresh rosemary, use 1½ teaspoons of dried rosemary, if you prefer.

Citrus Crescents

For a sweet treat, try these pretty crescent-shaped cookies, which have a lovely citrus tang to them.

NUTRITIONAL INFORMATION

Calories	72	Sugars	3g
Protein	1g	Fat	4g
Carbohydrate	10g	Saturates	2g

10 mins | 15 mins

MAKES 25

INGREDIENTS

- ⅓ cup butter, softened, plus extra for greasing
- ⅓ cup superfine sugar, plus extra for sprinkling (optional)
- 1 egg, separated
- scant 1½ cups all-purpose flour
- grated zest of 1 orange
- grated zest of 1 lemon
- grated zest of 1 lime
- 2–3 tbsp orange juice

1 Lightly grease 2 cookie sheets with a little butter.

2 In a mixing bowl, cream together the butter and sugar until light and fluffy, then gradually beat in the egg yolk.

3 Strain the flour into the creamed mixture and mix until evenly combined. Add the orange, lemon, and lime zests to the mixture, with enough of the orange juice to make a soft dough.

4 Roll out the dough on a lightly floured counter. Stamp out circles using a 3-inch/7.5-cm cookie cutter. Make crescent shapes by cutting away a quarter of each circle. Re-roll the trimmings to make about 25 crescents.

3

4

5

5 Place the crescents on the prepared cookie sheets, spacing them apart to allow room for spreading. Prick the surface of each crescent with a fork.

6 Lightly whisk the egg white in a small bowl and brush it over the cookies. Dust with extra superfine sugar, if using.

7 Bake in a preheated oven, 400°F/200°C, for 12–15 minutes. Transfer the cookies to a wire rack to cool and crispen before serving.

COOK'S TIP

Store the citrus crescents in an airtight container. Alternatively, they can be frozen for up to 1 month.

Lemon Jumbles

These lemony, melt-in-the-mouth cookies are made extra special by dredging them with confectioners' sugar just before serving.

NUTRITIONAL INFORMATION

Calories	50	Sugars	3g
Protein	1g	Fat	2g
Carbohydrate	8g	Saturates	1g

10 mins

20 mins

MAKES 50

INGREDIENTS

- ⅓ cup butter, softened, plus extra for greasing
- generous ½ cup superfine sugar
- grated zest of 1 lemon
- 1 egg, lightly beaten
- 4 tbsp lemon juice
- 2½ cups all-purpose flour
- 1 tsp baking powder
- 1 tbsp milk
- confectioners' sugar, for dredging

2

4

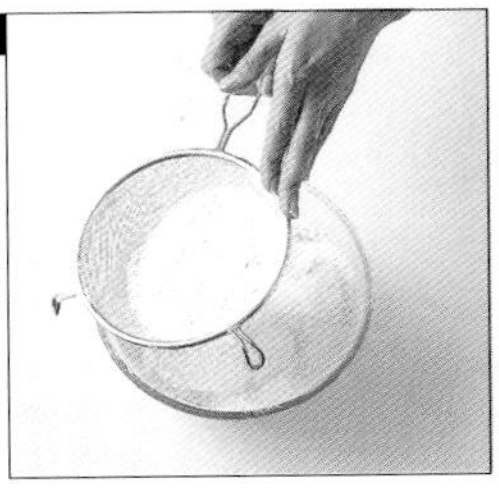

6

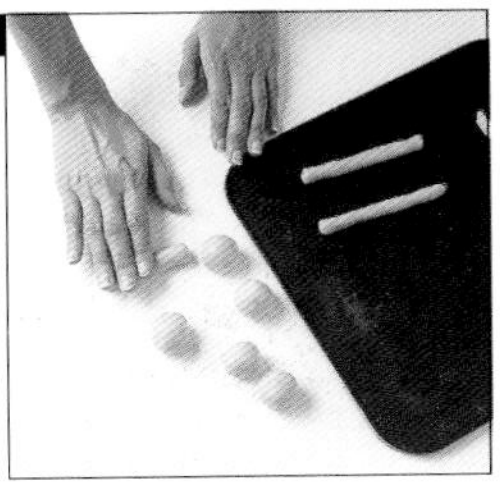

1 Lightly grease several cookie sheets with a little butter.

2 In a mixing bowl, cream together the butter, superfine sugar, and lemon zest, until pale and fluffy.

3 Add the beaten egg and lemon juice, a little at a time, beating well after each addition.

4 Strain the flour and baking powder into the creamed mixture and blend together. Add the milk, mixing to form a firm dough.

5 Turn the dough out onto a lightly floured counter and divide into about 50 equal-size pieces.

6 Roll each piece into a sausage shape with your hands and twist in the middle to make an "S" shape.

7 Place the cookies on the prepared cookie sheets and bake in a preheated oven, 325°F/170°C, for 15–20 minutes. Let cool completely on a wire rack. Dredge generously with confectioners' sugar before serving.

VARIATION

If you prefer, shape the dough into other shapes—letters of the alphabet or geometric shapes—or just make into round cookies.

Shortbread Fantails

These cookies are perfect for afternoon tea or they can be served with ice cream for a really delicious dessert.

NUTRITIONAL INFORMATION

Calories 248	Sugars 10g
Protein 3g	Fat 13g
Carbohydrate ...32g	Saturates 9g

40 mins

35 mins

SERVES 8

INGREDIENTS

- ½ cup butter, softened, plus extra for greasing
- scant ¼ cup granulated sugar
- 2 tbsp confectioners' sugar
- generous 1½ cups all-purpose flour
- pinch of salt
- 2 tsp orange flower water
- superfine sugar, for sprinkling

1 Lightly grease a shallow 8-inch/20-cm round cake pan with a little butter.

2 In a large mixing bowl, cream together the butter, the granulated sugar, and the confectioners' sugar, until light and fluffy.

3 Strain the flour and salt into the creamed mixture. Add the orange flower water and bring everything together to form a soft dough.

4 On a lightly floured counter, roll out the dough to an 8-inch/20-cm round and place in the prepared pan. Prick the dough well and score into 8 triangles with a round-bladed knife.

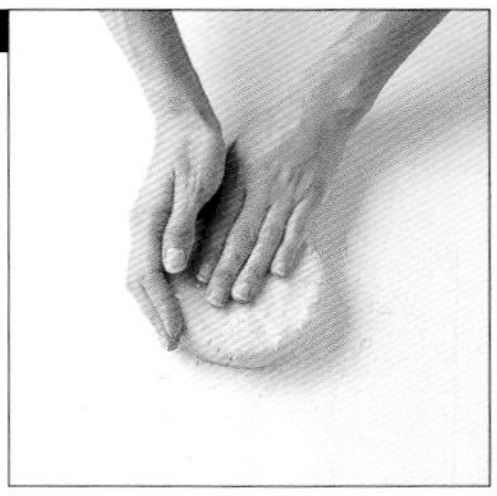
4

4

4

5 Bake the shortbread in a preheated oven, 325°F/160°C, for 30–35 minutes or until the cookie is crisp and the top is pale golden.

6 Sprinkle with superfine sugar, then cut along the marked lines to make the fantails.

7 Let the shortbread cool before removing the pieces from the pan. Store in an airtight container.

COOKS TIP

For a crunchy addition, sprinkle 2 tablespoons of chopped mixed nuts over the top of the fantails before baking.

Vanilla Hearts

This is a classic shortbread cookie which melts in the mouth. Here the cookies are made in pretty heart shapes which will appeal to everyone.

NUTRITIONAL INFORMATION

Calories 150	Sugars 9g
Protein 1g	Fat 8g
Carbohydrate ...20g	Saturates 5g

40 mins   30 mins

MAKES 16

INGREDIENTS

⅔ cup butter, cut into small pieces, plus extra for greasing

2 cups all-purpose flour

½ cup superfine sugar, plus extra for dusting

1 tsp vanilla extract

2

3
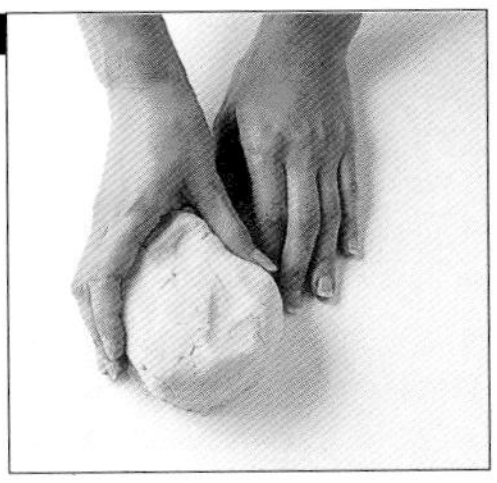

4

1 Lightly grease a cookie sheet with a little butter.

2 Strain the flour into a large mixing bowl and rub in the butter with your fingertips until the mixture resembles fine bread crumbs.

3 Stir in the superfine sugar and vanilla extract and bring the mixture together with your hands to make a smooth firm dough.

4 On a lightly floured surface, roll out the dough to a thickness of 1 inch/2.5 cm. Stamp out 12 hearts with a heart-shaped cookie cutter measuring about 2 inches/5 cm across and 1 inch/ 2.5 cm deep.

5 Arrange the hearts on the prepared cookie sheet. Bake in a preheated oven, 350°F/180°C, for 15-20 minutes until the hearts are a light golden color.

6 Transfer the vanilla hearts to a wire rack and let cool.

7 Dust the cookies with a little superfine sugar just before serving.

COOK'S TIP

Place a fresh vanilla bean in your superfine sugar and keep it in a storage jar for several weeks to give the sugar a delicious vanilla flavor.

Rock Drops

These rock drops are more substantial than a crisp cookie. Serve them fresh from the oven to enjoy them at their best.

NUTRITIONAL INFORMATION

Calories	270	Sugars	21g
Protein	4g	Fat	11g
Carbohydrate	41g	Saturates	7g

5–10 mins

20 mins

SERVES 4

INGREDIENTS

- ⅓cup butter, cut into small pieces, plus extra for greasing
- scant 1½ cups all-purpose flour
- 2 tsp baking powder
- ⅓ cup raw brown sugar
- ½ cup golden raisins
- 2 tbsp candied cherries, finely chopped
- 1 egg, lightly beaten
- 2 tbsp milk

1 Lightly grease a cookie sheet with a little butter and set aside.

2 Strain the flour and baking powder together into a mixing bowl. Rub in the butter with your fingertips until the mixture resembles bread crumbs.

3 Stir in the raw brown sugar, golden raisins, and candied cherries.

4 Add the beaten egg and the milk to the mixture and mix to form a soft dough.

5 Spoon 8 mounds of the mixture onto the prepared cookie sheet, spacing them well apart as they will spread while they are cooking.

6 Bake in a preheated oven, 400°F/200°C, for about 15–20 minutes until firm to the touch when pressed with a finger.

7 Remove the rock drops from the cookie sheet. Either serve piping hot from the oven or transfer to a wire rack and let cool before serving.

2

3

5

COOK'S TIP

For convenience, prepare the dry ingredients in advance and just before cooking, stir in the liquid.

Meringues

These are just as meringues should be—as light as air and at the same time crisp and melt-in-the-mouth.

NUTRITIONAL INFORMATION

Calories	183	Sugars	21g
Protein	1g	Fat	11g
Carbohydrate	21g	Saturates	7g

15 mins

1½ hrs

MAKES 13

INGREDIENTS

- 4 egg whites
- generous ½ cup granulated sugar
- generous ½ cup superfine sugar
- 1¼ cups heavy cream, lightly whipped
- salt

2

3

5

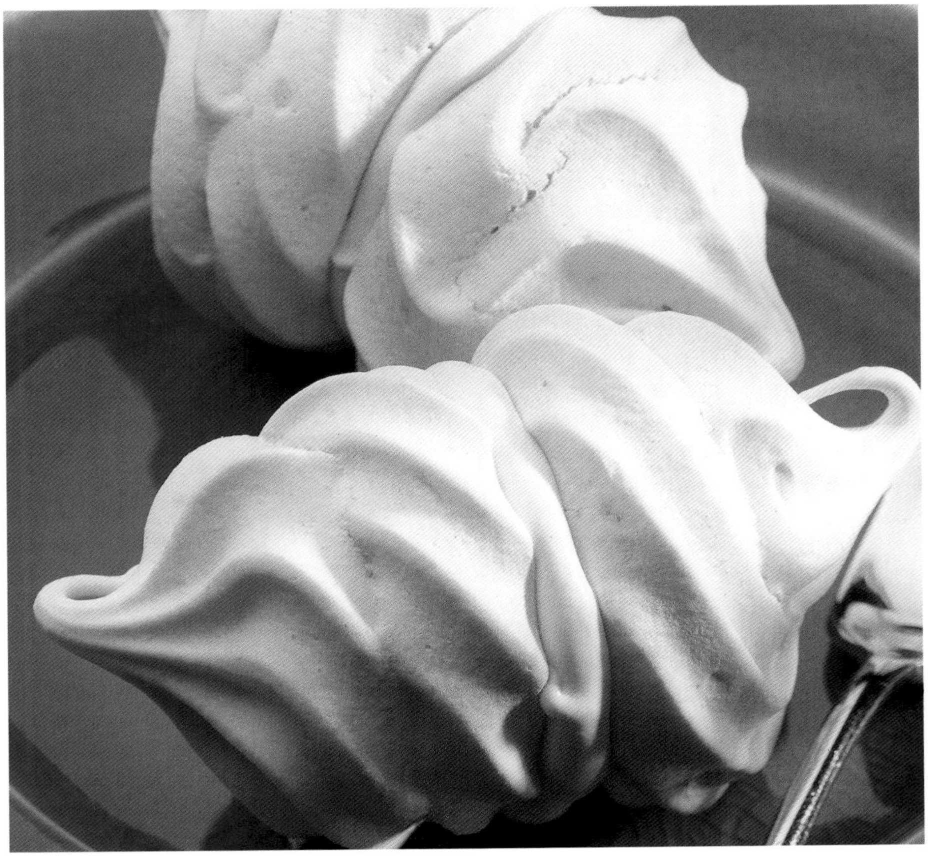

1 Line 3 cookie sheets with sheets of baking parchment.

2 In a large clean bowl, whisk the egg whites with a pinch of salt until they are stiff, using an electric hand-held whisk or a balloon whisk. You should be able to turn the bowl upside down without any movement from the egg whites.

3 Whisk in the granulated sugar, a little at a time; the meringue should start to look glossy at this stage.

4 Sprinkle in the superfine sugar, a little at a time, and continue whisking until all the sugar has been incorporated and the meringue is thick, white, and stands in tall peaks.

5 Transfer the meringue mixture to a pastry bag fitted with a ¾-inch/2-cm star tip. Pipe about 26 small whirls onto the prepared cookie sheets.

6 Bake in a preheated oven, 250°F/120°C, for 1½ hours or until the meringues are pale golden in color and can be easily lifted off the paper. Let cool in the turned-off oven overnight.

7 Just before serving, sandwich the meringues together in pairs with the whipped cream and arrange them on a serving plate.

VARIATION

For a finer texture, replace the granulated sugar with superfine sugar.

Index